DiscipleShape

DiscipleShape

Twelve Weeks to Spiritual Fitness

Dan R. Crawford

Foreword by Calvin Miller

HENDRICKSON
PUBLISHERS

Discipleshape: Twelve Weeks to Spiritual Fitness
© 1998 by Dan R. Crawford
Published by Hendrickson Publishers, Inc.
P.O. Box 3473
Peabody, Massachusetts 01961-3473

Printed in the United States of America

ISBN 1-56563-370-0

Second Printing–March 2000

Cover design by Veldheer Creative Services, Jenison, Mich.
Edited by Heather Stroobosscher

Library of Congress Cataloging-in-Publication Data
Crawford, Dan. R., 1941–
    Discipleshape: twelve weeks to spiritual fitness / Dan R. Crawford
        p.   cm.
    Includes bibliographical references and index.
    ISBN 1-56563-370-0 (cloth)
    1. Spiritual exercises. 2. Spiritual formation. I. Title
BV4832.2.C7   1998
248.4'6--dc21   98-14225
                                                                     CIP

Dedicated to
my spiritual coaches
who throughout the years have
trained me in being conformed to the image of Christ.

CONTENTS

Foreword

Semper *Fidelis* was Dan Crawford's benediction over his son, James Crawford, as he became a United States Marine. But the words are really a benediction over the discipline that his son achieved in making himself a Marine.

Dan Crawford is a *Semper Fidelis* kind of scholar. Dr. Crawford has never been an advocate of cheap grace. He has long understood the connection between the words *disciple* and *discipline.* Now in a wonderful new format, he discusses a twelve-week program designed to get the spiritually flabby into shape.

Discipline is the key to hardy discipleship. Marines do not become tough soldiers through lax lifestyles. Christians do not become rigorous and achieving servants through casual religiosity. Getting in shape demands a regimen. Staying in shape demands a lifestyle.

Dan Crawford has striven to be this kind of disciple. He has role modeled this discipline for two generations of students. Now comes the distillation of his devotional life and his life in ministry. This book is well written and will seem an easy read. But it will not be easy to put into practice. It is designed to teach discipline. To read this book will be easy. To do this book may be hazardous and will require all you are.

Professor Calvin Miller
Southwestern Baptist Theological Seminary
Fort Worth, Texas

Introduction

I was at the airport when my son, James, departed for Marine Corps boot camp and I saw young men of all shapes, sizes, and degrees of physical fitness. Some were grossly overweight, others had tried unsuccessfully to get in physical shape, still others were in good physical shape for ordinary life, but not for Marine Boot Camp. At the graduation ceremony three months later, I saw these same young men after an amazing physical transformation. Twelve weeks of training had molded these men into the best physical condition of their lives. In fact the opening statement of graduation, spoken by the commanding officer, was "These young men are in undoubtedly the finest physical fitness of their lives."

This statement along with the experience caused me to wonder that if twelve weeks of disciplined physical training could make such a difference, what could twelve weeks of disciplined spiritual training make? The answer was obvious, but so was the problem. I know few Christians who can take twelve weeks off for training at some retreat center. So the next, more practical question was: could this be done in the midst of a busy, hectic life? The answer is yes. The method is to schedule the training on a weekly basis. Similar to the twelve weeks of physical fitness training, this book offers a twelve-week guide to spiritual fitness. To read it in one setting is to miss the most effective way to train. Take two days to read a chapter, then spend five days with the Exercises for Spiritual Fitness. Physical muscle building takes time. So does spiritual muscle building. Spiritual fitness results in our lives being shaped in the image of Jesus Christ. As you become more spiritually fit, you become more Christlike in all areas of your life.

This was true in the lives of the disciples. The first disciples were selected before they were trained. They were recruits without knowledge or discipline. Because Jesus taught what he lived and lived what he taught, he became more than just an instructor. He became the incarnate model of what he taught. Because the New Testament writers lived what Jesus taught and taught what Jesus lived, they too became human instructors in spiritual fitness. Thus, in reality, the New Testament becomes a training manual on spiritual fitness written by the first recruits.

As a Christian, I have not yet "arrived" spiritually. I continually need spiritual training. The New Testament word *gumnasia* is variously translated "exercise," "discipline," or "train" and from this Greek word we derive the English word "gymnasium"—a place where physical training takes place. Paul uses this word when he writes, "discipline yourself for the purpose of godliness; for bodily discipline is only of little profit, but godliness is profitable for all things" (1 Tim. 4:7-8). Personally, I must constantly exercise to remain spiritually fit. I invite you to enter then into twelve weeks of basic training.

A news reporter asked a football coach, "What will you do if in the upcoming championship game you are entering the final few minutes and you are behind by a touchdown?" The answer was, "We will get back to the basics." The coach understood that games are not won or lost on fancy plays but by fundamental playing. Discipleship involves the consistency of the fundamentals more than the intensity of the fancy, thus, twelve weeks to spiritual fitness—*Discipleshape*.

A special thanks go to Helen Hanson, Madonna Krebs, and Beth Cochran for their disciplined preparation of this manuscript, and to my son, James Crawford, a physically fit United States Marine, who like many of the rest of us, is trying to be a spiritually fit disciple of Jesus Christ. *Semper Fidelis.*

phase one

BEING

IN SHAPE:

THE GOAL

OF A DISCIPLE

Being Blessed,
Being Poor in Spirit,
and Being Mournful

A FEW YEARS AGO in St. Petersburg, Florida, I watched the St. Louis Cardinals baseball team in spring training. The Cardinals were the defending World Series champions. For the first half-hour, the players exercised, ran the bases, and played catch. After what seemed an eternity, the players took their positions on the field. To my amazement, the World Series' Most Valuable Player, catcher Darrell Porter, practiced picking a runner off first base on a pitchout from the pitcher for thirty minutes. Before the morning was over, I watched the world champions practice bunting, sliding, and other skills that I had learned in Little League baseball. I left disappointed. I guess I had expected to see these heroes practicing to hit home runs in the bottom of the ninth with the score tied or sliding home on a crucial squeeze bunt. After several hours of reflection, I realized why they had won the World Series in October. They worked on the basics in March. Every so often Christians, like the Cardinals, need to get back to the basics. Little in the teaching ministry of Jesus is more basic than the beatitudes. For a spiritually fit

3

disciple, living out the truths of the beatitudes serves as a worthy goal.

The beatitudes of Jesus have also been called attributes, a more descriptive term. The word beatitude is a name derived from Latin, a rough translation of *beatus*, referring to a state of happiness or bliss. Attributes are defined as inherent characteristics. They are often used for identification purposes in a painting or a sculpture. Thus, this first week's focus is on a word portrait of a spiritually fit disciple. In scripture Jesus repeatedly (eight times in all) draws attention to some aspect of the character of the person who would follow him.

When you are born into a family, you inherit certain characteristics of that family. Likewise, when you enter the family of God, you become known by certain inherent characteristics or attributes. Jesus says his disciples are known by these inherent attributes or beatitudes.

Basic to any program of improvement is this fact: your view of yourself affects how you view everything else. If you desire to be physically muscle-bound, and see yourself as such, then everything in the weight room is viewed as a means to building physical muscle. Thus, we take a look first at who we are to be. We are to be Christlike. Christlikeness, then, is the goal of a spiritually fit disciple and the characteristics of Christ are listed in the beatitudes.

The first twelve verses of the Sermon on the Mount are phase one in the training manual for spiritual fitness. The Sermon on the Mount, of which these verses are a part, has been called the essence of the Christian life, the central document of the Christian faith, Christianity 101, Earth's Greatest Sermon, God's Magna Charta, A Pattern for Life, Christ's Inaugural Address, The Keys to the Kingdom, The Manifesto of the Kingdom, and many other eloquent descriptions. While this sermon contains ideas far ahead even of our advanced time, to the instructor and the instructed, it is basic and fundamental. If you want to be physically fit, you begin by developing your physical attributes. If you want to be spiritually fit, you begin developing your spiritual attributes. So, we begin, as Jesus began with his first disciples, with a look at spiritual attributes. "And when He saw the multitudes . . . " Jesus always saw people in the light of what they could become rather than in their present state. Like the drill instructor looking at raw recruits and seeing beyond their present condition to what they would become in twelve weeks of intensive training, so Jesus saw more in this crowd than any one else. So it is with us. Jesus looks beyond our pain to our possibilities, beyond the hazards to the hope, beyond the mire to the meaning and sees what we can become.

But, before beginning to speak, Jesus "went up on the mountain." Since Jesus was still in Galilee this could have been any of the many hills above the sea, yet the mountain does not dominate the message, the location does not dictate the lesson, the site is not paramount over the sermon. There Jesus "sat down" to teach his disciples. Often Jewish rabbis would teach their students while walking in the countryside or in the city streets. However, when official teaching was to be shared, it was always done from a seated position. Thus, synagogue sermons were delivered while seated (Luke 4:20). The fact that Jesus sat down underlines the significance of his teaching. No casual teaching was this, but crucial, strategic, official teaching.

Interestingly enough, when Jesus sat down, his disciples "came to Him." One of the major characteristics of Jesus was his approachability. No one ever needed to feel as though they could not or should not approach Jesus. Thus, these unfit, spiritually out of shape, poorly equipped disciples "came to Him." Then "He opened His mouth and He began to teach them." Having prayed all night the night before, Jesus was now ready.

BEING BLESSED

A rumor had spread among the people that Jesus was returning to Galilee. It was whispered from small group to small group, from home to home, and business to business.

5

Excitement grew. Suddenly, Jesus arrived, followed by his newly-called disciples and a multitude from Decapolis, Jerusalem, Judea, and beyond Jordan. Others from Tiberias, Bethsaida, and Capernaum would soon join them.

Together these new followers fell in line, leaving their places of business, their homes, their places of learning, their leisure activities. They followed him until they reached the summit of a dusty hill. There Jesus motioned for them to sit. Overwhelming anxiety gripped the multitude as they waited expectantly. His first word to them was "blessed," the Greek word being *markarios*, which is a complete, self-contained joy. Some, feeling the translation "blessed" to be too religious, have substituted the word "happy," but this translation is entirely too secular.

Happiness is a chief goal of humankind. Many philosophers have held that happiness is the *summon bonum*—the highest good in life. In writing the Declaration of Independence, Thomas Jefferson wrote about the "right to life, liberty, and the pursuit of happiness." This pursuit has caused humankind to look in many places and try numerous experiences to discover happiness.

One French philosopher said, "The whole world is on a mad quest for security and happiness." This quest has led to interesting pursuits. It was said that Leo Tolstoy, the Russian fiction writer and social reformer, was told by his older brother Nicholas that the secret of happiness is for everybody to love everybody else and the rules for such a life were written on a green stick buried in the forest under an oak tree near a deep, dark ravine. Ernest Newton in his book entitled, *This Book-Collecting Game*, states about one of his characters, "Gilbert White discovered the formula for complete happiness, but died before making the announcement." A book of famous quotations lists 137 quotes on the subject of happiness. The quest for happiness is universal, but for many happiness is elusive.

But happiness has within it the seeds of its own disqualification. The word is based on *hap*—a chance, a happenstance, whereas the kind of happiness referred to by Jesus means more than this. This "man of sorrows" knew the real meaning of happiness was based not on probabilities, but upon certainties.

Nor is the word *blessed* enough when judged by the popular use of the word. We tend to relate blessing to the material things of life, but this falls far short of the meaning as used by Jesus. This word *markarios* here refers more to an inward, distinctive joy and bliss. It is an inner joy that is untouched by the things of this world and unrelated to the outward accumulation of possessions.

The full meaning of *markarios* may perhaps best be understood when seen from the perspective of the Greeks themselves. They called the island of Cyprus, *hemarkia* (the feminine form of *markarios*) which literally meant *The Happy Isle*. So beautiful, lovely, rich, and fertile was Cyprus that the Greeks believed a person would never need to leave its shores to find genuine happiness. The climate, flowers, fruits, trees, minerals, and natural resources on Cyprus were everything anyone required. Thus, *markarios* describes a distinctive joy whose secret is within itself, untouchable, self-contained, independent of all the happenings of life.

This blessedness was superior to the blessedness known by persons in the past. Just as the Ten Commandments of the Old Testament summarize the Law, so these eight attributes of the New Testament summarize the gospel. Moses was a servant of God; Jesus was the Son of God. Moses came down from a mountain with ten statements engraved on stone tablets. Jesus spoke from a mountain eight statements that became engraved on human hearts and minds. Moses spoke of the law, judgment, and wrath. Jesus opened his mouth and said, "Blessed." The laws spoken by Moses related to outward conduct. The attributes spoken by Jesus related to an inward attitude. Moses spoke of the kind of life one must live to be godly. Jesus spoke of the blessedness of those who are godly. In contrast to the old words stands this new word: blessed.

Likewise, this blessedness is superior to the blessedness known in the present world. Over against the world's offer of quick-fix solutions is this word *blessed*. Over against the world's offer of delight through dependencies is this word *blessed*. Over against the world's offer of meaning through madness is the word *blessed*. Today the world's beatitudes might read like this:

Blessed are the movers and shakers,
>   for they get what they want in this world.
Blessed are those who insulate themselves with a hard shell,
>   for they never get hurt by life.
Blessed are those who gripe and complain,
>   for they seem to get all the attention.
Blessed are the apathetic,
>   for they never feel another's pain.
Blessed are the workaholics,
>   for they get results and promotions.
Blessed are they that explore outer space,
>   for they shall fill the inner void.
Blessed are they who place all their faith in hi-tech,
>   for the future belongs to them.
Blessed are the intellectuals,
>   for they know how to cope with life.
Blessed are the religious,
>   for they will know inner peace.

Finally, this blessedness is superior to what the world offers for the future. Today's voices loudly and confidently proclaim their promises of future hope: utopia reached through universalism, an eternity of eradication, an inheritance of annihilation, a future based on fatalism. "If you give today God will bless you tomorrow," proclaims a televangelist. Others have named it the "delayed gratification ethic." Contrast these offers to the words of Jesus concerning the future of spiritually fit disciples. Using the same word, *markarios*, Jesus speaks from heaven saying, "Blessed are the dead who die in the Lord . . . that they may rest from their labors" (Rev. 14:13).

Having pronounced his disciples "blessed," Jesus begins to list attributes or characteristics often called beatitudes. Eight times Jesus draws attention to an inherent characteristic of one who could be called truly blessed and in so doing outlines the attributes of the spiritually fit disciple.

BEING POOR IN SPIRIT

"Blessed are the poor in spirit" (Matt. 5:3). When Jesus spoke about being poor, he received the undivided attention of many who had come to listen that day. Few things get our attention and response faster than an empty wallet. Yet the poverty of which Jesus spoke was of the spirit. If we are honest with ourselves, we often go days, weeks, months, maybe even years with an empty heart. We are poor in spirit. For me, parts of my seminary education were like this. I would sometimes find myself so caught up in academics that I lost touch with devotion. I knew how to exegete scripture, but I didn't know how to exercise spirituality. It doesn't have to be either/or. It ought to be both/and. But for me, I was studying with an empty heart, spiritually bankrupt.

This particular attribute calls for a complete re-evaluation of true wealth. Surely, wealth is not achieved with the possession of things. Paul said of Jesus, "Though He was rich, yet for your sake He became poor, that you through His poverty might become rich" (2 Cor. 8:9). Concerning himself, Paul wrote:

> Whatever things were gain to me, those things I have counted as loss for the sake of Christ. More than that, I count all things to be loss in view of the surpassing value of knowing Christ Jesus my Lord, for whom I have suffered the loss of all things, and count them but rubbish so that I may gain Christ. (Phil. 3:7–8)

Those things that have constituted wealth and likewise those things that have constituted poverty must be re-evaluated in light of this attribute. Poverty in our day may be best described in this poem by Debbie Groves:

> Poverty is having many acquaintances
> and not knowing any of them.

Poverty is having so many clothes that
    you "haven't a thing to wear."
Poverty is eating so well
    you have to think about going on a diet.
Poverty is having every pill imaginable
    to cure your body's ills because
    you "can't afford to be sick."
Poverty is parents who keep their marriage together
    for your sake.
Poverty is being loaded down with toys
    at birthdays and Christmas
    and then being bored silly
    because there's nothing to do.
Poverty is having two cars, three TVs, and a dishwasher
    and then "roughing it" by going camping
    to get away from it all.
Poverty is the day-to-day going from one building
    to the next
    and never stopping
    to see the beauty
    in the world outside.
Poverty is spending money
    on makeup, deodorants, talcs, and colognes,
    and still being worried
    about the image you are projecting.
Poverty is never being curious
    about the world around you,
    never wanting to explore it
    or the people in it.
Poverty is of the soul as well as the body.

To be poor in spirit is to recognize our spiritual poverty apart from God, to declare spiritual bankruptcy, to realize our own inadequacy. It is to rearrange our résumé, emphasizing those attributes that are from God over those accomplishments that are from self. We may have houses and land and possessions of many kinds, but as a spiritually fit disciple we will possess these

things without allowing them to possess us. Indeed the realiza-
tion and admission that we are a no one, allows you to meet The
One who can make you a someone. As a young, inexperienced
preacher, I stood one Sunday with my well prepared yet prayer-
less sermon, and began to deliver it in my own spiritually unfit
strength. Early in this futile attempt to communicate I remember
thinking of the words to an old hymn by Augustus M. Toplady:

> Nothing in my hands I bring
> Simply to thy cross I cling;
> Naked, come to thee for dress;
> Helpless, look to thee for grace;
> Foul, I to the fountain fly;
> Wash me, Savior, or I die!

How then can we become poor in spirit? First, *recognize our
own spiritual poverty.* Admit that we have no hits in twenty times
at bat. Someone has said, "No man is so ignorant as he who
knows nothing and knows not that he knows nothing. No man
is so sick as he who has a fatal disease and is not aware of it.
No man is so poor as he who is destitute and yet thinks he is
rich."

Jesus told of a rich man who miscalculated his wealth:

> "I will say to my soul, 'Soul, you have many goods laid up for
> many years to come; take your ease, eat, drink and be merry.'
> But God said to him, 'You fool! This very night your soul is
> required of you; and now who will own what you have pre-
> pared?' So is the man who lays up treasure for himself, and is
> not rich toward God." (Luke 12:19–21)

In God's economy helplessness leads to power, emptiness
leads to filling, confession leads to freedom, dependence leads
to independence, and poverty leads to wealth.

Second, *see all gifts, graces, and benefits as being from God.*
Acknowledge that you scored a basket only because a teammate
fed you the ball. The word used by Jesus in this attribute is
ptochos and means a beggar who lives off the alms of another.

The same word described the beggar Lazarus in the parable told by Jesus in Luke 16:20. Like King David, we must acknowledge, "All things come from You" (1 Chron. 29:14), and like Job we must declare, "Naked I came from my mother's womb, and naked I shall return there. The LORD gave and the LORD has taken away. Blessed be the name of the LORD" (Job 1:21).

Third, *take no false pride in accomplishments, achievements, or awards.* Affirm that you won the race because God gave you the ability to run. The opposite of poor in spirit is proud in spirit. The story is told of a woodpecker who took great pride in the fact that while he was pecking on a tree, lightning struck and split the tree in half. And then there is the story of the ant and the elephant who walked dangerously over a hanging bridge. The bridge shook and squeaked and quaked but did not break. On the other side the ant commented, "Man, did we shake that bridge!" These are examples of false pride. James says, "God is opposed to the proud, but gives grace to the humble" (James 4:6).

Fourth, *compare yourself to no one but Jesus Christ.* Announce that your Most Valuable Player trophy looks small compared to a cross. Satan's strategy causes us to compare ourselves to others, especially those who are weaker. Whatever we are today, someone will be greater tomorrow; and whatever we accomplish today, someone will accomplish more tomorrow. Napoleon captured this earthly comparison with one statement: "I am doing now what will fill thousands of volumes in this generation. In the next, one volume will contain it all. In the third, a paragraph, and in the fourth, a single line." Comparison is only valid when we compare ourselves to our Lord. This comparison reminds us of our spiritual poverty.

Fifth, *exercise spiritual muscle.* Activate the abilities God has given you. In my early years of ministry an older minister counseled me, "Don't ever refuse an opportunity to speak for Jesus Christ." I've tried to the best of my time and health to follow his advice. The more you serve, the more you're reminded of spiritual poverty and total dependence on Jesus. C. H. Spurgeon said, "The way to rise in the kingdom is to sink in ourselves." John the Baptist said of Jesus, "He must increase, but I must decrease" (John 3:30).

Each attribute is followed by a promise. Each promise has an earthly and a heavenly application. For those who are poor in spirit, Jesus responded, "theirs is the kingdom of heaven" (Matt. 5:3). This phrase is a favorite of Matthew (appearing thirty-two times in his gospel account) and corresponds to the phrases "the kingdom" and "the kingdom of God" used by other gospel writers. It is a reference to part of a society where God's will is done on earth, even as in heaven.

This kingdom is both here and now as well as then and there. We who profess faith in Christ have dual citizenship. I am a citizen of the United States because I was born here. I am a citizen of heaven because I have been reborn. The phrase refers to a reign more than a region, to a presence more than a place and belongs uniquely to the followers of Jesus Christ. The full meaning of the word "theirs" is "theirs and theirs alone."

What a tragedy to be a follower of Jesus, an heir of the kingdom, and not understand its present reality in our hearts. Graham Kendrick captured this present tense kingdom with his words:

> The kingdom of our God is here.
> Heaven is in my heart.
> The presence of His majesty.
> Heaven is in my heart.
> And in His presence joy abounds.
> Heaven is in my heart.
> The light of holiness surrounds.
> Heaven in my heart.

There was something different about Morris Siegel. On the surface he seemed like an average Los Angeles street person— roaming about in dark alleys, sleeping outdoors, carrying all he owned in an old shopping cart. He died the way one expects a street person to die—in an alley. But something about him was different. Maybe it was his three bank accounts containing a total of $207,421.

Ten years earlier, Morris' father had died and left the money to him. When Morris did not claim it, the Division of Unclaimed Property tracked him down, and his family forced him to accept it. He did not show up at the ceremony when the cash was handed over. He took enough of the money to buy an old car, where he slept in bad weather. Relatives rented an apartment for him, but he never went there. He died December 14, 1989, with three dollars in his pocket and an untouched fortune in the bank.

Old Morris lived a wasted life and died a futile death, but we can't be too quick to point a finger at him. He was only dealing with the temporary while many of us are playing the same losing game with the eternal.

Finally, we can pray with Hannah, "The LORD makes poor and rich; He brings low, He also exalts. He raises the poor from the dust, He lifts the needy from the ash heap to make them sit with nobles" (1 Sam. 2:7–8). Those who come to God in spiritual poverty, with broken hearts, depart with spiritual wealth and mended hearts: "For thus says the high and exalted One who lives forever, whose name is Holy. I dwell on a high and holy place, and also with the contrite and lowly of spirit in order to revive the spirit of the lowly and to revive the heart of the contrite" (Isa. 57:15). When in admission of spiritual poverty we give up our own little kingdoms, God replaces them with the kingdom of heaven.

BEING MOURNFUL

"Blessed are those who mourn" (Matt. 5:4). Sorrow is described by nine different words in the New Testament, but the strongest of these words, *pantheo*, is used here. It refers to a grief so consuming that it cannot be hidden. The same word is used to describe the reaction of the disciples following the death of Jesus. When Mary Magdalene rushed to inform them of the resurrection, she found them "mourning and weeping" (Mark 16:10).

It seems strange to speak of the blessedness of the broken-hearted, the joy of sorrow, the gladness of grief, the treasure of tears. If you are blessed, why would you mourn? If you mourned, how could you be blessed? But this is God's plan and from it we learn not only how to cope with life's sorrows but also how to know and understand God better.

There is a story about a Jewish rabbi who was deeply loved by his students. One day an outgoing student rushed into the rabbi's office and exclaimed, "Do you know I love you?" The rabbi looked up from his books and asked, "Do you know what hurts me?" Confused, the student responded, "Your question is irrelevant." "No," returned the rabbi. "Only if you know what hurts me, can you really love me."

Through our mourning, we enter into a deeper understanding of the "man of sorrows" who was "acquainted with grief" (Isa. 53:3), and having learned from him, we can then bear our own sorrows. Robert Browning Hamilton wrote:

> I walked a mile with Pleasure.
>> She chattered all the way,
> But left me none the wiser
>> For all she had to say.
> I walked a mile with Sorrow.
>> And ne'er a word said she;
> But, oh, the things I learned from her,
>> When Sorrow walked with me!

There are three general areas in which we mourn: for human sorrows, for the evils of this world, and for the sin in our own lives. First, we mourn over human sorrow. Mourning occurs in those who have lost teenagers to peer pressure, a spouse to another love or to death, a job to someone more qualified, a home to fire, flood, or storm, a degree to financial or academic shortcomings, or an exercise program to an injury. The mourning takes place whether the reasons are justified or not.

Some mourning over human disappointment is needed. The musician Elgar heard a beautiful young girl give an almost flawless performance and then responded, "She will be great when something happens to break her heart."

Some mourning is so private we are prone to sing the words of the old Spiritual, "Nobody knows the trouble I've seen." Paul wrote to young Timothy concerning an unknown sorrow: "I constantly remember you in my prayers night and day, longing to see you, even as I recall your tears" (2 Tim. 1:3–4).

Perhaps the greatest of human sorrows is the mourning related to death. Following his wife's death, Abraham "went in to mourn for Sarah and to weep for her" (Gen. 23:2). The shortest verse in the Bible expresses the mourning of Jesus at the death of Lazarus: "Jesus wept" (John 11:35).

A woman in a church where I served as Interim Pastor lost her mother unexpectedly on a Friday following routine surgery. I conducted the funeral on Sunday afternoon. On Tuesday the woman's father died, and his funeral was held on Thursday. In six days she lost both parents. Apart from the comfort that is promised to those who mourn, she could not have borne this sorrow. In *Hamlet*, Shakespeare writes, "When sorrows come, they come not as single spies, but in battalions."

The Irish poet Thomas Moore, overwhelmed by the death of his oldest daughter, followed by the death of his youngest daughter wrote:

Come, ye disconsolate, where're ye languish,
Come to the mercy seat, fervently kneel,
Here bring your wounded hearts, here tell your anguish;
Earth has no sorrow that heav'n cannot heal.

A second area of life where we often mourn is in our relationship to the evils of this world: children of addicted parents, women abused, mental institutions, AIDS victims and their families, terminal cancer, divorce courts. While there are often innocent victims in each of these cases, we mourn the consequences of the evil that effects them. Abraham Lincoln said, "I feel sorry for the man who can't feel the whip when it is laid on the other man's back."

The captive children of Israel did not adapt to the conditions of Babylon and the injustices experienced there, but rather mourned for the return and restoration of Jerusalem. That which the world offers often leaves us in sorrow.

When Jesus thought of Jerusalem he lamented, "O Jerusalem, Jerusalem, who kills the prophets and stones those who are sent to her! How often I wanted to gather your children together, the way a hen gathers her chicks under her wings, and you were unwilling" (Matt. 23:37).

I have a pastor friend who drove to the top of a high hill over the city in which he served. As he thought of his city and the many injustices of it, he wept. He said he went there to pray but was overcome with the thoughts of evil in his city. His thoughts that day could have matched those of Frank Laubach who said, "Forgive me Lord for ever looking on my world with dry eyes."

The Greek word *mourn* was translated by Martin Luther into the German word *leidtragen*, meaning *sorrow-bearing*. Recently a drive-by shooting happened near my office. An eleven-year-old girl was accidentally killed by a bullet meant for another. While the little girl's mother was shown weeping, the television stations repeatedly aired a tape of a neighbor of the deceased, crying and asking why. She was "sorrow-bearing" for a fellow mother.

Still a third area in which we mourn is the area of sin in our lives. This is most likely the mourning Jesus had first in mind when he stated this attribute. It is here that the Christian life begins. Just as physical pain precedes physical birth so mourning over sin precedes spiritual birth. Just as conviction of sin must precede salvation, so you must grieve over your sin before asking Jesus to forgive you. As we continue to sin, we continue to mourn over our sin. Just as sore muscles precede physical fitness so confession precedes forgiveness and spiritual fitness. Yet how much better to mourn for sin and ask forgiveness than mourn because of the consequences of unforgiven sin.

Sin continues to pervade our life even though we have been saved. We continue to be tempted and we continue to yield to temptation. The closer we live with the Lord, the more we are conscious of our own sin. Isaiah became keenly aware of his sin when he came into the presence of God (Isa. 6:5). Standing unworthy in the presence of a holy God, standing unholy on holy ground, standing with unclean lips in the presence of holy perfection, Isaiah cried out with a mixture of confession and adoration.

One of the interesting studies in the life of Paul is how he viewed himself as his knowledge of Jesus increased. Around A.D. 48, Paul described himself as "an apostle (not sent from men nor through the agency of man, but through Jesus Christ and God the Father, who raised Him from the dead)" (Gal. 1:1). Around A.D. 55 Paul described himself as "the least of the apostles" (1 Cor. 15:9). In A.D. 63, Paul called himself "the very least of all saints" (Eph. 3:8). And finally, after years of missionary labor and years of walking with his Lord, Paul identified himself by saying, "Jesus came into the world to save sinners, among whom I am foremost of all" (1 Tim. 1:15).

The more we walk with and know the Lord, the more we are likely to mourn over our own sins. The 18th century missionary to the American Indians, David Brainerd, wrote in his journal on October 18, 1740, "In my morning devotions my soul was exceedingly melted and bitterly mourned over my exceeding sinfulness and vileness."

Following this attribute of mourning is the resulting promise, "they shall be comforted" (Matt. 5:4). The word for comforted is *parakalein* and it has four meanings. The first is the obvious idea of comfort, yet this is the rarest meaning. The second is helper or counselor. When Jesus told his disciples he was going away, he promised to send them "another Helper" (John 14:16), a reference to the Holy Spirit. The third meaning is encouragement or exhortation, that is, a challenge to get back in the midst of life having been temporarily sidetracked by sorrow.

Finally, the word comforted includes the idea of being invited to a banquet or celebration. Jesus said, "Blessed are you who weep now, for you shall laugh" (Luke 6:21). The Psalmist promised, "Those who sow in tears shall reap with joyful shouting" (Ps. 126:5) and "Weeping may last for the night, but a shout of joy comes in the morning" (Ps. 30:5). How many times have we seen the teammates of an injured athlete mourning over an injury. Then the same team, dedicates the game or the season to the injured colleague and eventually we are treated to the scene of a victorious locker room where someone reminds the world that they won for their fallen teammate. The grief had given way to celebration.

This much we know: whatever mourning exists in this life and to whatever degree our Lord comforts and relieves that mourning, it will someday end. In John's picture of heaven he says, "He will wipe away every tear from their eyes; and there will no longer be any death; there will no longer be any mourning, or crying, or pain" (Rev. 21:4). According to Matthew 5:3–4, the spiritually fit disciple is blessed. He or she is blessed by being poor in spirit and by mourning. The resulting promises are inheritance of the kingdom of heaven and the comfort and celebration of the Holy Spirit's presence.

DISCIPLESHAPE

EXERCISES FOR SPIRITUAL FITNESS

Day One Using terminology normally used to describe physical fitness, how would you describe the current status of your spiritual fitness? What goals would you set for your twelve week study? Record one goal here: _____

_____

Day Two What will it take to reach the above stated goal? Identify some preliminary steps to reaching this goal. What must you do first? _____

_____

Day Three Keeping in mind the meaning of *markarios*, what would have to happen today for you to feel genuinely blessed? Spend some time in prayer right now. Ask God to help you feel blessed today and to help you experience inner joy.

Day Four "To be poor in spirit . . . is to rearrange your résumé." Think about your résumé and how you want to be known. What are the priority characteristics on your résumé? Does "poor in spirit" appear? How could it be a part of your résumé?

Day Five Keeping in mind the meaning of *pantheo*, how long has it been since you mourned? List here one sin in your life over which you mourn. Commit it to God in prayer. _____

_____

Scriptural strengths to remember:
1. Matthew 5:3
2. Philippians 3:7–8
3. Matthew 5:4

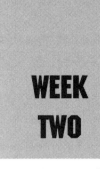

Being Meek, Being Righteous, and Being Merciful

SOMEONE, probably a frustrated teacher, has proposed the following scenario: Jesus took his disciples up on the mountain and began to teach them: "Blessed are the poor in spirit, for theirs is the kingdom of heaven. Blessed are those who mourn, for they shall be comforted."

Then Simon Peter asked, "Do we have to write this down?"

And Andrew said, "Will this be on a test?"

And Philip said, "I don't have a pencil."

And James said, "Do we have to turn this in?"

And John said, "This is not fair. The other disciples don't have to learn this."

And Judas said, "What does this have to do with real life?"

Then one of the Pharisees who was standing nearby said, "Where is your lesson plan and teaching outline of your main points? Where is your anticipatory set and learning objective in the cognitive domain?"

And Jesus wept.

Hopefully, after one week, none of the above questions are yours. As we move on in Matthew 5, we discover this week the attributes of meekness, righteousness and mercy.

BEING MEEK

"Blessed are the meek" (Matt. 5:5 KJV). The word translated by some as "meek" and others as "gentle" is *praus*. But this word does not mean today what it meant when Jesus uttered it. The idea of weak, soft, or mild is not at all the proper meaning. Given that meaning, what meek person ever inherited the earth? The Romans sought power and despised meekness. The Jews were looking for a military messiah. No one in Jesus' day had a category to describe meekness. It is the same in our day. Ask someone, "Who inherits the earth?" and names of powerful persons or countries come to mind as do board rooms and power politics. We are a people of power and might. No one has ever really lived in *Mr. Rogers' Neighborhood.*

In 1675 Sir Christopher Wren, the architect, laid the cornerstone for St. Paul's Cathedral in London after thirty-five years of construction. In 1710 Queen Anne paid a visit to the Cathedral. Wren waited anxiously for her reaction. Completing her tour, the Queen remarked, "It is awful, it is amusing, and it is artificial." The great architect breathed a sigh of relief. In 1710 awful meant awe-inspiring, amusing meant amazing, and artificial meant artistic. Words change in meaning. Such is the case with *praus.*

The word used by Jesus, *praus,* meant focusing on the needs of others rather than on the needs of self. Others' needs are of more importance than the things we possess or the ideas we defend or the achievements we accomplish. As others' needs become elevated, personal needs become relegated. Also, the one who is meek focuses on persons rather than things. Cultivating relationships is more important than collecting things. The status in life for a disciple is measured by the character of acquaintances rather than the amount of possessions.

Likewise, the one who is meek focuses on love rather than revenge. There is a story of an elderly minister who was awakened one morning to the sound of the tiles being torn off his roof and thrown to the ground by some of his enemies. He awakened his wife with instructions to fix a big breakfast. Inviting his enemies into the house, he insisted they eat since they had been working so hard. Prior to eating, the old minister prayed for his enemies and their families. Following breakfast, they went out and put the tiles back on the roof—a response to meekness when revenge was possible.

Often words are best understood when they become flesh. Two persons in the Bible are referred to as meek. One person is Moses who was anything but weak. Contrast this man who stands without his sandals before a burning bush in humility, submission, gentleness, tameness and patience with the man who confronted the mightiest ruler of his day with these words, "Thus says the LORD, the God of Israel, `Let My people go.'" (Exod. 5:1). It is the same man, Moses, of whom it was written, "Now the man Moses was very meek, above all the men which were upon the face of the earth" (Num. 12:3 KJV).

Jesus is the second person called meek in the Bible. Contrast this man who came into Jerusalem "meek, and sitting upon an ass [donkey]" (Matt. 21:5 KJV) with the man who twice drove the money changers out of the Temple and overthrew their tables (John 2:13–16; Luke 19:45–48). It is the same man, Jesus, who on one occasion said, "Take my yoke upon you, and learn of me; for I am meek and lowly in heart" (Matt. 11:29 KJV).

This contrast is further seen in the following poem by Harry Kemp:

> I saw the Conquerors riding by
>   With cruel lips and faces wan:
> Musing on kingdoms sacked and burned
>   There rode the Mongol Genghis Kahn;
> And Alexander, like a god,
>   Who sought to weld the world in one;

And Caesar with his laurel wreath;
>And like the thing from Hell, the Hun;
And leading, like a star the van,
>Heedless of upstretched arm and groan
Inscrutable Napoleon went,
>Dreaming of empire, and alone . . .
Then all they perished from the earth
>As fleeting shadows from a glass
And, conquering down the centuries,
>Came Christ, the Swordless, on an ass!

There are essentially five meanings of the word meek. First, it means gentleness. The world says, "might is right," "dog eat dog," and "the survival of the fittest." These secular philosophies are glamorized by movies, magazines and the media. In contrast, the spiritually fit disciple acts in gentleness even when he or she has the ability to act with severity.

Second, it means submissiveness. Again, the world says, "be in control," "wear clothes that show power," and "use hairstyles and makeup that demonstrate authority." In contrast, the spiritually fit disciple stands empty-handed before God in total dependence and self-surrender.

Third, it means tameness, coming from the idea of breaking the will of a wild animal so it can be used more efficiently. The world says "go wild," "live it up," and "party hearty." In contrast, the spiritually fit disciple allows God to break their sinful, selfish will and remake them into what they could never have been before.

Fourth, it means patience. The world says, "now," demonstrated by its quick-fix, fast food, instant copies, minute-lube, while-you-wait attitude. In contrast, the spiritually fit disciple is "quick to hear, slow to speak and slow to anger" (James 1:19).

Fifth, it means humility. The world says, "I've earned my keep," "What's mine is mine," and "I deserve more." In contrast, the spiritually fit disciple understands that everything is a gift from God, based on grace.

These five meanings of the word meek are personified in the life of George Frederick Handel. In his later days this stooped-shouldered old man could be seen shuffling through the dark streets of London. When his music was performed, the four decades of thrilling work was often broken up by street gangs. His small fortune was gradually depleted resulting in abject poverty. His health was broken and he was paralyzed on his right side. The medical doctors gave him no hope. But he worked, took hot baths for hours, exercised, and recovered. He completed four operas in rapid succession, but in the midst of renewed acclaim, again suffered major health problems. Once again he descended to poverty. With no more engagements, Handel appeared defeated and in despair.

This gentle, submissive, tame, patient and humble man would, however, write again. Coming home one evening from a purposeless walk, he found in his room a package—a musical score entitled, "A Sacred Oratorio" written by Charles Jennens. As Handel looked over its pages, God began to do what God can do with one who is meek. Without stopping, Handel charted score after score, often refusing to eat. Exhausted, he finally finished and expressed his elation: "I did think I did see all Heaven before me and the great God himself!" Handel collapsed into a seventeen-hour sleep, while on a nearby table lay the greatest oratorio ever composed, the *Messiah*. "Blessed are the meek."

The resulting promise for the meek is, "they shall inherit the earth" (Matt. 5:5). This is almost an exact quote from Psalm 37:11. In the Old Testament, the "earth" refers to the promised land while in the New Testament it refers to all the blessings of God.

I was recently involved in the settlement of an inheritance. Some time before death the relative became ill and in the midst of the illness changed the will. This was not known until after the relative's death when the will was probated. A few other relatives and myself were left out of the revised will. A contest of the will produced only a minimal out-of-court settlement, much of which went to attorney fees. I was deeply hurt. The monetary loss, although heavy, was secondary to the emotional trauma of being left out. The experience, even though painful, helped me appreciate the assurance of my inheritance as a member of the family of God. As a joint-heir with Jesus, I will "inherit a blessing" (1 Pet. 3:9).

The earth is not to be possessed, grabbed at, or fought over. It is to be inherited by those who through faith have become joint-heirs with Jesus Christ. "The earth is the LORD's, and all it contains" (Ps. 24:1). George McDonald said, "We cannot see the world as God means it in the future, save as our souls are characterized by meekness. In meekness we are its only inheritors. Meekness alone makes the spiritual retina pure to receive God's things as they are, mingling with them neither imperfection nor impurity."

The earth belongs to the powerless and disenfranchised disciples, and to us. Those who from time to time possess it by force will lose it, for "The kingdom of the world has become the kingdom of our Lord and of His Christ" (Rev. 11:15) and earth is the front porch of "a house not made with hands, eternal in the heavens" (2 Cor. 5:1). To inherit this earth is to also inherit, "a new heaven and a new earth" (Rev. 21:1).

Therefore, "Seek the LORD, all you meek of the earth" (Zeph. 2:3 NKJV).

BEING RIGHTEOUS

"Blessed are those who hunger and thirst for righteousness" (Matt. 5:6). Thousands of people threw themselves into the Tiber River to end their lives because of the famine in 436 B.C. in Rome. Similar famine struck England in 1005 and all of Europe in 879, 1016, and 1162. In the nineteenth century hunger attacked Russia, China, India, and Ireland. In recent years parts of India, Africa and Latin America have been devastated by hunger. Millions have died in this decade of hunger and it's related diseases.

On a recent three-week prayer journey, our team was to walk for several hours per day in some very hot climates. I tried my best to get in good physical shape before the experience. Even my best efforts were not enough. Nor was it enough to carry plastic water bottles every where I went. On a cloudless day, in a middle-eastern country, with the sum beaming down and sweat pouring off my face, I almost dehydrated. It was in this same area, in this same kind of climate, that Jesus talked about thirst to those who understood it's meaning.

In an overweight society, where people quench their hunger and thirst by opening the refrigerator door, hunger and thirst have only relative meaning. More than dictionary words, "hunger and thirst" are words that must be experienced—like the words "pain" and "love"—to be fully understood. In a country where the average wage was eight pence per day, the people had experiential knowledge of hunger and thirst. Jesus spoke this attribute to felt needs.

Just as physical hunger and thirst lead to physical necessities of life, so spiritual hunger and thirst lead to spiritual necessities of life. This attribute is not about luxuries. The Psalmist likened these drives to that of the little deer that thirsted for water, "As the deer pants for the water brooks, So my soul pants for You, O God. My soul thirsts for God" (Ps. 42:1–2).

The major difference between physical hunger and thirst and spiritual hunger and thirst is in capacity. In physical hunger and thirst consumption diminishes capacity. I re-learn this difference every time I eat at an all-you-can-eat buffet. When I am full, I can eat or drink no more until I become hungry and thirsty again. In spiritual hunger and thirst consumption increases capacity. The more I take in, the more I desire.

Jesus said he himself would be our spiritual food: "I am the bread of life; he who comes to Me will not hunger, and he who believes in Me will never thirst" (John 6:35). Likewise Jesus said he would supply our spiritual water: "Everyone who drinks of this water [from the well at Sychar] will thirst again; but whoever drinks of the water that I will give him shall never thirst;

but the water that I will give him shall become in him a well of water springing up to eternal life" (John 4:13–14). A popular chorus by Martha Stevens says:

> Come to the water, stand by my side;
> I know you are thirsty, you won't be denied.

Although the word righteousness (*dikaiosune*) sometimes means justice or justification, here the word refers to doing the things God is for and refraining from those things God is against. A family of dinner guests had just sat down at the table to eat when the spoiled little son noticed he didn't want any of the food on the table. Announcing his displeasure, he got up and stormed through a nearby door. Trying to ease the tension, the mother exclaimed, "Well, now that he's gone, we can enjoy this delicious meal in peace." To which the hostess replied, "Oh, he'll be back. He just went into a closet." If we are hungry and thirsty for anything other than what God has for us, we simply close ourselves off from God's best and close ourselves in to a lesser existence. Refusing the things of God is as foolish as the spoiled child storming into a closet.

There are some prerequisites to being truly hungry and thirsty for righteousness. First, *we can only be truly hungry and thirsty for righteousness if we are dissatisfied with ourselves spiritually.* We know the difference in getting up from a meal fully satisfied with good food versus getting up from a meal where we have eaten something we did not really want and that does not now agree with our digestive system. We are now dissatisfied with ourselves and eager to eat a good meal again. Someone who is self-satisfied spiritually is not a good candidate for desiring right-living with God. In fact, the person who least desires righteousness may be the one who needs it most. We must have a genuine desire to be emancipated from selfish concerns. Like Paul, we must conclude, "Wretched man that I am!" (Rom. 7:24). Surely, no person is so empty as the person who thinks he or she is full, but in reality is full of the wrong thing. Jesus spoke harsh words to a church in this condition, "You say

`I am rich, and have become wealthy, and have need of nothing,' and you do not know that you are wretched and miserable and poor and blind and naked" (Rev. 3:17).

Second, *we can only be truly hungry and thirsty for righteousness when we become free from dependence on external things for satisfaction.* At the conclusion of a football bowl game, I heard a member of the losing team say to a reporter, "Our fans weren't here and we weren't ever in the game." The athlete is not really hungry for victory until the roar of the crowd becomes secondary to winning. As long as the things of this world bring complete, lasting satisfaction, there can be no desire for righteousness. Paul so desired right living with God he was willing to set aside "a righteousness of my own derived from the Law" in order "that I may know Him" (Phil. 3:9–10). This was not the case with one of Paul's companions, Demas, of whom Paul said, "Having loved this present world, has deserted me" (2 Tim. 4:10).

Third, *we can only be truly hungry and thirsty for righteousness if we crave the things of God.* After a hard work-out, a long run, or a difficult competition, the physically fit athlete is anxious to eat. No one has to persuade them to eat. Those who are hungry and thirsty do not have to be called to the table repeatedly. Instead, like Isaiah, they cry, "At night my soul longs for You, indeed, my spirit within me seeks You diligently" (Isa. 26:9) and like the Psalmist they exclaim, "My soul is crushed with longing after Your ordinances at all times" (Ps. 119:20). The person who craves the things of God observes the things of the world and confesses, "Every good thing given and every perfect gift is from above" (James 1:17). Like dead persons who desire no food or water, the person who does not crave for the things of God is most likely "dead in . . . trespasses and sins" (Eph. 2:1). They go from one earthly side-show to another craving the wrong things.

Fourth, *we can only be truly hungry and thirsty for righteousness if we desire to be around the people of God.* Have you ever noticed how physical fitness buffs hang out together? They enjoy each other's company. They swap trade secrets and become more physically fit because of the support of like-minded friends. The biblical principal is, "Iron sharpens iron, so one man sharpens another" (Prov. 27:17). Godless friends provide a good challenge for evangelism and ministry but provide a poor substitute for Christian fellowship. Some of the saddest words written about any disciple are those written on the night of Jesus' resurrection when he appeared to the disciples, "But Thomas, one of the twelve, called Didymus, was not with them when Jesus came" (John 20:24). Among other things, Thomas missed the strength that comes from Christian fellowship. Somewhere Thomas, the doubter, was trying to make it alone.

One word of warning. Avoid impulsive eating or drinking. Instant gratification leads to long term debt. The disciple who desires spiritual fitness must learn to discern between what is spiritually healthy and what is spiritually unhealthy. Just as God made us with a physical appetite that tells us when we are really hungry, so God made us with a spiritual appetite that tells us when we need spiritual nourishment. No one has to explain to a baby that he or she is hungry. It is a created drive. Not so with impulsive eating and drinking. We learn how to yield to this temptation. While on Sabbatical leave in Boston, I discovered a Dunkin' Donut Shop every few blocks and in nearly every subway station. Because I ate donuts impulsively, both my weight and blood pressure went up. It took many months to correct this impulsiveness. We must be careful, spiritually, that we don't jump quickly to some apparent truth that offers instant gratification. It may give us spiritual indigestion.

The resulting promise for hungering and thirsting after righteousness is not a reward for achievement but rather a response to an attribute: "they shall be satisfied" (Matt. 5:6). The word for satisfied is *chortazesthia* and means to be stuffed, filled to capacity. This word is a passive verb. We do not satisfy ourselves; we are satisfied by God.

The promise is filling to satisfaction. In Greek mythology King Tantalus was punished for offending the gods. As punishment he was placed in a body of water up to his chin. Every time he tried to drink, the water receded. Furthermore, choice fruit hung just over his head. Yet when he tried to reach it, it too receded. He became the symbol of teasing and his name provided the root of our word, tantalize. Jesus offers real filling to satisfaction, not teasing. The Bible says "eat what is good, and delight yourself in abundance" (Isa. 55:2). Claire Cloninger and Martin J. Nystrom said it this way:

> Come to the table of mercy,
> Prepared with the wine and the bread
> All who are hungry and thirsty,
> Come and your souls will be fed.

The encouraging part of this attribute is that spiritual filling is offered not to the one who is already righteous, but to those who are hungry and thirsty for righteousness. The possession is available to those still on the pathway.

Even though we still may hunger and thirst along the way, ultimately we will feast at the marriage supper of the Lamb (Rev. 19:9) in a place where "They will hunger no more, neither thirst any more" (Rev. 7:16). In that day we shall truly be spiritually fit disciples. Until then we join with that Welsh Methodist, William Williams in singing:

> Guide me, O thou great Jehovah,
> Pilgrim through this barren land;
> I am weak, but thou art mighty;
> Hold me with thy powerful hand;
> Bread of heaven, Bread of heaven,
> Feed me till I want no more,
> Feed me till I want no more.

BEING MERCIFUL

"Blessed are the merciful" (Matt. 5:7). In the Old Testament the parallel word is *chesedh*, translated ninety-six times as "mercy," thirty-eight times as "kindness," and thirty times as "lovingkindness." Indeed, "The earth is full of Your loving kindness, O LORD" (Ps. 119:64). Again, God "delights in mercy" (Mic. 7:18 NKJV). God showed mercy to Lot in the escape from Sodom (Gen. 19:19) and to Jacob as his life was protected (Gen. 32:10). Furthermore God extended mercy to Joseph as he rose to power in Egypt (Gen. 39:21) and to David by giving him a son to succeed him as King (2 Sam. 7:12). The Children of Israel experienced God's mercy as they were directed by God (Ps. 106:7).

The word for mercy in the New Testament is *eleos* which is used twenty-seven times. Whereas in the Old Testament the idea was outgoing kindness, in the New Testament the idea contained in this word is outgoing love, the opposite of self-centeredness. It is not just an emotion, but emotion with action. "God so loved" is an emotion, but "God so loved the world, that He gave His only begotten Son" (John 3:16) is actualized outgoing love. Michael W. Smith wrote:

> Great is the Lord, He is faithful and true;
> By His mercy He proves He is love.

Jesus further illustrated this attribute in the parable of the Good Samaritan when he said of the Samaritan, who had discovered a beaten man by the road:

> "A Samaritan, who was on a journey, came upon him; and when he saw him, he felt compassion, and came to him, and bandaged up his wounds, pouring oil and wine on them; and he put him on his own beast, and brought him to an inn and took care of him." (Luke 10:33–34)

Mercy is shown to the one who is wrong, as in the story of the unmerciful slave (Matt. 18:23–35) and also shown to the one who is in need, as in blind Bartimaeus crying, "Jesus, Son of David, have mercy on me!" (Mark 10:47). Further, the New Testament teaches us that God is "rich in mercy, because of His great love with which He loved us" (Eph. 2:4); that God invites us to, "draw near with confidence to the throne of grace, that we may receive mercy" (Heb. 4:16); that we have a living hope, "according to His great mercy" (1 Pet. 1:3); and finally that we are to "Be merciful, just as your Father is merciful" (Luke 6:36).

Mercy does not characterize our world. Today the world prefers to insulate itself against the pain and hurt of humanity. Today the world exacts revenge and shuns forgiveness.

Napoleon was moved by a mother's plea for a pardon on behalf of her son. Napoleon responded that it was the young man's second offense. The second offense and justice demanded death. The mother responded, "I do not ask for justice, I plead for mercy." To which Napoleon replied, "But he does not deserve mercy." "Sire," she cried, "it would not be mercy if he deserved it, and mercy is all I ask for." Napoleon granted the pardon on the basis of mercy.

A student of mine shared a story from his days as a High School quarterback. It was the biggest football game of his senior season. His team was behind by four points with time enough for only one play before the first half ended. The coach called for a pass play. My student, the quarterback, rolled out and threw a perfect pass to the wide receiver. The opposing player who was defending this wide receiver, fell down. The wide receiver was wide open and all alone. No one was between him and the goal line. A half-time lead was in everyone's minds. But the wide receiver dropped the ball. All through the half-time break, no one in the locker room spoke to the wide receiver. He was sure that his playing days were over. As the team prepared to leave the locker room for the second half, the coach surprised everyone by announcing that this same wide receiver who cost his team a half-time lead would be starting at wide receiver in the second half. He deserved justice. He received mercy. He also scored the winning touchdown late in the game to give his school the victory.

When the reality of our mistakes begin to overwhelm us, the truth of God's mercy rescues us. The old hymn by William R. Newell says it this way:

By God's Word at last my sin I learned;
Then I trembled at the law I'd spurned,
Till my guilty soul imploring turned
To Calvary.

Mercy there was great and grace was free;
Pardon there was multiplied to me;
There my burdened soul found liberty
At Calvary.

How then can we who are recipients of such outgoing love show mercy to others? First, *we show mercy through concern for others*. Because we have experienced God's great mercy, we should be concerned for those who never or seldom experience it. Even on the cross, Jesus showed merciful concern to the repentant thief (Luke 23:43) who with dry throat and collapsing muscles was painfully paying for his crime against society. Then he showed mercy to his mother (John 19:26–27) whose grief was mixed with thoughts of an uncertain future with no husband and now no oldest son. Finally he showed mercy to those who were killing him (Luke 23:34) who even in their military discipline may have questioned the implementing of these orders.

Second, *we show mercy by striving to right social wrongs*. Jesus fed the hungry, restored the disenfranchised, condemned the corrupt leaders, befriended the friendless, healed the sick, and challenged the prejudiced. Can we do any less? Mercy allows us to see from another's perspective, think with another's mind, and feel with another's emotions. It is much deeper than sympathy. It is empathy followed by action on another's behalf. It "seasons justice" as William Shakespeare wrote in *The Merchant of Venice*:

The quality of mercy is not strain'd,
It droppeth as the gentle rain from heaven
Upon the place beneath: it is twice bless'd;
It blesseth him that gives and him that takes:
'Tis mightiest in the mightiest; it becomes

The throned monarch better than his crown;
His sceptre shows the force of temporal power,
The attribute to awe and majesty,
Wherein doth sit the dread and fear of kings;
But mercy is above the sceptred sway,
It is enthroned in the hearts of kings,
It is an attribute to God himself,
And earthly power doth then show likest God's
When mercy seasons justice.

Third, *we show mercy by sharing the gospel with the unsaved.* When humankind fell, God immediately activated a pre-arranged plan of redemption, culminating in the greatest act of outgoing love, the death of Christ on the cross. Paul says, "He saved us, not on the basis of deeds which we have done in righteousness, but according to His mercy" (Titus 3:5). That saving mercy is available to all. When our lives are touched by the magnificent mercy of God, we should willingly share it with others.

The resulting promise here is that the one who is merciful "shall receive mercy" (Matt. 5:7). Later in this same sermon Jesus said, "In the way you judge, you will be judged" (Matt. 7:2) and James added, "Judgement will be merciless to one who has shown no mercy" (James 2:13).

This then is God's way: If you would have truth, you must be true; if you would have love, you must love; if you would have friendship, you must be a friend; if you would have mercy, you must be merciful. Your willingness to show mercy is part of the prerequisite in receiving it.

An inscription on a tombstone in an Aberdeen churchyard speaks of mercy received and mercy given.

Here lie I, Martin Elginbrodde;
Ha'e mercy o' my soul, Lord God;
As I wad do, were I Lord God,
An' ye were Martin Elginbrodde.

In his plays *Adronacles and the Lion*, George Bernard Shaw portrays his character walking through a jungle and meeting a lion in great pain with an infected thorn in its paw. Due to his condition, the lion was too weak to be dangerous. The man took out the thorn, poured alcohol in the wound, and went on his way. Years later the man, a Christian, was thrown into an arena of lions. One lion recognized him, nestled up against him, and protected him from the others. Mercy was shown to the merciful.

Ultimately, in addition to the mercy we are shown on this earth, Jude encourages us to "keep yourselves in the love of God, waiting anxiously for the mercy of our Lord Jesus Christ to eternal life" (Jude 21).

Earlier we saw that the spiritually fit disciple is blessed by being poor in spirit and by mourning. To these two attributes we have now added three more: meekness, righteousness and mercy, with their resulting promises of inheritance of the earth, filling to satisfaction and obtaining mercy. Three more attributes await us in the next week.

EXERCISES FOR SPIRITUAL FITNESS

Day One Keeping in mind the meaning of *praus,* what evidences are there of meekness in your life? List one evidence here: _____

_____

Day Two How desperately do you hunger and thirst for righteousness? Can you cite one example of your hunger and thirst? Write it here: _____

_____

Day Three Keeping in mind the meaning of *dikaiosune,* what is there in your life that God is "for"? _____

_____

And "against"?_____
In prayer, commit these to God today.

Day Four Keeping in mind the meanings of the words translated as merciful, what is one way you can express mercy to someone else today? Write it here and seek to fulfill it: _____

_____

Day Five How have you received mercy this week from God?

_____

From another person? _____

_____

Give thanks right now for mercy received.

Scriptural strengths to remember:
1. Matthew 5:5
2. James 1:19
3. Matthew 5:6
4. Matthew 5:7

WEEK THREE

Being Pure in Heart,
Being a Peacemaker,
and Being Persecuted

THE MIGHTY MISSISSIPPI RIVER winds 2,350 miles from its beginning near the U.S.–Canada border to its ending at the Gulf of Mexico. In comparing its size and majesty to other rivers they knew, the Native Americans named it the "great river." More than a mile in width in some places, it digs to a bed of 100 feet in other places. With more than 250 tributaries, the Mississippi is one of the longest river systems in the world. As great as the Mississippi River is, it all begins as a two-foot deep, narrow stream, flowing out of Lake Itasca in north central Minnesota.

Likewise the volumes that have been written about the Sermon on the Mount begin in these eight statements of Jesus called attributes or beatitudes of spiritually fit disciples. We have explored five. Now we turn to the final three. This week we will discover a spiritually fit disciple is pure in heart, is a peacemaker, and can rejoice under persecution.

BEING PURE IN HEART

"Blessed are the pure in heart" (Matt. 5:8). The word pure, *katharos*, means clean, unmixed, unadulterated, unalloyed. The word appears twenty-eight times in the New Testament and refers to rightness of mind and singleness of motive. This attribute begins by saying, blessed are those whose thoughts and motives are absolutely unmixed, free from foreign matter, and therefore pure.

The significance of purity vs. impurity is illustrated by Alfred Lord Tennyson's two knights of the Round Table. Impurity barred the vision of Sir Lancelot and kept him from seeing the Holy Grail, the cup thought to be the symbol and vehicle of the blood of Jesus. Tennyson says of Lancelot, all that was "pure, noble, and knightly" in him "twined and clung 'round that one sin, until the wholesome flower and poisonous grew together, each as each, not to be plucked asunder." Because what is in our heart determines what we see, Lancelot was not even able to see the Holy Grail when he came to Castle Carbonek, but as he looked in its direction, "a stormy glare, a heat as from a seven-times heated furnace, blasted and burnt and blinded him."

On the other hand, Tennyson has Galahad, the pure knight say, "My strength is as of ten, because my heart is pure." While Lancelot was brave in battle, Galahad was pure in heart.

The Bible speaks of six different kinds of purity all of which relate to spiritual fitness. There is that *divine purity* that exists only in and is essential to God's character. Similar to divine purity is *created purity* such as God established in creation prior to the fall of humankind. *Imputed purity* is given to us at the time of our conversion. This kind of purity is often called right-eousness in the New Testament (Rom. 4:5; 2 Cor. 5:21) and in the songs we sing like the one by Don Harris:

> Lord, make me pure in heart.
> Make my heart faithful and true.
> So when you look at me
> It's your righteousness You see.
> Lord, make me pure in heart.

Along with imputed purity God gives *renewed purity*. In other words, as we sin against God, God allows us to be renewed again and again (Rom. 6:4–5; 8:5–11; Col. 3:9–10; 1 Pet. 1:3). There is also a *shared purity* mentioned in the New Testament, in which we participate with God in our own purity. Paul calls us to "cleanse ourselves from all defilement of flesh and spirit, perfecting holiness in the fear of God" (2 Cor. 7:1) and Peter adds, "Do not be conformed to the former lusts which were yours in ignorance, but like the Holy One who called you, be holy yourselves also in all your behavior" (1 Pet. 1:14–16).

Finally, there will be *rewarded purity* which we will experience in heaven for "we will be like Him, because we will see Him just as He is" (1 John 3:2).

The idea of pure in heart puts all else in proper priority. You can't live a pure life without a pure heart. Many try to work this formula backwards, but pure life does not result in a pure heart. Rather a pure heart results in a pure life; that is, a life that is unmixed with evil. Just as pure gold is without alloy and pure water is free from other liquids or matter, so a pure heart is one with no mixture. Thus, it is single-minded and focused. As Kierkegaard reminds us, "Purity of heart is to will one will."

We live in a day of enormous knowledge and concern about the human heart. This rugged, four-valved, four-chambered pump organ handles 5,000 gallons of blood per day, enough to fill a railroad tank car. This amazing organ supplies the human circulatory system through 12,000 miles of vessels. In the course of an average lifetime it beats 2,500,000 times.

We speak often of the heart in phrases like "his heart is in the right place," referring to motives; "have a heart," referring to emotions; "open up your heart," when appealing to someone to not be harsh or hard; "hard-hearted," when referring to personality; "she's got heart," when referring to energy or activity or describing one as being non-passive; "think about this in your heart," when referring to the mental. Thus, "heart" becomes a synonym for the whole person.

In the New Testament times, medical science was still of the belief that blood carried thought, concluding then that all thought originated in the heart. Thus, to the Hebrew, the heart included intellect, emotions, and will. This led to the biblical idea, "For as he thinks in his heart, so is he" (Prov. 23:7, NKJV). As well as the question of Jesus, "Why are you thinking evil in your hearts?" (Matt. 9:4). Likewise the question, "Why are you reasoning about these things in your hearts?" (Mark 2:8). Of the 148 uses of the New Testament word heart, *kardia*, almost all refer to the inner person.

Even in our day, with so much emphasis on heart care, heart by-pass, and heart transplants, there is so little concern for heart purity. The Bible is clear in its statements concerning the importance of heart purity: "Watch over your heart with all diligence"(Prov. 4:23) implores the writer of the Proverbs. The Psalmist prays, "Create in me a clean heart, O God" (Ps. 51:10), and Jesus adds, "For from within, out of the heart of men, proceed the evil thoughts" (Mark 7:21).

Again, purity of heart is an inward thing. In the world of Jesus' day purity was a matter of ritual observance, obedience to a list of rules and regulations, a ceremonial matter. On the Day of Atonement, the high priest washed his entire body five times and his hands ten times. Before a meal, orthodox Jews first poured water over their hands with fingers pointed upward, then with fingers pointed downward, then washed each palm by rubbing it with the fist of the other hand.

Jesus set the proper order by beginning purity on the inside. Nothing on the outside can change us on the inside— not government, not family, not education, not morality, not religion, not behavior modification, not twelve steps, not rehabilitation, and not therapy—only that which is in our heart. No wonder the writer of the Proverbs implored us to "watch over your heart with all diligence, for," he adds "from it flow the springs of life" (Prov. 4:23). Unfortunately, this wellspring of life has become a polluted spring that only God can make pure.

Purity of heart comes by allowing God to control your thoughts. Early in human history, "the Lord saw that the wickedness of man was great on the earth, and that every intent of the thoughts of his heart was only evil continually" (Gen. 6:5). Temptations are brilliant but often deadly, scenery is bewitching but often corrupting. We must allow no thought to remain in our mind that taints or defiles God's purity. We must heed Paul's encouragement, "whatever is true, whatever is honorable, whatever is right, whatever is pure, whatever is lovely, whatever is of good repute . . . dwell on these things" (Phil. 4:8). I have found it helpful to turn to prayer when an impure thought tries to invade my mind. This places God back in control of my thoughts. Robert Browning said it well: "Thought is the soul of the act."

Likewise, *purity of heart comes by allowing God to control your affections.* We must love. We have been created to love. But we must not allow our affectionate love to stray to those to whom we ought not give it whether this be expressed in monopolizing friendships, exclusive relationships, or adulterous involvement. Common sense, if followed, will lead us away from impure affections.

Purity of heart comes also by allowing God to control your will. Impurity often springs from the lack of a resolute will or a wavering on decisions. Like the front wheels of a front-wheel drive vehicle, a will controlled by God must steer our course and set our direction.

As God controls our thoughts, our affections, our wills, and makes our hearts pure our actions will become pure. Just changing the filters in your air conditioning system will not help much if the source of the air is polluted. Neither will a variety of activities produce pure action unless the heart is puri-fied by God. Spiritual fitness must have purity of heart.

We are not talking about sinless perfection. The Bible tells of Noah getting drunk, Abraham deceiving King Abimelech, Moses disobeying God, Job cursing the day of his birth, Elijah fleeing in fear, Peter denying Christ, and Paul confessing his tendency to evil when he wanted to do good. None were perfect or sinless, but all were pure in heart. Just because an athlete makes a costly mistake does not make him or her any less a member of the team. Likewise, even though a spiritual athlete sins, they are still a part of the faith team.

The resulting promise is "they shall see God" (Matt. 5:8). While impurity obscures our vision of God, purity enhances that vision. To see God must surely be one of the ultimate purposes of a disciple. Yet it is only the disciple, the pure in heart, who can see God. The impure of heart see everything but God. What one is determines what one sees, and that which we miss seeing stems from the things we miss being. The more God-like we become, the more of God we see in other people, in creation, and obviously in the scripture.

So the pure in heart do see God, because of who we are. This has always been true—what one sees is determined by what one is. In Jesus' day the rich man could purchase an unblemished lamb for sacrifice while the poor man purchased a dove. But whether rich or poor, the pure in heart were the ones who worshiped God. Physical eyes saw lambs and doves. Spiritual eyes saw the Lord. Yard workers see trees as leaf producers. Golfers see trees as obstacles. However, Joyce Kilmer wrote:

> I think that I shall never see
> A poem as lovely as a tree.

Perhaps the point is best illustrated by the poem of the pussycat who went to London. Upon return, the cat was asked:

> Pussy cat, pussy cat, where have you been?
> I've been to London to visit the Queen.
> Pussy cat, pussy cat what saw you there?
> I saw a little mouse under a chair.

Cats are cats. They see mice, even in the presence of royalty. The spiritually unfit disciple who is impure of heart sees the impure, even in the midst of purity. They even come to church and complain of not experiencing God there. Only the pure in heart see God. They see wonder in each week, deity in each day, holiness in each hour, majesty in every moment, and the sacred in each second.

It was the desire of Old Testament saints to see God. Moses cried, "I pray You, show me Your glory!" (Exod. 33:18). David exclaimed, "As the deer pants for the water brooks, So my soul pants for You, O God" (Ps. 42:1). Job confessed, "I have heard of You by the hearing of the ear; But now my eye sees You" (Job 42:5). We join their desire in wanting to see God. It is absolutely amazing to me the ends to which people will go to see God. They will crawl on bloody knees, starve themselves, endure seasons of separation from friends, and grasp at any fresh idea, just to see God. Even in our music we acknowledge our desire to see God. Keith Green wrote:

> O Lord, You're beautiful.
> Your face is all I seek.
> For when Your eyes are on this child,
> Your grace abounds to me.

The promise of seeing God is both present and future. John assures us, "Beloved, now we are children of God, and it has not appeared as yet what we will be. We know that when He appears, we will be like Him, because we will see Him just as He is" (1 John 3:2). Again, John tells us "He is coming with the clouds, and every eye will see Him" (Rev. 1:7). Once again, of those in heaven John says, "They will see His face" (Rev. 22:4). F. F. Bullard has expressed the ultimate goal of spiritual fitness by writing:

> When I in righteousness at last
> Thy glorious face shall see;
> When all the weary night has passed,
> And I awake with Thee,
> To view the glories that abide,
> Then and only then will I be satisfied.

What will it be like for us to see Jesus? We will see a brow where a crown of thorns once pierced the skin. We will see a face from which some of the beard was plucked out. We will see hands and feet that were once pierced with nails. We will see a side once opened with a sword. We will see eyes that never saw a person beyond hope. We will see lips through which came words so meaningful, that volumes have been written to explain them. We will see ears worthy of hearing our praise. We will see our joint-heir to the Kingdom. We will see our adversary with the Father. We will see the One whom to see is to see the Father. We will see the One who did not leave us comfortless. We will see the object of all our hallelujahs. We will see what we have been striving to become. We will be spiritually fit.

Alfred Lord Tennyson was once asked, "What is your greatest wish?" He responded, "A clear vision of God." Perhaps this is why, on his deathbed, he instructed his oldest son to see that "Crossing the Bar" would be the final poem in any future collection of his works. The poem ends:

> For tho' from out our bourne of Time and Place
>> The tide may bear me far,
> I hope to see my Pilot face to face
>> When I have crossed the bar.

BEING A PEACEMAKER

"Blessed are the peacemakers" (Matt. 5:9). Used eighty-eight times in the New Testament, the word *peace* appears in all twenty-seven books. Indeed the Bible opens with peace in the Garden of Eden and closes with peace in the eternal city. The gospel opens with peace as the multitude of the heavenly host praise God, saying, "Glory to God in the highest, and on earth peace among men" (Luke 2:14). Before his death, Jesus' last will and testament left "peace" to the disciples (John 14:27) and in one of his first resurrection appearances Jesus greeted his disciples with the words, "Peace be with you"

(John 20:19). The Bible is a book of peace, best modeled by Jesus himself.

In all the New Testament, the word peacemaker, *eirenopolis*, appears only here. In the first six attributes, blessedness was dependent on an inward condition. Here blessedness is linked to a pro-active involvement. A peacemaker is one who seeks to make peace, not one who simply and passively endures in a posture of peace. This calls for toiling laboriously, living dangerously, fighting sacrificially, and enduring painfully. The tasks of peace are more difficult than those of war, for it is easier to defeat an enemy than to defeat his enmity, easier to stop a fight than to solve the disagreement.

We must remember also that the world in which Jesus first spoke these words was not in peace. It was marked by mutual hatred between Jews and Romans. The Province of Galilee was a revolution waiting to happen. Now the disciples are told they must not only have peace, which they received when they received Jesus as Messiah, but they must also make peace in a troubled world. The spiritually fit disciple pays the price to make peace.

The disciples would begin, where we must begin, by *making peace with self*. While it appears this attribute has more to do with conduct than character, it assumes a peacemaker to be a possessor of the attitude of peace. This explains why purity of heart precedes peacemaking. Thomas á Kempis said it well: "First keep thyself in peace, and then thou shalt be able to keep peace among others."

So, not only must disciples make peace with self, but likewise *make peace with others*. In a day when many are concerned with piece-making (diversity), disciples must be caught up in peacemaking (unity). We are called to be arbitrators for the Almighty, mediators for the Master in the home, work place, community, church, and place of leisure. We must combat prejudice, competition, jealousy, and envy. There is a New Year's Eve custom in Scotland called "first-footing it." This refers to the first person to enter one's house after midnight to

wish a happy new year. It relates to aggressive discipleship—
"first-footing it" for peace.

But the disciple must also *make peace with God*. Henry David
Thoreau was asked near the end of his life if he had made peace
with God. He replied, "We never quarreled." I don't know how
many of us can say that, but we all should be at peace with
God. The Bible instructs us, "do not stiffen your neck like your
fathers, but yield to the LORD and enter His sanctuary which He
has consecrated forever, and serve the LORD your God, that His
burning anger may turn away from you" (2 Chron. 30:8). We
must surrender to God. We must stop fighting God and begin
serving God if we would be at peace with God. We are not sons
of God because we make peace, rather we make peace because
we are sons of God.

When we are at peace with self, others, and God, there will
be a greater chance for peace in the world. A Chinese proverb
says, "If there is righteousness in the heart, there will be beauty
in the character. If there is beauty in the character, there will be
harmony in the home. If there is harmony in the home, there
will be order in the nation. And when there is order in the
nation, there will be peace in the world."

So then, how do we go about making peace? First, *we must
control our verbal response to situations*. Sometimes what we desire
to say needs to remain unsaid. Other times what we desire to
say needs to be softened and tempered. Our words can disrupt
or soothe depending on when and how we use them. An
ancient proverb says, "If you talk with a soft voice, you do not
need a thick stick." Solomon said it this way, "A gentle answer
turns away wrath, but a harsh word stirs up anger" (Prov. 15:1).
James instructs, "Every one be quick to hear, slow to speak and
slow to anger" (James 1:19).

Second, *we must control our response to unpeaceful situations*.
To be used as a peacemaker is often costly. The world's ultimate
peace, the peace that passes all human understanding, came
from a costly cross: "For it was the Father's good pleasure for all
the fullness to dwell in Him, and through Him to reconcile all

things to Himself, having made peace through the blood of His cross" (Col. 1:19–20). The hands that reach to calm the storm were nail-pierced. The feet that go before and pave the way to peace are likewise, nail-pierced.

Martin Luther often told the story of two goats who met on a narrow bridge over deep water. "They could not go back; they durst not fight. After a short parley, one of them lay down and let the other go over him, and thus no harm was done. The moral is easy: Be content if thy person be trod upon for peace's sake. Thy person, I say, not thy conscience." Peacemakers are more concerned with principles than their own person.

Response often finds us reaching out to persons who are resistant to us. Being blessed as peacemakers, we are prone to take the opposite view of others and say, "cursed are the peace-breakers." But this is not the way of the cross. Edwin Markham, author of the poems "The Man with the Hoe" and "Lincoln," was once asked what he considered his greatest poem. Without hesitation he responded, "I wrote four lines which I treasure more than all else I wrote during my entire life:"

> He drew a circle that shut me out—
> Heretic, rebel, a thing of flout.
> But love and I had a wit to win:
> We drew a circle that took him in.

Markham's lines show the spirit of a peacemaker and a goal of spiritual fitness.

The resulting promise is "They shall be called sons of God" (Matt. 5:9). One emphasis is on the word "called." We become sons of God at the time of our conversion, but we shall be called sons of God as we pass on the peace we find in Christ. To be made a son of God is to be renewed in God's image and likeness. To be called a son of God is to be recognized and honored as such.

Note we are "sons," *huiroi*, not children of God. In Jewish thought sons bore the meaning of "partaker of the character of." To be called "Sons of Thunder" as James and John were

(Mark 3:17) meant they possessed characteristics of thunder. Thus, a son of God possesses God's character.

God is a God of peace. Paul calls God, "the God of peace" (Rom. 16:20, 2 Cor. 13:11, Phil. 4:9) repeatedly as does the writer of Hebrews (Heb. 13:20). Perhaps there is nothing so God-like as to be a maker of peace. When we lose sight of the Fatherhood of God, it effects the brotherhood of man. When we make peace with our brothers and sisters, we exalt the Fatherhood of God, as sons.

Interestingly enough, the adjective used in this attribute for peacemaker is the same word used in verb form for the Son of God "establishing peace" in Ephesians 2:15 and "having made peace" in Colossians 1:20. In other words as sons of God and peacemakers, we celebrate our identity also as joint-heir with the Son of God who likewise makes peace and who "Himself is our peace" (Eph. 2:14).

"Sons of God" is more than just a present label or name since it has future implications as well. "Shall be called" is a continuous future passive tense indicating that throughout eternity, we will be called "sons of God." While we may have a lack of peace here on earth, there awaits for earth's peacemakers an eternity of peace. So we pray with Francis of Assisi:

> Lord, make me an instrument of Your peace:
>> Where there is hatred, let me sow love;
>> where there is injury, pardon;
>> where there is doubt, faith;
>> where there is despair, hope;
>> where there is darkness, light; and
>> where there is sadness, joy.

> O divine Master, grant that I may not so much seek
>> to be consoled as to console;
>> to be understood as to understand,
>> to be loved as to love;

For it is in giving that we receive;
   it is in pardoning that we are pardoned; and
   it is in dying that we are born to eternal life!

BEING PERSECUTED

"Blessed are those who have been persecuted" (Matt. 5:10). The word persecuted, *dioko*, means "put to flight, driven away and pursued." It is a natural follow-up to making peace. The blessed one is the one who endures hardship rather than the one who weakly abandons convictions. Some believe this attribute was addressed only to the twelve disciples since they alone would understand its full meaning. Nevertheless, one who lives consistently according to the first seven attributes eventually experiences this eighth attribute. There is no spiritual fitness apart from persecution.

Jesus told his disciples at a later time, "If you were of the world, the world would love its own: but because you are not of the world, but I chose you out of the world, therefore the world hates you. . . . If they persecuted Me, they will also persecute you" (John 15:19–20). Paul added, "For to you it has been granted for Christ's sake, not only to believe in Him, but also to suffer for His sake" (Phil. 1:29). And again Paul wrote, "All who desire to live godly in Christ Jesus will be persecuted " (2 Tim. 3:12).

What had been written and spoken came to pass. The early Christians were hated because they were different. Their religion was declared illegal. Because they refused to acknowledge Caesar as Lord, their faith was considered subversive. They lost their jobs, homes, families, and were imprisoned and martyred for their belief. Their goodness was a constant, unspoken condemnation of others' way of life. Just as those who are physically fit offer a silent condemnation to those who are physically unfit, so it is in spiritual fitness.

The only one of the eight attributes to be expounded on by Jesus was done to prepare his disciples for future persecution and even death by the time of Acts 7. Jesus promised it, the disciples experienced it, the New Testament documents it, and the early church felt it. Nor did the persecution end with the disciples.

In his account of Nero's persecution, Tacitus tells of some of the horrors faced by early believers: "Besides being put to death, they were made to serve as objects of amusement; they were clad in the hides of beasts and torn to death by dogs; others were crucified, others set on fire to serve to eliminate the darkness of the night."

In *The Martyrdom of Polycarp*, a voice from heaven spoke to the aged saint as he was being brought to the stadium to die: "Be strong Polycarp, and play the man." When the Proconsul urged the old man to curse Christ and live, Polycarp replied, "Eighty and six years have I served him, and he hath done me no wrong, how then can I blaspheme my king, who saved me?" Before nailing him to the stake the Proconsul threatened Polycarp with wild beasts and with fire. Rejecting all threats, Polycarp proclaimed, "Let me be as I am. He that granted me to endure the fire will grant me also to remain at the pyre unmoved, without being secured with nails."

Adoniram Judson suffered greatly in stocks while imprisoned in Burma. After his release he asked the King for permission to preach in a particular city. The King responded, "I am willing for a dozen preachers to go to that city, but not you. Not with those hands. My people are not fools enough to listen to and follow your words, but they will not be able to resist those scarred hands." Persecuted, he bore in his body the marks of Jesus.

Few have understood persecution better than Dietrich Bonhoeffer. After much suffering, he was executed by direct order of Heinrich Himmler in April of 1945 in the Flossenburg concentration camp only a few days before it was liberated. Bonhoeffer had written, "Suffering, then, is the badge of true discipleship. The disciple is not above his master. Following Christ means . . . suffering because we have to suffer."

Martin Luther considered suffering among the marks of the true church, and one of the memoranda drawn up in preparation for the Augsburg confession defines the church as the community of those "who are persecuted and martyred for the gospel's sake" and martyred they were.

So many believers were martyred for their faith that by the end of the first Christian century the word for witness and the word for martyr had become the same Greek word, *martus*. A witness in that day had every chance to become a martyr. In fact the "Gloria Patri" is based on the march-to-death song of the early Christian martyrs.

Then Jesus broadened the scope of persecution with the words, "Blessed are you when people insult you, and persecute you, and falsely say all kinds of evil against you" (Matt. 5:11). This personalizes persecution—no longer the third person "those" of verse 10, but the second person "you" of verse 11.

More than physical torture, this persecution now includes character assassination, insult, spoken malice, ridicule, belittling, and a host of other indignities suffered in families, work places, recreation locations, classrooms, and even churches. Modern disciples are reviled like Moses (Exod. 5:21, 14:11, 16:2, 17:2), Samuel (1 Sam. 8:5), Elijah (1 Kings 18:17, 19:2), Micaiah (2 Chron. 18:17), and Nehemiah (Neh. 4). Like the stoning of Stephen, the imprisonment of Peter and John, and the beheading of John the Baptist, today's disciples are persecuted. On a recent three-week prayer journey through the unreached people groups of the world, I visited with pastors, lay-leaders, and new Christians who had been persecuted for their faith. They told stories of friends and fellow-workers who have disappeared and are assumed to be in prison or dead. Many others are presently suffering from lesser forms of persecution.

Yet persecution is a compliment, twice-blessed by our Lord. Persecution means someone takes you seriously. No one persecutes an ineffective, indecisive person. It comes only to those who are considered by others as dangerous and gives the disciple an opportunity to demonstrate he or she is not ashamed of the gospel. Even though we may never become a

martyr or even endure heavy persecution, we must agree with
W. C. Burns who wrote, "Oh, to have a martyr's heart if not a
martyr's crown," and with Isaac Watts who asked:

Must I be carried to the skies
On flowery beds of ease,
While others fought to win the prize,
And sailed through bloody seas?

Spiritual fitness often comes at the price of persecution.

It is not just persecution or being reviled and spoken
against, for many endure this, but "for the sake of righteousness" (Matt. 5:10) and "because of Me" (Matt. 5:11) says Jesus.
Persecution in and of itself brings no blessing. It is the object
that blesses. We are blessed because of "righteousness" and
"because of"of our loyalty to Jesus. We suffer not in vain, for
"even if you should suffer for the sake of righteousness, you are
blessed" (1 Pet. 3:14).

It is for righteousness sake that we endure persecution not
for lack of wisdom or discernment, not for foolish actions, not
for playing with temptation, not for being a fanatic, not even for
being faithful to church activities, not for a cause, not for a pet
project, not for being good or noble or self-sacrificing, but for
righteousness we suffer.

Our commitment is to a person, not a principle; to a man,
not a method; to a Savior, not a system; to a Lord, not a list; to
a Christ, not a creed. And so, "because of" Jesus, we endure
persecution. This, in turn, builds spiritual muscle just as aerobic
exercises of resistance build physical muscle. Spiritual muscle
will then help us not only resist Satan's attacks, but also stand
firm in the midst of further persecution.

"For so they persecuted the prophets who were before
you" (Matt. 5:12). There is a plaque at Boulder Dam upon
which are listed the names of those who died during its construction. It reads, "These have made the desert to blossom
like a rose." Many are blessed because some suffer. The joy
of the difficult way lies in its fellowship. The pathway of

persecution is hallowed by the footsteps of God's saints and God's Son, who "endured the cross, despising the shame" (Heb. 12:2).

"Rejoice, and be glad" (Matt. 5:12). Jesus endured his persecution, "for the joy set before Him" (Heb. 12:2). Peter tells us, "to the degree that you share the sufferings of Christ, keep on rejoicing" (1 Pet. 4:13). How do we respond to our persecution? We do not sulk like a child, nor lick our wounds like a dog, nor grin and bear it like a Stoic, nor pretend to enjoy it like a masochist. We rejoice.

We rejoice like Paul because "we are afflicted in every way, but not crushed; perplexed, but not despairing; persecuted, but not forsaken; struck down, but not destroyed; always carrying about in the body the dying of Jesus, that the life of Jesus also may be manifested in our body" (2 Cor. 4:8–10).

The resulting promises were, "For theirs is the kingdom of heaven" (Matt. 5:10); and "for your reward in heaven is great" (Matt. 5:12). Here is the final reward but with present connotations. We do not enter the kingdom of God because of our successful endurance of persecution. We are persecuted and will ultimately enjoy the reward because we are presently a part of the kingdom of heaven. There is no reward in self-sought persecution or martyrdom. He who is thrown to the lions is a persecuted martyr on his way to great heavenly reward. He who jumps into the den is a self-seeking egotist who already has his reward.

Make no mistake, there is a reward! Paul promised, "We suffer with Him so that we may also be glorified with Him" (Rom. 8:17) and "If we endure, we shall also reign with Him" (2 Tim. 2:12). Moses chose "rather to endure ill-treatment with the people of God than to enjoy the passing pleasures of sin, considering the reproach of Christ greater riches than the treasures of Egypt; for he was looking to the reward" (Heb. 11:25–26).

A most unusual evergreen tree grows in Yellowstone National Park, the lodgepole pine. Like other pines, its cones remain on the tree for years. Even when they do fall off, they usually remain unopen. They open only when exposed to extreme heat such as a forest fire. Frequently, following a devastating fire, the first tree to grow again in the fire-ravaged area is the lodgepole pine. What devastates some, brings life to others. Out of heavy persecution, comes the disciple's reward of eternal life.

We have explored eight attributes of a spiritually fit disciple. These define what it means to be in shape spiritually. Having identified what it means to be in shape, we now are ready to investigate the process of getting in shape.

EXERCISES FOR SPIRITUAL FITNESS

Day One Review the different kinds of purity in the Bible. What are your needs related to renewed purity? Related to shared purity? Ask God what is necessary for each to be enhanced in your life today. Write your impressions here. _____

_____

Day Two How have you seen: wonder in this week? _____

_____

deity in this day? _____

_____

holiness in this hour? _____

_____

majesty in this moment? _____

_____

Day Three A peacemaker is one who seeks to make peace, not one who simply and passively endures in a posture of peace. What have you done or hope to do this week to be pro-active for peace? _____

_____

Day Four Keeping in mind the meaning of the word *dioko*, persecuted, how have you experienced this in the past few days? _____

_____

Day Five What is one way you can rejoice right now in the midst of your persecutions? _____

_____

Scriptural strengths to remember:
  1. Matthew 5:8
  2. Matthew 5:9
  3. Matthew 5:10–12

phase two

GETTING

IN SHAPE:

THE OBJECTIVE

OF A DISCIPLE

WEEK FOUR

Walking

NOW THAT WE KNOW what being in shape looks like, it's time to get in shape. There is no rush, no need to begin at any level other than the first. There is no fast-track to discipleshape, no short cut to shaping-up. So, let's begin by walking.

On the physical level, walking is an excellent way to get in shape. You don't need special clothing, a health club membership, or even athletic talent. Walking can strengthen bones, lungs, heart, and muscles; make joints more flexible; and burn fat and calories. In addition, walking can keep you mentally and emotionally fit as well. You really can "walk your blues away" and relieve anxieties.

Walking has certain advantages. It is low-impact, so joints, muscles and bones are unlikely to become injured. It is easy to sustain, so walkers tend to walk longer than runners run or swimmers swim. It's convenient since you can walk in many places and under many conditions—in your neighborhood, at the park, in the mall, or on a treadmill.

Many years ago our ancient ancestors ensured their survival and food supply by moving forward, constantly walking. This produced a never-ending series of reward mechanisms which are available to us today. Physical fitness experts assure us that forward motion connects the mind, body, and spirit, which makes us feel whole. Walking improves our attitude as we begin to feel better and more in control of self. Physiologists tell us if we walk long enough we'll shift into our right brain, opening up an unlimited supply of creative solutions to problems and inspirational thoughts. Walking offers vitality and energy in all areas of life.

Just as walking has obvious physical and less obvious mental and emotional benefits, likewise it has spiritual benefits. The recently popularized practice of prayer-walking is one example. The mind seems to function more clearly when the physical juices are flowing. In other words, movement motivates and facilitates prayer.

For our purposes, we are looking at spiritual walking rather than physical walking. The apostle Paul encourages us to "walk by the Spirit, and you will not carry out the desire of the flesh" (Gal. 5:16) and again, "If we live by the Spirit, let us also walk by the Spirit" (Gal. 5:25).

WALKING THROUGH WANT: CONVICTION

Just as physical walking begins with a conviction of need, so does spiritual walking. While the conviction for physical walking may come from a medical doctor, a spouse, or a friend the conviction for spiritual walking comes directly from the Holy Spirit. The Holy Spirit convicts. In what one has referred to as the "last will and testament of Jesus," our Lord described this work of the Holy Spirit for his disciples when he said, "and He, when He comes, will convict the world concerning sin and righteousness and judgment" (John 16:8). Since conviction must always precede conversion, the Holy Spirit takes the initiative in evangelism. Whenever individual Christians attempt to fill the role of the convicting agent, we find ourselves out of place, the Holy Spirit displaced, and the power thwarted. Conviction of sin has been assigned only to the Holy Spirit of God. The only thing a human being can do in relationship to conviction, apart from the Holy Spirit, is to impose guilt upon the nonbeliever. Human-imposed guilt apart from the Holy Spirit, can be human relieved guilt in the life of that non-Christian. Only the Holy Spirit can impose genuine conviction of sin in the life of the nonbeliever.

When the Holy Spirit brought conviction in our life, probably he used an individual or an event that was orchestrated by God. No matter how God brought it about, remember the source. Conviction always comes from God's Holy Spirit.

However, the Holy Spirit uses Christians to assist in his role of conviction. This might be likened to light bulbs and electricity. Light bulbs have no power in themselves. Their power is only in relationship to the current which they touch. Likewise, with Christians, our power in convicting of sin is related to the activity of the Holy Spirit. Sometimes the Holy Spirit may not use a particular Christian because the light is too dim. Dim lights do not reveal much. They allow for mistakes. Likewise, if a light is too bright, it may not be used by the Holy Spirit to convict of sin. Bright lights tend to blind and create oversight. When our light is too dim or too bright, when others see us as too carnal or too spiritual, we may thwart the power of the Holy Spirit. Only when we are properly attached to the power current of the Holy Spirit can we illumine the convicting power of that Spirit.

One of my hobbies is railroading. I collect the antiques when I can afford them and ride on the trains when it is practical—which is not often. Several years ago I was in Chicago and needed to be in Washington, D.C. I had the time so I took the train. There were a lot of reasons for doing that. For one, I could relax. I didn't have to land within minutes of take off. When I went to the dining car, I didn't have to worry about people being in a hurry because I wasn't going anywhere in a hurry. So, when I sat down with whomever they placed me with (it's always random), I had plenty of time to talk. I didn't have to worry about "approaching our final descent" about the time I got to the plan of salvation. So, I enjoy it.

I went to the dining car that evening. They seated me across the table from a young man. As we began to talk, I discovered he worked for the railroad. He asked me what I did and where I was going. I told him I was traveling for the Southern Baptists and I was on my way to speak at a retreat for single adults.

"Isn't that interesting," he said. "My divorce was finalized last week."

"Well, about half those present this weekend will be divorced," I answered. He began to talk about his children and how he missed them. He shared the same kind of story I had grown accustomed to hearing. Then he asked, "What are you going to tell these single adults?"

I talked about Jesus Christ, what he meant to me, and what he could mean in the lives of other people.

"You know, that's very interesting" he said. "My former wife was a believer. She was always talking to me about accepting Christ. I never did." We talked a little further. He said, "Just last night I was watching television. There was a movie on about a priest. I watched the whole thing."

You say coincidence. No, it was conviction. The Holy Spirit of God had begun to work on him. He had worked through people. He had worked through feelings. He had worked through mistakes. He had worked through a television movie about a priest. The Holy Spirit had used several ways to nudge this man toward faith in him.

I first felt the Holy Spirit's nudge when I stole a baseball card from a friend's collection. I had been trying without success to get this particular card. He had two of them and wouldn't trade one of them to me. So, I just took the desired card when he wasn't looking. At first I felt proud. I now possessed the card I had long desired. That same night, I had trouble sleeping. I began to feel guilty. I knew I had done wrong.

I tried to rationalize my act. Still no sleep. The next day, I found a way to slip the stolen card back into the collection of it's rightful owner. I would later come to understand that it was the Holy Spirit convicting me of a wrongful act in my life. Still later, I would understand that wrongful act to be sin. That led to the beginning of my understanding of my need for a Savior who could forgive my sin and save me. I discovered that conviction, while never comfortable, leads to the comfort of sin forgiven and a found Savior.

WALKING TO DECISION: CONVERSION

In addition to conviction, the Holy Spirit works toward and accomplishes conversion in the life of the nonbeliever. When talking with Nicodemus, Jesus underlined this activity of the Holy Spirit when he said, "Truly, truly, I say to you, unless one is born of water and the Spirit, he cannot enter into the kingdom of God. That which is born of the flesh is flesh, and that which is born of the Spirit is Spirit" (John 3:5–6).

After we become convicted by the Holy Spirit of our need for salvation, we make a decision. While Christianity has used various terminology to describe this decision, what happened was we basically decided to turn from our present way of living, invite Jesus Christ into our lives, and begin living (or walking) like and for him. This is called conversion. It is the beginning of the new walk.

Conversion is change. The very word means to turn around or turn toward. More than just a decision of the mind or will, conversion is a determination to walk a new and different way.

The Psalmist wrote, "Restore to me the joy of Your salvation, and sustain me with a willing spirit. Then I will teach transgressors Your ways, and sinners will be converted to You" (Ps. 51:12–13).

Even more direct are the words of Jesus, "Truly I say to you, unless you are converted and become like children, you will not enter the kingdom of heaven" (Matt. 18:3).

The early Christians record Paul and Barnabas as "being sent on their way by the church . . . passing through both Phoenicia and Samaria, describing in detail the conversion of the Gentiles" (Acts 15:3).

These are representative of the twelve times (five in the Old Testament and seven in the New Testament) this word "conversion" is used in the Bible.

In addition to meaning change, *conversion is also singular*. Change happens to each one of us uniquely. There are no assembly line, photocopy believers. Conversion is one-to-one, the person-to-Jesus. Therefore, in a group of believers there will be a diversity of conversion accounts.

On one extreme there will be those who dramatically came to faith in Jesus like Paul on the road to Damascus (Acts 9). On the other extreme will be those like Lydia who listened to Paul at a riverside near Philippi while the Lord quietly "opened her heart to respond" (Acts 16:14). And all varieties in between these two extremes will likewise be experienced by believers.

A news story told of a hotel fire where a man jumped from a high window into the fire fighters' net, while another descended the stairs and walked out through the lobby. Both men were saved—one dramatically, one routinely. So it is with spiritual salvation—varieties of experience, all singular, all valid.

Not only is conversion change and singular, *conversion is likewise continual*. Consider the case of Simon Peter. Having found Jesus Christ for himself, Andrew then found "his own brother Simon and said to him, 'We have found the Messiah' [which translated means Christ]. He brought him to Jesus" (John 1:41–42). Later, Jesus was walking on the shore of the Sea of Galilee and "saw two brothers, Simon who was called Peter, and Andrew his brother, casting a net into the sea; for they were fishermen. And He said to them, 'Follow Me, and I will make you fishers of men'" (Matt. 4:18–19). When Jesus asked to be identified at Caesarea Philipi, Peter responded with a declaration of faith, "You art the Christ, the Son of the living God" (Matt. 16:16). In the upper room, Jesus said to Peter, "Simon, behold, Satan has demanded permission to sift you like wheat; but I have prayed for you, that your faith may not fail; and you, when once you have turned again, (The King James Version says, "when thou art converted") strengthen your brothers" (Luke 22:31–32). After three times denying that he was a disciple of Jesus, Peter "went out and wept bitterly" (Matt. 26:75). After the resurrection of Jesus, Peter was asked three times, "do you love Me?" (John 21:15–17).

When was Peter converted? At some point in his relationship with Jesus, Peter was individually and uniquely changed, but there is evidence that his conversion reflected continual change. Conversion is not static. It has a beginning point, but it continues. We were converted. We are being converted.

Finally, *conversion is completable*. We will ultimately and finally be converted. This final phase is often called glorification. It is a culmination of the process of redemption. Speaking of the end, Paul writes, "Now salvation is nearer to us than when we believed" (Rom. 13:11). The writer of Hebrews says Jesus will "appear a second time for salvation" (Heb. 9:28). John "heard a loud voice in heaven, saying, 'Now the salvation, and the power, and the kingdom of our God and the authority of His Christ have come" (Rev. 12:10). Some day, your conversion will be complete. Conversion is change, singular, continual, and completable.

DEAD MEN WALKING

I had been out of seminary about four years and in full-time ministry when I discovered the concept of dead men walking. It would be another twenty-five years before a movie by a similar name would be released. Any similarity is accidental. I had learned the lesson early, but I had learned it only in the mind. I had not learned it through experience. Frustrated because I had just reached the point of running out of seminary momentum and had begun to grasp for what else I might find to please people, to feed people, and to grow personally. I was struggling.

During a break at a conference in Houston, I went out into the parking lot and sat on the curb. I refused to go back in because I was so frustrated. The things I had heard weren't finding fertile soil in my life because of my own struggles. Sitting out there in that parking lot God brought to mind a verse that I had memorized as a teenager and had long since forgotten: "Unless a grain of wheat falls into the earth and dies, it remains by itself alone; but if it dies, it bears much fruit"(John 12:24).

That day I made a commitment to go back to my place of ministry and die to myself, to become a dead man walking; to plant my life literally in the fertile soil of that place and to water that soil with tears until God brought about a harvest. The next two years of my ministry were the most fruitful years up to that point.

Paul said, "I have been crucified with Christ; and it is no longer I who live, but Christ lives in me" (Gal. 2:20). Somewhere along the way we must learn the truth that until we are willing to die to self and make Jesus Christ the Lord of all, fruit will not grow. All the work and the deeds and the momentum and the energy we can generate in our lives cannot alone produce spiritual fruit. It can only be produced by the Holy Spirit, who is freed to work in us because we have yielded ourselves totally to the Lordship of Jesus Christ. Many believers are fruitless because self has not died. For the most part, although gathered together in the family of faith, they abide alone.

Having died to self, we must walk away from the old-creature, and crucify the flesh. Indeed, "those who belong to Christ Jesus have crucified the flesh with its passions and desires" (Gal. 5:24). Likewise, Paul admonishes us to "lay aside the old self" (Eph. 4:22). The act of crucifying the old self has already happened if we are a Christian. The old self, old nature, old creature is dead, *but* its influence continues to affect us— just like all influences go on beyond death. So let us look at the continuing expressions of the old nature.

Paul lists the *physical expressions of the old nature* in Galatians 5:19: "Now the deeds of the flesh are evident, which are: immorality, impurity, sensuality." Putting these physical expressions of the old nature together, Paul mourns over "those who have sinned in the past and not repented of the impurity, immorality and sensuality which they have practiced" (2 Cor. 12:21).

There are also *religious expressions of the old nature* which relate to the religious area. Two are mentioned in Galatians 5:20: "idolatry, sorcery." Paul encourages us to "flee from idolatry" (1 Cor. 10:14), and in Revelation 21:8, sorcerers are listed with others who will "be in the lake that burns with fire and brimstone, which is the second death."

Then there are *social expressions of the old nature* and the remainder of the list in Galatians 5:20–21 is social: "enmities, strife, jealousy, outbursts of anger, disputes, dissensions, factions, envying, drunkenness, carousing." Concerning social evils, Paul counsels young Timothy to "flee from these things, you man of God, and pursue righteousness, godliness, faith, love, perseverance and gentleness" (1 Tim. 6:11). Contrast this list of fleshly deeds with what Jesus said comes out of the disobedient heart: "evil thoughts, murders, adulteries, fornications, thefts, false witness, slanders (Matt. 15:19). Again Paul encourages us to "put . . . aside: anger, wrath, malice, slander, and abusive speech . . . since you laid aside the old self with its evil practices" (Col. 3:8–9).

These descriptions of the old, crucified self remind me of the garbage-laden barge of 1987. Labeled the "gar-barge," the floating trash bin contained 3,186 tons of New York City sewage sludge. The barge traveled in the Atlantic and the Gulf of Mexico for five months rejected by coastal states all the way to Texas and by Mexico, Belize, and the Bahamas before it returned home to be dumped in a Long Island landfill.

Similarly a few years later a trash train with forty-three cars traveled for four weeks from New York through the Midwest to Kansas and back with no one willing to accept it. The "P. U. Choo Choo" carrying 2,200 tons of rotting garbage was rejected in city after city by mayors, city councils, judges, and enraged citizens. No one would have anything to do with all that old rotting trash.

You must decide. Do you yield to these expressions of the old nature and walk in decaying flesh, or do you resist and flee, seeking the path of righteousness on which to walk? No military unit can capture an island without first establishing a beachhead. Satan's forces cannot capture us, cannot even influence us until they establish a point of entry, a beachhead in our lives. That point is established through temptation. Each person is stronger on some fronts than on others. There are some things that are extremely tempting for you but may not affect me at all. While I am not in the least bit tempted by certain items, there are other things that almost constantly tempt me. These temptations of mine may not bother you at all. We are all vulnerable somewhere. That vulnerable spot is where Satan can establish his point of entry into our life and influence our walk in the Spirit. But Satan can't get in unless he finds a vulnerable spot, a deed of the flesh. The way to eliminate these vulnerable spots is a more consistent walk in the Spirit. The end result of this consistent walk will be the production of spiritual fruit.

At the conclusion of this list of expressions of the old nature Paul adds, "I have forewarned you, that those who practice such things shall not inherit the kingdom of God" (Gal. 5:21). Now relax. This does not mean because a Christian slips and falls back into one of these deeds of the flesh and commits a sinful act, salvation is taken away. It has to do, not with isolated acts, but with lifestyle. The key word is "practice," meaning "to make a habit of." He, who makes a habit of these deeds of the flesh and whose lifestyle revolves around these things, is the one who cannot inherit the Kingdom of God. It is one thing for a Christian to slip into sin, or as we used to say "backslide." It is all together another thing for someone to have their lives totally dominated by the practice of these deeds of the flesh. He who is born of the Spirit has a desire and tendency to walk in the Spirit. None of us are perfect. While we may slip back into these deeds of the flesh from time to time, it does not mean we have lost our salvation.

However, if your lifestyle centers around these deeds and they dominate you and control your life, it may well be that you've never had a genuine conversion experience. You may have thought you did, but the Spirit of God was never born inside you, never began to live in you. If the Spirit of God lives in you, you walk in the Spirit. If the Spirit of God does not live in you, you have no desire to walk in the Spirit. You walk in the deeds of the flesh.

We do not just walk away from the expressions of the old nature, the deeds of the flesh, but we also began walking as a new creature. We "put on the new self" (Eph. 4:24). The imagery is that of putting off an old, soiled garment and putting on a new, fresh garment. In our new nature, symbolized by our new garment, we begin producing Spirit-fruit: "love, joy, peace, patience, kindness, goodness, faithfulness, gentleness, self-control" (Gal.5:22–23).

I call your attention to the singular dimension of Spirit-fruit. While the "deeds of the flesh" are plural, there is but one "fruit of the Spirit." The verse does not say the fruits of the Spirit *are*. If we want plural (fruits), we'll have to change the grammar. We will either have to change the "is" to "are," and "fruit" to "fruits"; or we will have to accept the grammar as is and then concentrate on the meaning behind the text, which is singular: "the fruit of the Spirit is . . . "

Yet, the list of what appears to be "fruits" poses a problem. Since the punctuation marks were not inspired in the original biblical text, G. Campbell Morgan suggests changing the punctuation to read like this: "The fruit of the Spirit is love;—joy, peace, longsuffering, kindness, goodness, faithfulness, meekness, temperance." Perhaps a colon after "love" would be even better.

Fruit is an outward expression of the inward. Apples are outward expressions of the "appleness" of the tree. Okra is an outward expression of the "okraness" of the vine. That which is produced is an expression of that which produces. To make a fruit salad you do not find a fruit salad tree. That's plural. To make a fruit salad you must find an apple tree, an orange tree, a cherry tree, and some other kinds of fruit trees and pull one type fruit off each tree to blend them together into a fruit salad. This text is singular: "The fruit of the Spirit *is* . . . " As the fruit is a singular expression of what is inside, so the Spirit of God produces one fruit.

To discover the supreme definition of Spirit-fruit, you just have to add one word: "The fruit of the Spirit is *love*." Love is that which takes priority over all else. It is *the* fruit of the Spirit. If you have love, there is the potential of having the other eight mentioned in the list. Love precedes all of the others listed.

If you have not love, whatever degree to which you experience the other eight will be empty, void, and without meaning for of what real, lasting value would any of those be apart from God's love? Is it possible to have patience without love? Is it possible to be faithful without love? Is it possible to have gentleness without love? On the other hand, if you have love, is there no possibility of being patient, being faithful, being gentle?

The fruit of the Spirit is love, as seen in Paul's writings. After listing a number of wonderful gifts, qualities, abilities, and characteristics, Paul says, "The greatest of these is love" (1 Cor. 13:13). Christianity has not taken full hold upon your life until your life is love-mastered, love-motivated, and love-matured.

The fruit of the Spirit is love, as seen in the words of Jesus who said, "Abide in Me, and I in you. As the branch cannot bear fruit of itself unless it abides in the vine, so neither can you unless you abide in Me" (John 15:4). If we abide in Jesus, our fruit bears the likeness of him. Just as apples express the "appleness" of the apple tree, the fruit of the Spirit expresses the nature of Christ himself. What is the nature of Christ? It was he who said, "Greater love has no one than this, that one lay down his life for his friends" (John 15:13). He loved his friends. Love was the fruit produced in his life. Again he said, "You have heard that it was said, 'You shall love your neighbor, and hate your enemy.' But I say to you, love your enemies and pray for those who persecute you." (Matt. 5:43–44). He also loved his enemies. The fruit of the Spirit produced in the life of Jesus Christ was love for friends, neighbors, and enemies. It was a love that carried him through a diversity of experiences all the way to a cruel cross. On that cross he laid down his life voluntarily, not because he was joy, or peace, or patience, or goodness, or faithfulness, or gentleness, or self-control, but because he was love. In the life of Jesus, the fruit of the Spirit is love.

There are then eight secondary expressions of Spirit-fruit like a head of wheat, barley, or oats that might have eight separate and distinct kernels upon it. They are still a part of one stalk, one plant, one product. Each has its own size, shape, and content. Like a cluster of grapes—different sizes, shapes, and content. Some may be sweeter, more desirable, or larger but they are all grapes. So, what some would refer to as "fruits" of the Spirit is in reality "fruit" of the Spirit, all clustered around the same product which is love. Love expresses itself as follows:

> LOVE'S FEELING is joy.
> LOVE'S ASSURANCE is peace.
> LOVE'S DISCIPLINE is patience.
> LOVE'S ACTION is kindness.
> LOVE'S INSPIRATION is goodness.
> LOVE'S COMMITMENT is faithfulness.
> LOVE'S RESERVE is gentleness.
> LOVE'S VICTORY is self-control.

Now, in the table on the next page, look at 1 Corinthians 13:4–7, the love chapter, and compare it with the expressions of the fruit of the Spirit:

I Corinthians 13:4–7	Galatians 5:22–23
"Love is patient"	"patience" (love's discipline)
"love is kind and is not jealous"	"kindness" (love's action)
"love does not brag and is not arrogant"	"gentleness" (love's reserve)
"does not act unbecomingly; it does not seek its own"	"self-control" (love's victory)
"is not provoked"	"peace" (love's assurance)
"does not take into account a wrong suffered"	"goodness" (love's inspiration)
"does not rejoice in unrighteousness, but rejoices with the truth"	"joy" (love's feeling)
"bears all things, believes all things, hopes all things, endures all things"	"faithfulness" (love's commitment)

When we walk in the Spirit as a new creature, the Spirit produces fruit in our life. The supreme fruit of the Spirit is love. The secondary expressions of love are joy, peace, patience, kindness, goodness, faithfulness, gentleness, and self-control. When these are being produced in our lives, we have a story to tell. David W. Morris wrote:

> Walking in the Spirit,
> Abiding in His mercies,
> In the presence of the Lord is great joy.

Walking in the Spirit,
Abiding in His mercies,
At His right hand are pleasures forevermore.

WALKING THE TALK: TESTIMONY

Few people are more anxious to tell their experiences than those who have just begun a new walking program. It seems, the more they walk, the more they talk. That's the way it ought to be with physical fitness, and that's the way it ought to be with spiritual fitness also.

Someone said, "When you walk the walk, you can talk the talk." A testimony is talking the walk. Here are a few suggestions for preparing a testimony.

Our testimony is unique. Among other reasons, our testimony has within it the added dimension of the Holy Spirit's power. If I share my personal testimony of a recent trip to Europe, it would have no power other than that which I might generate. My presentation of the details of that trip might be so persuasive that you would decide to go to Europe, but no outside power would participate in the telling of that testimony. Now, if I share with you what God has done and is doing in my life, power operates at two levels. For one, the Holy Spirit indwells and empowers the testimony as I voice it; second, the Holy Spirit convicts as the hearer hears it. A personal testimony is unique.

Our testimony is authoritative. In the United States, it takes only one reputable eyewitness to prove or disprove a case in our courts. In a country that places that much authority on one eyewitness testimony, allowing a person to be imprisoned or even executed based on it, your personal testimony has authority. We should share it with God-empowered authority.

Our testimony is relevant. That which we share of our relationship with God will be rooted in the past as we tell of life before Christ, and relay our conversion experience, and early Christian growth. However, our testimony must not emphasize the past to the extent that it de-emphasizes the present. If, in sharing with you the personal testimony of my marriage, I told you that I was married to Joanne Cunningham of San Antonio, Texas, on August 8, 1964, at 3:00 P.M. in the Trinity Baptist Church of San Antonio, and in the year 2014 we plan to celebrate our fiftieth anniversary, what helpful information would you know about my marriage? You know about as much as I would know of your Christian testimony if you told me that you became a Christian at age ten and you plan on going to heaven when you die. A relevant testimony is up-to-date and meaningful, as my marriage testimony would be if I shared how God is working in our family now. We should update our testimony as God continues to work powerfully in our life.

Our testimony should avoid excessive details and negative statements. Whereas the details make it personal, rather than a Xerox copy of someone else's testimony, excessive details tend to become boring to an uninformed listener. Unless it was Billy Graham or some other well-known person, the name of the person preaching in the service where we made a public profession of our faith is excessive since the listener would not know the preacher. Too many references to self, especially pre-conversion references to self, make the testimony negative. We should share what life was like before Christ but not to the extent that we glorify the non-Christian lifestyle and present a negative Christian testimony. I grew up in a day when some youth evangelists so glorified their lives of sin before they met Christ and spent so little time on their positive Christian experiences, that some of my peers decided to go out and "get a testimony." The effect was negative because the emphasis was on self rather than on Jesus Christ. We need to share a positive, persuasive testimony.

Our testimony should be in the language of the people. Christians are loaded with in-church terminology. We understand what we mean when talking to each other; but non-Christians, especially if they have not been raised in a church, do not understand our language. When a doctor shares the results of an examination in medical terms, it confuses us.

That is the way non-Christians feel when, looking at them as "prospects," we "share" with them the "grace" of God, urging them to get under "conviction" and "invite Jesus into their hearts," so that they can "get saved" out of "the world in which they live," get "washed in the blood of the Lamb," and join the "fellowship of the saints." I understand every part of that statement, but do non-Christians with whom we are trying to communicate the good news of Jesus Christ? We must be prepared to share our testimony in a terminology that can be understood.

Our testimony is important enough to prepare. A call to share is a call to prepare, thus we should write out our testimony. We might allow a Christian friend to read it or listen as we read it for the purpose of constructive criticism. We should read our testimony in light of the preceding suggestions, then rewrite it again until we have a testimony that communicates. Preparation will also allow us to cover the important facts as we condense our testimony. If we prepare a condensed version, we can elaborate as time and interest allow. On the other hand, if we have a long testimony, we may not be able to share it in a brief encounter. I have jokingly said that I have two testimonies—an elevator testimony and a coast-to-coast flight testimony. What I really mean is that I have a condensed version that can be given in less than two minutes and a long version that can be given at whatever length the listener is interested in hearing. Having prepared our testimony, we should share it in the power of the Holy Spirit.

Our testimony is a part of a larger plan. Since "we are witnesses of these things; and so is the Holy Spirit" (Acts 5:32), let's define the responsibilities. God has assigned to the Holy Spirit numerous tasks, some of which we would rather do ourselves. Most Christians enjoy that part of witnessing that convicts the non-Christian. We can easily elaborate on "all have sinned" (Rom. 3:23) and even get specific. Likewise, most Christians enjoy that part of witnessing that converts the non-Christian to Christ. We can so strongly emphasize "Behold, I stand at the door and knock" (Rev. 3:20) that we almost open the door for them. Both of these tasks—conviction and conversion—have been assigned to the Holy Spirit (John 16:7–15). Our testimonies fit into this larger plan as we share what God has done in our life and what God can do in another's life. We must allow the Holy Spirit to do his work, understand that others will also be a part of the witnessing process, share faithfully our testimony and the plan of salvation, and let God's power generate the results. We should not claim, "I led him (or her) to Christ," with emphasis on the "I." It's more correct to say, "I was a part of a greater plan that resulted in him (or her) becoming a Christian." We must understand our role in a larger plan.

One of the most intriguing statements in the Old Testament is a simple statement about Enoch. It's right in the middle of all those genealogical accounts. It's that section of the Bible where we likely quit when we are reading through the Bible in one year. So and so begat so and so, and they lived so many years, and they begat so and so. One preacher called it the history of *nobodyism*. We seldom if ever hear of any of those people. So, we conclude we'll not read that section. Yet there is an interesting statement there: "Enoch walked with God; and he was not, for God took him" (Gen. 5:24). That's the perfection of the walk. I would hope that it could be said of each one of us that we walked with our Lord and one day we "were not" because God just walked us right on into heaven.

A worthy goal of our lives as Christians is to so let the Spirit of God live within us that when we have walked in that Spirit to that last earthly step, the next step into heaven would be a baby step instead of a giant step. Washington Gladden wrote:

> O Master, let me walk with thee
> In lowly paths of service free;
> Tell me thy secret—help me bear
> The strain of toil, the fret of care.
>
> Help me the slow of heart to move
> By some clear, winning word of love;

Teach me the wayward feet to stay
And guide them in the homeward way
Teach me Thy patience: still with Thee
In closer, dearer company,
In work that keeps faith sweet and strong,
In trust that triumphs over wrong.

In hope that sends a shining ray
Far down the future's broadening way,
In peace that only Thou canst give,
With Thee, O Master, let me live.

It has been my observation that some disciples of Jesus will only walk. Some walk because they do not know how to run. Having begun to walk, other believers left them alone to progress on their own or perhaps they had an unteachable spirit. Others walk because they have no desire to run. Walking has become comfortable and they have grown complacent. Perhaps the early excitement of discipleship has worn off and they have become spiritually unfit. A few will forget how to walk as they get more and more involved in running. They will begin to see themselves as advanced disciples. Some day, when they need again to walk, they will have to re-learn. Still others will walk and run. If you're ready to run, read on.

EXERCISES FOR SPIRITUAL FITNESS

Day One Describe what it was like prior to your conversion when you first felt Holy Spirit conviction:_____

_____

_____

Day Two Describe your conversion experience: _____

_____

_____

Day Three How have you found strength to resist the deeds of the flesh and is there a particular one that has been extra difficult for you? _____

_____

_____

Day Four Which expression of the fruit of the Spirit do you see most clearly in your life today? _____

_____

_____

Day Five In completing the above questions, you have just outlined your own testimony: life before Christ (conviction), accepting Christ (conversion), current events in your Christian walk (tempting deeds of the flesh and evidence of Spirit-fruit). Work on your testimony by sharing it with at least one other Christian this week and seeking their critique.

Scriptural strengths to remember:
1. John 16:8
2. Psalm 51:12–13
3. Galatians 5:22–23
4. Acts 5:32

WEEK FIVE

Running

A T THE GOLDEN AGE of fifty, I determined it was time for me to begin a physical fitness program that included running. Please understand that while I had spent the earlier portion of my life involved in various athletic endeavors and even at fifty was fairly fit, I had never before run consistently. I decided if I was going to be successful, I would need a goal. I looked at the race schedules in the local paper and entered a one-mile race several Saturdays in advance. This would motivate me to get in shape.

On that memorable Saturday, I lined up with a host of others (mostly children and elderly women, some with their dogs on leash), having never before run "against a clock" or in competition. On the way to winning that race in my age division (there were only two of us), I learned several lessons. First, I learned I could run in front of the group but only if I decided to do so; it didn't happen by accident. Second, I learned I could run behind the group and there was some comfort in following. Third, I learned I could run with the group and actually sense a kind of camaraderie. Finally, I learned I could run in place if the conditions dictated it. These same lessons apply to spiritual fitness.

RUNNING AHEAD: DECISION MAKING

Spiritual fitness is a gift from God. It is not the self-generated state that many seem to believe. Nor is it a program created by church leaders. When we have done all we can do, fitness still comes from God. On the other hand, we must do all we can do. You will not become spiritually fit without deciding to work at it, to employ God-created discipline.

Paul wrote about the discipline needed to run a race. First Corinthians 9:24–27 says:

> Do you not know that those who run in a race all run, but only one receives the prize? Run in such a way that you may win. Everyone who competes in the games exercises self-control in all things. They then do it to receive a perishable wreath, but we an imperishable. Therefore I run in such a way, as not without aim; I box in such a way, as not beating the air; but I discipline my body and make it my slave, so that, after I have preached to others, I myself will not be disqualified.

For the spiritually fit leader to run ahead, good decision-making skills must be developed and implemented. We live in a decision making society. The average grocery store has 36,000 items for sale. Crest has 36 different sizes, shapes, and flavors of toothpaste. Revlon has 158 colors and shades of lipstick. Levi makes over 70,000 products. Cable TV systems offer 50-to-80 channels. There are 200-to-300 new magazines and newspapers published each year. And the choices are not limited to the secular. Literally thousands of new Christian books and tapes are published each year. Brochures advertising helpful conferences arrive in my mailbox almost weekly. When I get on the religious internet, the choices are astonishing. How can you make the right decision every time?

Let's look at a case study in decision-making. Several hundred years before the birth of Christ, a prophet by the name of Jonah lived in the village of Gath-hepher (2 Kings 14:25). One day he received a call from God to go to Nineveh and preach judgment (Jon. 1:1–2). Nineveh was an ancient city with an unhappy past. While there were many people there, it was not a popular assignment for an up-and-coming prophet with an impressive resume. So Jonah had a decision to make: run to Nineveh, capital of the Assyrian empire or run somewhere else.

Jonah decided to run the opposite direction. He ran to Joppa, a port on the Mediterranean seacoast and boarded a ship to Tarshish, a commercial outpost on the southwest coast of Spain and the farthest point west for the Phoenician traders. Jonah attempted to run as far from God's chosen destination as he could get. Besides, Tarshish was more exciting, exotic, and adventurous. It was a resort city of great wealth. Every three years, King Solomon had received ships from Tarshish loaded with gold, silver, and ivory (1 Kings 10:22).

Jonah faced two choices: God's way and the world's way. God said Nineveh; the world said Tarshish. God's choice is not always as unattractive as Nineveh but the world's choice is always tempting. Having decided to run the world's way, Jonah was thrown into the sea to be swallowed by a large fish. This was God's way of protecting Jonah until he could make the right decision. Crying out to God (Jon. 2:1–10), Jonah was given a second chance. This time Jonah made the right choice and went to Nineveh (Jon. 3:1–3).

God allows us the freedom to make decisions. When wrong decisions are made, God often protects us. Sometimes second chances are offered by God in decision making. *The Living Bible* paraphrase of Proverbs 2:9 is significant: "He shows how to distinguish right from wrong, how to find the right decision every time."

Following are some questions that we might ask ourselves as we try to "find the right decision every time":

1. Is the decision one that is in harmony with God's Word? (See Ps. 119:105.)
2. Is the decision one I'd want everyone to know? (See Prov. 10:9; James 4:17; Rom. 14:14.)
3. Is the decision one that will make me a better person? (See 1 Cor. 10:23; 1 Cor. 6:12.)
4. Is the decision one that will harm anyone else? (See Rom. 14:12–13; Rom. 15:1–2.)
5. Is the decision one that is supported by trusted friends? (See Prov. 18:1.)

There are some errors to avoid in decision-making. A few of these are listed here:

1. Avoid an unwillingness to think ahead. (See Deut. 32:28–29.)
2. Avoid an unwillingness to take advice. (See Prov. 12:15.)
3. Avoid an unwillingness to suspect oneself. (See Ps. 139:23–24.)
4. Avoid an unwillingness to discount personalities. (See 1 Cor. 16:12.)
5. Avoid an unwillingness to learn from past experiences. (See Prov. 26:11.)
6. Avoid an unwillingness to wait on the Lord. (See Ps. 27:14.)
7. Avoid an unwillingness to follow guidance already given by God. (See Phil. 3:16.)

What happens when you make a wrong decision? For Jonah, although the path back was traumatic, God protected, gave him second chance, and blessed him. However, he had to live with the circumstances—the image, the trauma, the memory. While God forgives, restores, and blesses, God does not remove the consequences of the wrong decision.

Running ahead through the making of right decisions is a quality of the spiritually fit disciple, but we must not always run ahead. Sometimes we must follow.

RUNNING BEHIND: FOLLOWING GOD'S WILL

To seek, find, and follow the will of God is the most challenging and at the same time most rewarding task of a disciple. W. O. Cushing wrote:

> Follow! Follow! I would follow Jesus!
> Anywhere, everywhere, I would follow on!
> Follow! Follow! I would follow Jesus!
> Everywhere he leads me I would follow on!

Paul discovered that following God's will occasionally meant setting his own will aside and following "anywhere, everywhere." Consider these words from Acts 16:6–10:

> They passed through the Phrygian and Galatian region, having been forbidden by the Holy Spirit to speak the word in Asia; and after they came to Mysia, they were trying to go into Bithynia, and the Spirit of Jesus did not permit them; and passing by Mysia, they came down to Troas. A vision appeared to Paul in the night: a certain man of Macedonia was standing and appealing to him, and saying, "Come over to Macedonia and help us." When he had seen the vision, immediately we sought to go into Macedonia, concluding that God had called us to preach the gospel to them.

Paul was in the midst of following what he perceived to be God's will. The original purpose of this second missionary journey was to revisit and strengthen the churches visited on the first journey. God closed the door and redirected Paul through a night vision. "Immediately," implying, they may have run or at least hurried, the group left for Macedonia. From Troas to Samothrace, a rocky island, to Neapolis, the seaport city for Philippi and on to Philippi where on the plains below, Augustus and Anthony fought the great battle against Brutus and Cassius. Here in Philippi Paul started the first Christian church in Europe and the gospel turned westward. Fortunately, Paul was ready to follow God's will.

Following God's will means being ready for God's interruptions. Paul learned this lesson on the Damascus road. As he journeyed on his way to persecute Christians, God intervened and Paul was converted to Christianity. Now Paul was not the first to experience God's interruption.

Thirteen times in the gospels Jesus extends the imperative— "follow me." This type of command offered in the imperative mood required immediate and complete obedience. Walking by the Sea of Galilee, Jesus called out "follow Me" to two brothers, Peter and Andrew (Matt. 4:18–19). A bit further, Jesus called two other brothers, James and John and they "followed Him" (Matt. 4:21–22). As Jesus passed by Matthew, he interrupted his life with the command, "Follow Me" (Matt. 9:9). Later, to his disciples, Jesus said, "If anyone wishes to come after Me, he must deny himself, and take up his cross and follow Me" (Matt. 16:24). To the rich, young, ruler Jesus said, "Follow Me" (Matt. 19:21). To one along the road, Jesus said, "Follow Me" (Luke 9:59). Still later Jesus said, "If anyone serves Me, he must follow Me" (John 12:26).

Nor is this interruptive command limited to the gospels? When Peter was in prison, an angel appeared to him and said, "Wrap your cloak around you and follow me" (Acts 12:8). And now, through a vision, God calls Paul to travel westward to Macedonia. If you desire to follow God's will, be ready for God's interruptions.

Following God's will also means being ready for God's revelations. When God closed one door for Paul, another door was opened and God revealed the next step. How does God reveal the next step to us today? Let me suggest four ways. Surely there are others, but these I've experienced.

God reveals through the Bible his overriding will for humankind. You cannot know God's will apart from God's Word. God will be consistent with the Word. A correct understanding of the Bible is our best authority and likewise our best commentary on God's will.

Second, God reveals through the Holy Spirit. The indwelling Spirit of God prompts us as he did Paul, sometimes in a vision, more often in less dramatic ways.

Third, God reveals through other people. The advice of trusted friends and even on occasion, unknown friends, often helps clarify insight into the interpretation of God's will.

Finally, God reveals through circumstances. Events that happen to or around us often apply to our search for God's will.

These four ways need to complement each other. God is not an author of confusion, but of harmony and peace (1 Cor. 14:33).

Some of the most miserable people I know are those who are overruling God's interruptions and tuning out God's revelations. I have a friend who enrolled in a Baptist college to prepare for a vocational ministry to which he felt called. Upon graduation, he entered a secular field and spent a career there. He admitted to me recently that he had been miserable most of his life. On the other hand when we allow for God's interruptions and listen to God's revelations, we experience the next step. When God interrupts and reveals, then God directs.

Following God's will means being ready for God's directions. God sent Paul west instead of east. Had Paul resisted and continued eastward, the gospel might never have made it to the west. God directs geographically as well as intellectually and emotionally. Wherever God directs, disciples are to go. Indeed, "the steps of a man are established by the Lord" (Ps. 37:23).

Perhaps it would be good to see some of the errors made in understanding and following God's directions. Sometimes we are *resistant to God's long-range planning.* True, God does not often let us in on knowing the long range, but he always has more for us than we see. God's immediate direction can only be understood in light of the long-range direction. Many of the children of Israel probably wondered why they were wandering in the wilderness. The reason was long-range. God was preparing them for the promised land (Deut. 32:28–29).

Another error we make is to *place too much weight on personal feelings.* We are just not that smart or pure. Personal agendas and impure thoughts crowd our understanding of God's directions.

The Psalmist asked God to search his thoughts to see if there were any hurtful ways in him and to lead him in the way everlasting (Ps. 139:23–24). God may need to remind us as Isaiah was reminded, "My thoughts are not your thoughts, nor are your ways My ways" (Isa. 55:8).

Our *unwillingness to wait on God* is the last error. There is often great time distance between God's interruption and God's directions. Impatient disciples run on ahead. The Psalmist encouraged us to "Wait for the Lord" (Ps. 27:14). Waiting may be the most difficult instruction of all. It no doubt was for the excited disciples who had just seen the resurrected Lord yet heard him say, "Stay in the city until you are clothed with power from on high" (Luke 24:49).

God has plans for every believer. Our responsibility is to discover what God's will is and then apply it to our lives. In the midst of following God's will, some may experience God's call to vocational ministry. Not everyone will but those who do, do so in the context of following God's will.

How can you discern God's call? Here are several suggestions. First, *identify where you are in the process*. Are you asking questions? Beginning to have an interest? Feeling uneasy about your own plans for the future? Responsive to God's directions? Committed to God's plan for your life?

Second, *study how God called men and women in the Bible*. Especially helpful are the methods God used to call Abraham, Moses, Joshua, Ruth, David, Esther, Isaiah, and Amos in the Old Testament and the disciples, Paul, and Timothy in the New Testament.

Third, *consider the calls of others in ministry such as your pastor, a missionary, a church staff member, or other minister friend*. How did God make them aware of the call? While each experience is unique, there are some experiences common to all.

Fourth, *evaluate whether this potential call to ministry is in harmony with what God has been doing and is presently doing in your life*. God's consistency is to be preferred over the world's intensity.

Fifth, *seek the advice and counsel of trusted friends, family members, and associates.* Many times, those who know you best spiritually and have watched you in action will have discerned your call before you do.

Sixth, *spend much time with God in prayer.* God's calling is not that hard to discover for those who talk with God faithfully and obediently.

God's directions come in God's way, as a part of God's larger agenda, on God's time schedule. Meanwhile, follow what you know to be God's will as it applies to you, right now. Ira F. Stamphill helped us understand the extent to which we must be willing to follow:

> I traveled down a lonely road
>   and no one seemed to care,
> The burden on my weary back
>   had bowed me to despair;
> I oft complained to Jesus
>   how folks were treating me,
> And then I heard Him say so tenderly:
> "My feet were also weary
>   upon the Calvary road,
> The cross became so heavy,
>   I fell beneath the load;
> Be faithful weary pilgrim,
>   The morning I can see—
> Just lift your cross
>   and follow close to Me."
>
> "I work so hard for Jesus"
>   —I often boast and say—
> "I've sacrificed a lot of things
>   to walk the narrow way;
> I gave up fame and fortune
>   —I'm worth a lot to Thee!"
> And then I heard Him gently say to me:

"I left the throne of glory
  and counted it but loss,
My hands were nailed in anger
  upon a cruel cross;
But now we'll make the journey
  with your hand safe in Mind—
So lift your cross
  and follow close to Me."

O Jesus,
  if I die upon a foreign field someday,
'Twould be no more than love demands
  —No less could I repay;
"No greater love hath mortal man
  than for a friend to die—"
These are the words He gently spoke to me:
"If just a cup of water
  I place within your hand,
Then just a cup of water
  is all that I demand;"
But if by death to living
  they can Thy glory see,
I'll take my cross
  and follow close to Thee.

When you've learned to run ahead in decision making and run behind in following God's will, you are ready to run with God's people in fellowship.

RUNNING WITH: FELLOWSHIP

In Hebrews 12:1–2 the writer speaks of "running with":

Therefore, since we have so great a cloud of witnesses surrounding us, let us also lay aside every encumbrance, and the sin which so easily entangles us, and let us run with endurance the race that is set before us, fixing our eyes on Jesus, the author and perfecter of faith, who for the joy set before Him endured the cross, despising the shame, and has sat down at the right hand of the throne of God.

The passage is plural, using the pronouns "we," "our," and "us" a total of six times.

We run side-by-side in the fellowship of other believers. The King James Version translates the word "surround" as "compassed." Like a compass, we are surrounded on the north, east, south, and west with "witnesses." Therefore, we run, as it were, on a circular track, surrounded on every side. As we run in circular fashion, we run alongside other runners; we pass and are passed by them. There is fellowship on the track. Paul understood this and wrote, "recognizing the grace that had been given to me, James and Cephas and John, who were reputed to be pillars, gave to me and Barnabas the right hand of fellowship" (Gal. 2:9).

The fellowship of other believers *provides support.* In the Special Olympics, a group of Downs Syndrome children were running the 100 meter dash. At the 75 meter mark, one child fell down. Spontaneously, all the children in the race stopped and then ran to the injured child. They helped their friend up, brushed the dirt off, and together, they all ran the final 25 meters. That's the way the spiritual race ought to be run—in fellowship and mutual support.

The fellowship of other believers likewise *provides accountability.* As we run together we must hold each other accountable in the race. I have an accountability group of Seminary students with whom I meet weekly. My accountability group has ten questions we ask each other:

1. Are you experiencing quality time alone with God?
2. Are you thinking pure and wholesome thoughts?
3. Are you living in obedience to God's will as best you understand it?
4. Are you experiencing sexuality within God's plan for male and female?
5. Are you using power and authority properly?

6.   Are you managing money wisely?
7.   Are you giving proper time and attention to family?
8.   Are you honoring God's call related to Seminary studies?
9.   Are you sharing your faith consistently?
10. Are you lying about any of the previous questions?

We all need such a group. Use our questions or develop your own, but be accountable to others and hold them accountable.

The fellowship of other believers *provides discipline.* Jesus said, "If your brother sins, go and show him his fault in private; if he listens to you, you have won a brother. But if he does not listen to you, take one or two more with you . . . if he refuses to listen to them, tell it to the church." (Matt. 18:15–17). For many, discipline is a missing ingredient in their life. When there is no discipline, there is no discipleship, no learning and no growth. Discipline is the responsibility of the disciple group. Neglect it and there is no spiritual fitness.

The fellowship of other believers *allows us to hurt together.* Derek Redmond had to drop out of the 1988 Olympic 400 meter race ninety seconds before the first heat. Hamstring problems had caused him to defer his dream of Olympic gold until 1992. The British runner trained hard for the '92 Barcelona Summer Games. In the race of his life, Derek was leading at the first turn. Then a sharp pain in the back of his thigh threw him to the track in agony with a torn hamstring muscle. Determination caused Derek to rise, wave off the medical assistance, and continue the race with no hope of winning a medal. However, even the tenacity of this dedicated runner could not get him to the finish line alone. As Derek hobbled down the final stretch, his father, Jim Redmond, pushed aside the security guards and made his way on to the track. Arm in arm, shoulder to shoulder, father and son finished the race together to the standing ovation of an awestruck crowd. *Sports Illustrated* wrote, "Derek didn't walk away with the gold medal, but he walked away with an incredible memory of a father who, when he saw his son in pain, left his seat in the stands to help him finish the race." Blessed are those who learn how to hurt together.

The fellowship with other believers *allows us to wait* together. One of the more difficult activities for a disciple, especially in an impatient society, is to wait. Yet there are times of waiting. When Mary received the announcement that she was to give birth to Jesus, she went to Elizabeth who likewise was waiting for the birth of John the Baptist: "When Elizabeth heard Mary's greeting, the baby leaped in her womb; and Elizabeth was filled with the Holy Spirit. And she cried out with a loud voice and said, 'Blessed are you among women, and blessed is the fruit of your womb'" (Luke 1:41–42). Mary stayed with Elizabeth for three months (Luke 1:56) and during this time these two young women affirmed each other's waiting. They model for us the fellowship of waiting together.

Support one another, hold others accountable, and be held accountable, share discipline, hurt together, and wait together. This is part of what it means to run with the fellowship of others.

We also run with the fellowship of "a cloud of witnesses." The writer has mentioned some by name in the preceding chapter and others by groupings—"men of whom the world was not worthy" (Heb. 11:38). While the scripture does not say they are watching us, it does imply they are encouraging us on. Like them we are to "also lay aside every encumbrance and the sin that so easily entangles us" and then, we are to run the race before us.

They have already run their race and of them the writer says, "All these, having gained approval through their faith, did not receive what was promised, because God had provided something better for us, so that apart from us they would not be made perfect" (Heb. 11:39-40). We belong together—we and the cloud of witnesses. Let us run *with* their support as they cheer us on.

As we run with other believers and with the encouragement of a cloud of witnesses, we are to run with endurance. The idea is patience. Anyone can quit in a man's race, but not this race. This is God's race and it must be run with endurance. Look at Jesus. He "endured the cross, despising the shame." He did not quit. He endured. So must we.

American Gail Devers won the 100-meter dash by only six one-hundredths of a second over her four top competitors in 1992. Gail suffers from Grave's disease. Just one year before she won the Olympic gold, Gail came within two days of having both feet amputated. After surviving that scare, she began to train and push herself toward her goal. Her determination and persistence won the day. Who would have thought the fastest woman in the world was the same woman who almost lost her feet. This showed the triumph of the Olympic spirit. As you run with similar persistence and endurance, you will show the triumph of the Christian spirit.

We are to run with our eyes fixed on Jesus. Don't just glance at him. Don't just offer an occasional look. Fix your eyes on him. You will run well in a human race by fixing your eyes not at the crowd, nor at the other runners, but directly toward the goal. The writer of Proverbs says, "Let your eyes look directly ahead and let your gaze be fixed straight in front of you" (Prov. 4:25).

When you look at Jesus you see the "author and perfecter of faith" who ran his own race with a combination of "joy" and endurance and has, "sat down at the right hand of the throne of God"—our finish line. John Fawcett wrote:

> Blest be the tie that binds
> Our hearts in Christian love;
> The fellowship of kindred minds
> Is like to that above.

RUNNING IN PLACE: REST

Not even the greatest athlete can run all the time. Rest is as much a part of fitness as is activity. Likewise the spiritually fit disciple must find time for rest. And yet we do not. We remain busy. In a commentary of our day, Henri Nouwen once said, "One way to express the spiritual crisis of our time is to say that most of us have an address but cannot be found there." In contrast, the Bible says, "The sleep of the working man is pleasant" (Eccles. 5:12). Yet rest doesn't mean quitting or even ceasing to serve. Perhaps "running in place" is a good description of disciple rest.

Jesus had difficulty finding time to rest. He understood that sometimes we have to rest on the move—run in place. On one occasion, Jesus "went away . . . to the region of Tyre. And when He had entered a house, He wanted no one to know of it; yet He could not escape notice" (Mark 7:24). The nonbelievers and the seekers in his day seemed to always know where he was. Resting on-the-run was the pattern of his life. Always on the go may be the pattern of our life, but we must rest, even if it is on-the-run.

The wrong kind of rest was experienced by Jesus' disciples. It was to be for them one of the most exciting and best remembered nights of their lives. They had been asked to pray with Jesus. Judas and the soldiers were coming with swords and clubs to take him. This was the night of preparation. The prayers of this night would ensure the endurance of the cross. And the disciples fell asleep! Coming to them Jesus asked, "Are you still sleeping and resting?" (Mark 14:41).

Sometimes we hit very strategic times in our service when the task calls for the best we have in us only to find ourselves sleepy. We wanted very much to awaken on a given day to meet the excitement of the day with gusto only to find that the lateness of the bedtime hour on the preceding night prevented us from doing so? We needed very much to pay attention to what someone was saying only to find the lack of sleep caused our minds to wander?

This last week of Jesus' earthly life had been a hectic time, and the pace must have been intense, but surely these disciples could have found a better time to sleep. It would have been far easier for the disciples to have stayed awake in the crucial time had they gotten the necessary sleep at its proper time. Sometimes the most crucial thing you can do is sleep. Then when the Lord says to us, "Get up, let us be going" (Mark 14:42), not only will our mind and heart be ready, so will our body.

It might help to know that while we sleep, "He who keeps you will not slumber" (Ps. 121:3). Rest is a part of God's plan for your ministry: "The sleep of a labouring man is sweet, whether he eat little or much" (Eccles. 5:12 KJV).

This is not an encouragement to the lazy. Jesus' promise to give rest to his disciples was preceded by, "Come to Me, all who are weary and heavy-laden, and I will give you rest" (Matt. 11:28). The lazy do not become weary nor do they get heavy-laden. This is a promise to active, working disciples. To disciples who take his yoke upon themselves and learn from him, Jesus promises, "You will find rest for your souls" (Matt. 11:29). Lazy rest is a sedative. Running rest is a stimulant. One is an enemy of strength; the other is its hidden resource.

So, all disciples must rest—the most spiritual to the least spiritual, the most fit to the most out-of-shape, those on a pedestal and those in a pit. How then, do we rest?

One way is to "find a place for the Lord" in our rest. The Psalmist says, "Surely I will not enter my house, Nor lie on my bed; I will not give sleep to my eyes Or slumber to my eyelids, Until I find a place for the Lord" (Ps. 132:3–5). Ignoring God at bedtime is a sure path to insomnia. On the other hand, reading God's word and communicating with God at bedtime beats sleeping pills.

When rest is interrupted, we can pray ourselves back into rest. God may awaken us in the night in order that intercession may be offered for someone on the other side of the world who, in the daylight hours, stands in need of prayer. While our minds are not racing with work, God may remind us of a prayer concern. In the quietness of our rest, we can pray.

Glory in godly rest. Those who in their work flaunt their sinfulness and deny their need for God, encounter turbulence in their rest. Selfish, work time demands, become rest time demons while the selfless, God-honoring disciple finds, "times of refreshing . . . from the presence of the Lord" (Acts 3:19). If we desire God to be our comfort in rest, we must allow God to be our companion in work.

So, in a day when ministry is a high-stress assignment, when spiritual warfare terminology is freely used, when burnout is descriptive of active Christian servants, when there is more work than time at the end of the day, we better learn how to run in place, to rest.

We have walked and we have run, but we are not yet in spiritual shape. Many stop here. After all, walking is enjoyable for the most part. It takes little energy and a minimum amount of discipline. Those who don't walk admire those who do. Running is invigorating and challenging. It even creates a kind of spiritual high. Even more to be admired is the faithful and consistent runner. But for the majority, enough is enough. "Seriously now," they reason, "we don't want to be fanatical about this business of spiritual fitness." But we have only just begun. Take a deep breath and get ready for the next step. Getting in discipleshape includes pressing on and we must press on!

EXERCISES FOR SPIRITUAL FITNESS

Day One   Have you ever had an experience of resistance like Jonah had? If so, what positive lessons did you learn? _____

_____

_____

Day Two   There is a list of questions on page 84 to help you find the right decision and also a list of errors to avoid in decision making. What would you add to either of these lists? _____

_____

_____

Day Three Have you ever experienced one of God's interruptions? If so, describe your feelings about it then and now. _____

_____

_____

Day Four   I share ten accountability questions on pages 91–92. Can you add another or improve on one of the ten listed? _____

Day Five   What does it mean for you to run in place (rest) this week? _____

_____

_____

Scriptural strengths to remember:
        1. 1 Corinthians 9:24–27
        2. Psalm 139:23–24
        3. Hebrews 12:1–2
        4. Matthew 11:28

Pressing On

THE OLYMPIC MOTTO includes three words that have motivated the athletes of the world throughout the decades. *"Citius, Altius, Fortius"* or "Faster, Higher, Stronger" pushes athletes beyond their previous best. It is a call to preparation that peeks at performance time. Paul called it *pressing on*.

For most people, walking is a natural exercise, done with very little effort. While running requires more discipline, as well as energy, it is still possible for many. Pressing on is different. It is a level beyond walking and running, measuring full-grown adulthood rather than developing youth. Having both walked and run, Paul singles out this exercise: "one thing I do . . . I press on" (Phil. 3:13–14).

Paul desired to lay hold of the "prize of the upward call of God in Christ Jesus." It was a prize of which he "was laid hold of by Christ Jesus." In other words Paul sought to grasp that which had grasped him, (Phil. 3:12–14) and so twice he says, "I press on" (Phil. 3:12, 14).

For what prize has God called us, grasped us, laid hold of us? Press on to that purpose. Forget what is behind, what distracts, and press forward. In a recent 200 meter run, a USA runner in Olympic competition glanced back at the finish line only to see a fellow runner lunge at the line and win the race. Don't look back, press on.

PRESSING ON THROUGH PRIORITIES

Paul was impressed with priorities. He said, "One thing I do" (Phil. 3:13) indicating his ability to focus on the crucial and lay aside the trivial. In his Sermon on the Mount, Jesus likewise emphasized focusing on the crucial. He said, "Seek first His kingdom and His righteousness" (Matt. 6:33).

What are kingdom priorities and what does God's righteousness look like? God's priority always seemed to be the gathering of a people—whether it be a nation, a family, a group of disciples or a church—to glorify God's own name and fulfill God's own purpose in the world. As you seek to become a more spiritually fit disciple and make disciples of others you get caught up in God's priorities.

I have seen hundreds of agendas: in churches, in associations, and on campuses; at international, national, state and local levels; in committee meetings, in faculty meetings, in staff meetings. I have watched men and women fight over things that are not even on the fringe of God's agenda. I've observed supposedly mature believers play spiritual trivial pursuit. Only rarely have I seen a tear, heard a sob or a voice quiver over the lostness of people and the immaturity of believers. Yet this is God's agenda, God's priority—making disciples who make disciples.

How do we balance a busy, demanding schedule in order to make time for our priorities and God's? No time management system works for everyone. We have different personality types, different work ethics, different schedules, and different outside demands. Some are feelers, others are thinkers. However, all of us fall victim to certain myths of time management. Let's look at some of these myths.

Myth #1: *"I just need more time."* The truth is we have all the time we need to do what God has designed us to do. God does not mock us by giving us more to do than we have God-given time to accomplish. The problem comes when we try to do more or less than God asks. We can not burn out doing God's will. We can and possibly will burn out doing more or less than God's will. We don't need more time, we need more discipline of the time God has given us.

Myth #2: *"If I work longer, I'll accomplish more."* The truth is we lose time in the small units first. Minutes are lost before hours are lost, hours lost before days. The solution is not adding more work time on the end of the normal work day. The solution is making better use of gaps of time that would otherwise be lost—ten minutes between conferences, five minutes before a meeting, the time before a meal. We don't need to work longer, we need the discipline of working smarter.

Myth #3: *"If I work harder, I'll accomplish more."* While hard work is certainly to be commended, working harder usually means working through break or relaxation times. Down time is an absolute necessity for the proper functioning of the body. We need to divert daily, withdraw weekly (the Biblical concept of the Sabbath allows for this), and take an intermission intermittently (as in vacation time). We don't need to work harder; we need the discipline of balancing retreat and charge.

Myth #4: *"I can manage my time."* The truth is we can't manage time, we can only manage ourselves. Everyone has twenty-four hours per day. We don't need time management; we need the discipline of self management.

So, without imposing another system of time management on us, here is a collection of suggestions that should assist all of us in managing ourselves and making the priority, the priority:

1. Pray for effective use of time.
2. Make a list of things that need to be done.
3. Prioritize the list.

4. Complete at least one task early in the work day.
5. Delegate tasks to others.
6. Set goals—short-term, immediate and long-term.
7. Learn to say no.
8. Use prime time for prime tasks.
9. Try to avoid perfectionism.
10. Combine activities where possible.
11. Handle interruptions quickly but courteously.
12. Understand some interruptions become priorities.
13. Take a break.
14. Break large projects down into smaller steps.
15. Go high tech if it is more efficient.
16. Read and respond to mail at the same time.
17. Play waste basketball and slam dunk outdated material.
18. Meet others on their turf. It's easier to leave.
19. Don't put off difficult jobs; they'll get bigger.
20. Create a filing system and use it.

The writer of Ecclesiastes indicated there was a time for many activities (Eccles. 3:1–8). Remember that God created time as we know it (Gen. 1:14). God sent Jesus in a fullness of time (Gal. 4:4). God will someday call time (Rev. 10:5–7). In the meantime, God wants us to redeem the time (Eph. 5:15–16; Col. 4:5). Leslie Weatherhead, in his book *Time for God*, mathematically calculated a schedule which compares a lifetime of "three score and ten" years with the hours of a single day from 7:00 A.M. to 11:00 P.M. It works like this:

> If you're 15 years old, it's 10:25 A.M.
> If you're 20 years old, it's 11:34 A.M.
> If you're 25 years old, it's 12:42 P.M.
> If you're 30 years old, it's 1:51 P.M.
> If you're 35 years old, it's 3:00 P.M.
> If you're 40 years old, it's 4:08 P.M.
> If you're 45 years old, it's 5:16 P.M.
> If you're 50 years old, it's 6:25 P.M.

If you're 55 years old, it's 7:34 P.M.
If you're 60 years old, it's 8:42 P.M.
If you're 65 years old, it's 9:51 P.M.
If you're 70 years old, it's 11:00 P.M.

No matter how old we are, it's later than we think and the priorities lie ahead. But, we will not need to tackle them in our own strength. There is power available.

PRESSING ON WITH POWER

Several years ago, my wife and I attended the Rose Parade in Pasadena, California. In the midst of it, a flower-covered vehicle stopped. Mechanics worked feverishly to discover the problem. It was discovered that the vehicle was out of gas. To make matters worse, the float was sponsored by a major oil company. Sometimes disciples learn the hard way that we who advertise to be disciples of the living God must draw our power, our energy from that same God. The God who calls us to discipleship supplies the power for us to function as disciples.

Paul had been writing about making spiritually fit disciples in the previous verses when he concluded, "For this purpose also I labor, striving according to His power, which mightily works within me" (Col. 1:29). Paul was "striving," or pressing on in the work of his calling, but not in his own power. Paul discovered a power for the priority and so can we. He who "works within" is the Holy Spirit. Holy Spirit power is described in the following paragraphs.

We have already established in an earlier chapter that the Holy Spirit *convicts* and *converts*. He convicts of sin because people do not believe in Jesus Christ. He convicts of righteousness, a right pattern of conduct modeled by Jesus because Jesus was going back to the Father to be seen no more. He convicts of judgment because the prince of this world, Satan, is judged. Having convicted of sin, righteousness, and judgment (John 16:9–11), the Holy Spirit then converts and guides people "into all the truth" (John 16:13).

The Holy Spirit also *consecrates* or sanctifies. After a brief description of the unrighteous, Paul told the Christians in Corinth "such were some of you; but you were washed, but you were sanctified, but you were justified in the name of the Lord Jesus Christ and in the Spirit of our God" (1 Cor. 6:11). When writing to the church at Thessalonica, Paul said he was thankful for this church because "God has chosen you from the beginning for salvation through sanctification by the Spirit" (2 Thess. 2:13). Simon Peter indicated that our obedience to Jesus Christ was through "the sanctifying work of the Spirit" (1 Pet. 1:2).

The Holy Spirit *clarifies* or guides us to the truth. In that last message to his disciples, Jesus reminded them that "when He, the Spirit of truth, comes, He will guide you into all the truth" (John 16:13). Due to an extensive weekend conference schedule and interim pastorate ministry, I frequently find myself driving back to my home in Fort Worth, Texas, in the late night or early morning hours. Usually (especially if I have been away for several days and am experiencing some homesickness) I tune my car radio dial to WBAP 820 AM, Fort Worth, Texas—a 50,000 watt "clear channel station." This not only gives me music and news from home, it also gives it to me clearly—even hundreds of miles away. Being a clear channel station means that the transmitting power is great enough that one can hear the signal from a distance. When the weather is bad, I can get the station, but it is sometimes clouded with static. Turbulent weather affects even a clear channel station. The Holy Spirit clarifies or guides the disciple to truth.

Related perhaps most closely to conviction is the fact that the Holy Spirit *climatizes* (i.e., sets the climate and the surroundings in which the disciple can bear witness effectively). We should learn a lesson from advertising. Advertisers are masters at catching the attention of potential customers. The advantage Christians have over the advertising world is that we are not solely responsible for creating the climate in which to witness. The Holy Spirit climatizes our surroundings for effective evangelism. If we live in touch with the work of the Holy Spirit, we will function in a climate that is conducive to spiritual fitness.

The Holy Spirit *comforts*. Jesus told His disciples, "I will ask the Father, and He will give you another Helper [comforter], that He may be with you forever" (John 14:16). While there is comfort in knowing the presence of the Holy Spirit in our lives, there is a tendency to become comfortable. This is not what Jesus had in mind by leaving us a Comforter. Some take comfort in the presence of the power of the Holy Spirit in their lives; others have become so comfortable that they appear to be asleep. An abundance of comfort is a proper priority in the cemetery, but not in a spiritually fit disciple, who is alive and on mission for Jesus Christ in the power of the Holy Spirit.

The Holy Spirit *compels* rather than repels (i.e., pushes people toward Jesus Christ rather than pushing people away from him). When my son was twelve, he came home from summer camp and informed us he had been "repelling." His mother was upset to hear that our son had not been well-received. I explained that he had been *rappelling*, not "repelling." Rapelling is an exciting, adventurous technique for rapidly descending a steep incline or mountain by sliding down a rope secured around the body.

When my son told us they let him rappel down a seventy-foot cliff, my wife and I shuddered. I imagined my boy seven stories up, dangling from a rope. I could picture his young legs shoving him away from the mountain over and over as he slid toward the ground. His propelling thrusts away from the outcrop soon lost their force, and the laws of physics compelled him back to the stony cliff again and again.

This comparison of rappelling (and repelling) to the work of the Holy Spirit is apt. While our human questions cause us to "bounce off" Jesus several times in the process of reaching a "grounded" knowledge of him, the power of the Holy Spirit compels us back to the truth. The work of the Holy Spirit draws sinners toward Jesus Christ despite our comparatively feeble efforts to kick at the Rock.

The Holy Spirit *controls* the spiritually fit disciple. At a recent baseball game, I sat behind a man who drank at least one beer per inning and in long innings, he consumed more than one. Watching him get drunk helped me to understand the parallel that Paul was trying to make in Ephesians 5:18: "do not get drunk with wine . . . but be filled with the Spirit." From his conversation, I learned that this man had undergone a frustrating day at work. I'm not sure how many drinks he had before arriving at the baseball game, but by the third inning, I noticed that he was losing control. For one thing, his speech became louder, more constant, and more bold. Whereas, in the first inning he did not like the umpire, by the third inning he wanted to kill the umpire. At the beginning of the game, he knew nobody around him. By the fourth inning, this semi-intoxicated fan was talking to everyone around him, even those of us who did not care to listen.

Who of all persons should be more under control by an outside force than the believer under control of Holy Spirit power? The Holy Spirit power should control our speech, making us more invincible, more constant, and even more bold.

The Holy Spirit *carries* the disciple. Recently, I found myself with a tight schedule. I was to speak at Ridgecrest, North Carolina, on Saturday morning and at Glorieta, New Mexico, on Sunday morning. There was no way in my own power that I could make both responsibilities. But after completing my assignment in Ridgecrest, I boarded a jet, sat back, and relaxed, submitting to another power source, and in just a few hours was in Glorieta in time to get a short night's sleep before my Sunday speaking responsibility. Jet power is greater than human power, but it is also more dangerous, involving more risk. Some people are scared of jet power and never submit to it. They will never reach certain destinations by depending upon their own power. I have learned when I run the risk of submitting to a power greater than my own—that of the Holy Spirit—I am able to cover more territory, both physical and spiritual.

Finally, the Holy Spirit *charges* or energizes. One Christmas I received a Dustbuster as a gift. This gadget reaches places where it is difficult to use a normal vacuum cleaner. The hint was overwhelmingly obvious—I needed to clean the trunk of the car, which was a task I had been putting off because it was so much trouble to take the vacuum cleaner out to the garage. As with most gifts requiring batteries or recharging, someone else in the family played with the gift before I got around to using it for its real purpose. While I was busy cleaning up those little bits and pieces of trash in the trunk, the Dustbuster made a slow, whirring, grinding sound and then stopped. I had at least two options. I could continue cleaning the carpet in the trunk by using a magnifying glass, tweezers, and trash can. Or, I could take the Dustbuster back in the house, use the attachment provided with it to plug into an electrical outlet, and reenergize its power. If I chose that option, I could relax with a glass of iced tea while it recharged and then complete my job with relative ease. In this case the choice was obvious. Unfortunately, in the spiritual realm, the options are not so easily chosen. Christians are prone to try to serve in their own power—even when that power runs low due to their lack of close relationship to the Holy Spirit. When we find ourselves running low on energy or power, we have the same two options. We can continue the work in our limited human power, or we can relax, get back in touch with the source of power, and become reenergized for a fresh approach to being a spiritually fit disciple of Jesus Christ.

In Colossians 1:29 Paul uses the Greek word *energeia* to speak of the Holy Spirit's power. This word is used nine times in the New Testament, each time by the apostle Paul. Never used to describe human power, this word, from which we obviously get our English word energy, is always used to describe divine power in action. In these nine uses, we can see the potential of God's power, the use of God's power, and the misuse of God's power. *Energeia* is variously translated power, might, and work.

How much power does God have? Of the nine uses of *energeia*, five are related to the potential of God's power. In Ephesians 1:19–20, Paul asked this question concerning the potential of God's power, then gave one answer: "What is the surpassing greatness of His power toward us who believe? These are in accordance with the working of the strength of His might which He brought about in Christ, when He raised Him from the dead and seated Him at His right hand in the heavenly places" (Eph. 1:19–20). Using the word *energeia* twice in this reference, Paul states that God's power raised Jesus from the dead. In another letter, Paul makes a similar reference: "For when you were baptized, you were buried with Christ, and in baptism you were also raised with Christ through your faith in the active power of God, who raised him from death." (Col. 2:12, GNB). In addition to God's power being used to raise Jesus from the dead, there are other examples of the potential of God's power.

How much power does God have? In writing to the church in Ephesus, Paul identified, Christ as the head of the body because in him "the whole body grows (strong) and builds itself up through love" (Eph. 4:16, GNB). The power of God is what holds the body, the church, together. A fifth use of the word *energeia* indicates the power of God is that which changes the human body at the end of this life: "For our citizenship is in heaven, from which also we eagerly wait for a Savior, the Lord Jesus Christ; who will transform the body of our humble state into conformity with the body of His glory, by the exertion of the power that He has even to subject all things to Himself" (Phil. 3:20–21). Now we need to look at the ways God allows divine power to be used.

How can we use God's power? The very same word, *energeia*, which described the potential of God's power was also used twice to describe how Paul used God's power in his ministry. Paul writes, "I was made a minister, according to the gift of God's grace which was given to me according to the working of his power" (Eph. 3:7). It was through God's power that Paul found his strength for service: "For this purpose also I labor, striving according to His power, which works mightily within me" (Col. 1:29). Paul found strength for his work in the power of God. As we serve God and work the work that God has given us to do, we have at our availability *energeia*—the kind of power that God used to raise Jesus from the dead, to hold the church together, and to change earthly bodies into heavenly bodies. The implementing of that kind of power is certain to arouse Satan's curiosity.

How does Satan attempt to use God's power? If you don't know by now, you will soon learn that anytime God has something good working, Satan always tries to get in on it. So it is with *energeia*. Twice in the Scriptures, the word *energeia* is used to describe the activity of Satan. Paul writes: "The Wicked One will come with the power of Satan and perform all kinds of false miracles and wonders, and use every kind of wicked deceit on those who will perish. They will perish because they did not welcome and love the truth so as to be saved. For this reason God sends the power of error to work in them so that they believe what is false" (2 Thess. 2:9–11, GNB). Even though Satan is allowed to misuse the power of *energeia*, it is obvious that it is God who supplies the power and allows the misuse of it. In so doing, God continues to control *energeia*. With God as the source of power, it is available to be used in ministry, all the way to the finish line.

PRESSING ON TOWARD THE FINISH

Parade magazine carried the following story out of the 1968 Olympic Games. At 7:00 P.M. on the evening of October 20, 1968, a few thousand spectators remained in the Mexico City Olympic stadium. It was cool and dark as the last of the marathon runners were carried off in exhaustion to first-aid stations. More than an hour earlier, Mamo Wolde of Ethiopia, looking as fresh at the finish line as when he started the race, won the grueling twenty-six mile event. His teammate, the legendary Abebe Bikila, winner of the two previous Olympic marathons in Rome and Tokyo, had been forced to retire from the race after ten miles because of a broken leg bone.

As the lingering spectators prepared to leave, those sitting near the marathon gates suddenly were aroused by the sound of sirens and policemen blowing whistles. Confused, the spectators looked toward the gate. A lone figure entered the stadium wearing the colors of Tanzania. His name was John Stephen Akhwari. He was the last man to finish the marathon. His leg was bloodied and bandaged, and he grimaced with each step. He had severely injured his knee in a fall. He painfully hobbled around the 400-meter track.

The spectators who remained rose and applauded the courage of this man as if they were receiving the winner. Akhwari painfully crossed the finish line. Without turning to the cheering crowd he slowly walked off the field.

Asked why he had not quit, since his task was so painful and he had no chance of winning a medal, he said, "My country did not send me seven thousand miles to start the race. They sent me seven thousand miles to finish it."

Likewise, you and I were not called to be spiritually fit disciples in order to just begin a race, or just run a race, but also in order to finish a race.

Not everyone presses on to the end. Their failure is not due to some fault along the way but a faulty beginning. When there is no faith commitment at the beginning, there is no faithfulness along the way and no victory at the finish line. This truth is seen in three men who sought to follow Jesus but stumbled out of the starting blocks.

As Jesus and his disciples traveled along a road, "someone said to Him, 'I will follow You wherever You go'" (Luke 9:57). The response of Jesus was, "The foxes have holes and the birds of the air have rests, but the Son of Man has nowhere to lay His head" (Luke 9:58). Since we never hear of this man again, we may assume that he, like the second and third man in the account, chose not to follow Jesus. He had heard Jesus teach, knew who he was and was impressed enough to want to follow, but he had not yet counted the cost of discipleship. The idea of nowhere to lay his head was too high a price for this man.

Simply hearing of Jesus and being impressed with Jesus is not sufficient to equip one to press on to the end.

A second man did not volunteer, but by his presence must have indicated an interest. It seems around every group of believers there are those who just exist on the fringes, interested, curious, but not committed. To this man, Jesus said, "Follow Me" (Luke 9:59). The man responded "Permit me first to go and bury my father" (Luke 9:59). Likely the man's father had not yet died and the response was that he would follow Jesus after the father's death and burial. Jesus would not accept discipleship on those terms but demanded immediate obedience. Following Jesus must be on Jesus' terms not on ours.

A third man said, "I will follow You, Lord; but first permit me to say good-bye to those at home" (Luke 9:61). Jesus responded "No one, after putting his hand to the plow and looking back, is fit for the kingdom of God" (Luke 9:62). This man was willing to call Jesus, "Lord" but denied his Lordship over all, insisting on calling the shots himself. Convenience is a wonderful thing, but it is secondary to obedience. Convenience calls us to look back, and looking back calls us to go back and Jesus will not allow going back. The commitment is made in the starting blocks, and it must be a life commitment.

Pressing on is tough. As I was writing this week's chapter, a minister friend came by my office. After asking what I was writing, he shared his burden. He and his wife had separated and he was moving back to his parent's home to give her some freedom to decide if she really wanted the divorce she had requested. He happens to be a weight lifter. His conclusion, knowing what I was writing, was, "It is easier for me to bench press 400 pounds, than work through this separation." Physical fitness, while sometimes demanding, is far easier than spiritual fitness. With both, if the initial commitment is not adequate, the journey will end short of the mark.

One who did press on to the end was Paul. In his latter days, he wrote to young Timothy:

I am already being poured out as a drink offering, and the time of my departure has come. I have fought a good fight, I have finished the course, I have kept the faith; in the future there is laid up for me the crown of righteousness, which the Lord, the righteous Judge, will award to me on that day; and not only to me, but also to all who have loved His appearing. (2 Tim. 4:6–8)

For those whose initial commitment was solid, who press on to the end, there waits a glorious victory celebration. Nearly anyone can make it 100 meters or perhaps even a mile, but discipleship is a marathon.

> Ne'r think the victory won
> Nor lay thine armor down.
> The work of faith will not be done,
> Till you obtain the crown.

At the end of the way, the record of your life will be celebrated in Heaven. Nine times the Bible makes reference to a book, a record, a remembrance of our earthly deeds (Exod. 32:32–33; Ps. 69:28; Dan. 12:1; Mal. 3:16; Luke 10:20; Phil. 4:3; Rev. 20:12; Rev. 21:27). These deeds will be revealed. Heaven will celebrate a fight fought to the finish, a race run rewardingly, a faith kept faithfully.

What kinds of deeds are being recorded in your heavenly record? In his book *Measure Your Life*, Wesley Duewel helps us with scripture suggestions:

Your whole life:	Rom. 14:10–12; 1 Cor. 3:11–15; 2 Cor. 5:10; 1 Pet. 4:5
Your words:	Ps. 19:14; Mal. 3:16; Matt. 12:36–37
Your thoughts:	Prov. 15:26; Ps. 19:14; 94:11; 139:2, 23; Isa. 55:7; Matt. 9:4; 15:19; Rom. 2:15–16; Heb. 4:12

Your secrets:	Eccles. 12:14; Rom. 2:16
Your motives:	Prov. 16:2; 1 Cor. 4:5
Your tears:	Ps. 56:8
Your prayers:	Ps. 5:8; 8:3–4
Your gifts to God:	Phil. 4:17–18; Heb. 13:16
Your helping others:	Matt. 25:34–40
Your visiting those who need you:	Matt. 25:34–40

So, press on. The trip will not be easy. No promise was ever made that it would. But there is a promised presence that makes the walking, running, pressing worth it all. As for me I want to join with Johnson Oatman, Jr. in proclaiming:

> I'm pressing on the upward way,
> New heights I'm gaining every day;
> Still praying as I onward bound,
> "Lord, plant my feet on higher ground."

You're getting in shape. It is the objective of a spiritually fit disciple. The spiritual muscles may ache, but the prize will be worth the pain. Once you get in shape the challenge changes. Now, you need to stay in shape. Read on!

EXERCISES FOR SPIRITUAL FITNESS

Day One   Paul pressed on toward the "prize of the upward call of God in Jesus Christ." For what "prize" has God called you and what distractions are you currently experiencing?_____

Day Two   Page 101 lists four myths of time management. Which one (or perhaps an added one not listed there) has the greatest negative effect on you? What could you do this week to correct it? _____

Day Three   Share one recent experience of feeling the Holy Spirit's power in a ministry you performed or share why you think you're not experiencing the Holy Spirit's power. _____

Day Four   If you knew for certain that God would energize you for a particular ministry, what would you attempt? _____

Day Five   Review the scripture suggestions of deeds that are recorded in heaven. What is one deed that may have been recorded out of your life last week and what is one you'd like to have recorded out of next week?

Scriptural strengths to remember:
1. Philippians 3:13–14
2. Colossians 1:29
3. 2 Timothy 4:6–8

phase three

STAYING

IN SHAPE:

THE CHALLENGE

OF A DISCIPLE

WEEK SEVEN

Communicating

THE CHALLENGE of staying in shape begins with your faithfulness in communicating with both our Lord and other people, continues with your ability to pace yourself, and faces its strongest test with your boldness in standing firm at the face of Satanic opposition.

The day in which we are living has been called the Golden Age of Communication. This need to communicate with each other around town and around our world has captured our imaginations. We desire to hear and to be heard, to understand one another and to be understood. More information has been generated in the last three decades than in the previous 5,000 years. Over 4,000 books are published every day. One weekday edition of *The New York Times* includes more information than the average person encountered in his entire lifetime in seventeenth century England. Twenty years ago, there were only 300 on-line databases; now over 8,000 such databases store literally billions of bits of information.

It is fitting this week that we consider our communication with God and with nonbelievers. When you have talked with God fully, you will come away with a burden for nonbelievers because this is God's burden. Further, you should never talk with a nonbeliever about God without first talking to God about the nonbeliever. Thus communication with both God and nonbelievers fits well together.

COMMUNICATING WITH GOD

When I was young, I lived with my grandparents. It was during World War II and my grandmother's favorite song was "In the Garden." In the chorus, C. Austin Miles writes of Jesus:

> And He walks with me, and He talks with me,
> And He tells me I am His own;
> And the joy we share as we tarry there,
> None other has ever known.

More than the fact that Jesus would walk with me, I was impressed with the idea that Jesus would talk with me. As we think about communicating with God, let's look word-for-word at the line "and He talks with me."

The word "and" speaks of what precedes it. It means "in addition to" and it connects with the next few words. Before we focus on communication, we need to be reminded that our Lord created us in his image, protected us in his love, saved us by his grace, forgave us by his power, filled us with his spirit, perfects us with his presence, will come for us in his glory "and" communicates with us through prayer.

In addition to everything else we receive from the Lord, we need to receive and implement this gift of communication in order to stay in shape spiritually.

Prayer begins with the Lord. It is *he* that talks with me. In the beginning, with the Father and the Holy Spirit, prayer was his idea, not an idea created by either our casual or crisis needs. Because it's his idea, prayer means more to him than it does to us. Like parents accepting long distance collect calls from their children, even though it cost them money, the conversation will mean more to the parent than the child.

The priority is on him, not on our ability to pray to him. Someone once said, "More things are wrought by prayer than this world dreams of." Not so. More things are not wrought by prayer. Rather more things are wrought by the Lord, through prayer, than this world dreams of.

Prayer was of extreme importance to Jesus. It was more important than teaching and healing. When great multitudes came to Jesus he withdrew to pray (Luke 5:15–16). Prayer was more important to Jesus than rest. Jesus would often get up long before day to pray (Mark 1:35) and on occasion would pray through the night (Luke 6:12). Prayer was more important to our Lord than miracles. When Satan asked permission to sift Peter like wheat, rather than miraculously sparing Peter, Jesus prayed for him (Luke 22:32). Prayer was more important to Jesus than missionary and evangelistic strategy. Jesus' one prayer request to the church was to pray to the Lord of the harvest to send workers into the harvest (Matt. 9:38). Prayer must have meant more to Jesus than preaching since it is never recorded that he taught his disciples to preach, but did teach them to pray (Matt. 6:5–15; Luke 11:2–4).

Prayer was so important to Jesus that Luke used the Greek word *proseuchomai*, meaning "to pray," thirty-five times (nineteen in the gospel of Luke; sixteen in Acts). Jesus began his ministry with prayer at his baptism (Luke 3:21–22). He prayed before calling his first disciples (Luke 6:12–16). Jesus was praying when he was transfigured (Luke 9:28–31). Before he taught his disciples and in the Garden of Gethsemane Jesus prayed (Luke 11:1–4). It was the pattern of his earthly ministry and the pattern of his resurrected life. The writer of Hebrews reminds us that "He always lives to make intercession" (Heb. 7:25).

It is significant that *he* (Jesus) talks with me for he (Jesus) is the supreme role model for praying disciples. He taught his disciples the model prayer, commonly referred to as The

Lord's Prayer (Matt. 6:9–13; Luke 11:2–4). He also gave his disciples another model by praying aloud what is often called, The High Priestly Prayer (John 17). The spiritually fit disciple would do well to model after the following three divisions of this prayer.

In the first division, our Lord begins by praying for himself John 17:1–5). Because his time had come Jesus prayed, "Father . . . glorify Your Son, that the Son may glorify You" (v. 1). Six times in this prayer Jesus referred to God as Father. It was his most often used name for God. Once more in verse five Jesus repeats, "glorify Me," but the purpose of the personal petition was that God might ultimately be glorified. This must be the goal of personal requests. It's all right to pray for self but personal prayer must never be selfish.

Having briefly prayed for himself, Jesus turns the attention of his prayer, in the second division, toward intercessory requests on behalf of the disciples (v. 6–19). "I ask on their behalf; I do not ask on behalf of the world" (v. 9). Then Jesus requests, "keep them in Your name . . . that they may be one" (v. 11). There are two requests here. Being kept in God's name is not the same as being united with other believers. Too often those in God's name are not at peace with one another. Yet both are necessary for effective discipleship. Our intercessory prayer for others should seek to relate them properly to God and to fellow man.

Finally, in the third division of John 17, Jesus makes requests for the church (v. 20–24). As he had prayed for his present disciples, so now he twice prays for all future disciples, "that they may all be one" (v. 21–22) and then prays, "that they may be perfected in unity" (v. 23). There is a reason Jesus desires this unity. It is so, "the world may believe" (v. 21) and so, "the world may know" (v. 23). While it seems improbable if not impossible that today's church could ever be one along doctrinal or even organizational lines, it can be one in prayer. So when you pray with or for believers of different doctrinal or denominational persuasion than you, pray for the church's united witness to the world.

In the last two verses (v. 25–26), Jesus concludes his prayer with a desire for God's love to fill the disciples. May love be the motivating and driving force of your prayer life.

Prayer continues as we *talk* with him. Our Lord began creation by talking with Adam and Eve in the Garden of Eden (Gen. 3:8–19). On Mt. Sinai, "Moses spoke and God answered him" (Exod. 19:19). David, describing his deliverance from his enemies and from Saul, said, "The Lord thundered from heaven, and the Most High uttered His voice" (2 Sam. 22:14). The Psalmist said of God, "He raised His voice" (Ps. 46:6). Isaiah said, "I heard the voice of the Lord" (Isa. 6:8). To Jeremiah, the word of the Lord came saying, "Call to Me and I will answer you" (Jer. 33:3). Jesus, the Good Shepherd, said of the shepherd, "sheep follow him because they know his voice" (John 10:4). The writer of Hebrews quotes the Psalmist saying, "Today if you hear His voice, do not harden your hearts" (Ps. 95:7–8; Heb. 3:7–8).

Few hear an audible voice but all spiritually fit disciples should hear his voice. I was with a tour group observing Abraham's Gate at Tell Dan on the northern border of Israel. It was presidential election day in Israel and the atmosphere was tense. Earlier that day, several Israeli soldiers had been killed when their jeep hit a land mine. However, we did not know this as we prayed a few feet from the Lebanon border. There was a loud explosion, that shook the ground. The prayer leader immediately said, "Amen." There was a unanimous responsive "amen" from the crowd as we headed toward the bus. On the way down the mountain, someone near me said, "When God says it's time to stop looking at Abraham's Gate, I'm ready to get on the bus." Well, I'm not sure if the boom was from God or the big guns or a sonic boom, but it got our attention. Wherever this boom came from, it is true that God communicates, sometimes with unique methods.

I was participating in a conference at the Glorieta Baptist Conference Center in the beautiful mountains east of Sante Fe, New Mexico. Seated in the glass-walled auditorium on Sunday morning, I noticed the clear sky to the west and the dark sky to the east. A storm was coming. The speaker for the session was in the midst of his opening prayer when he said, "Lord, we are thankful for every manifestation of your presence in this place and we anticipate hearing from you today." Just then, the thunder began to roll in the mountains to the east and did not stop until it had rolled over the auditorium and off to the west. The glass rattled, the walls shook, and the lights blinked. For a few seconds everyone waited in hushed expectation. Then the speaker continued his prayer, "Thanks, Lord, for letting us hear from you."

Prayer is two-way communication. This is its uniqueness. Many people talk to me, at me, over my head. Some try to talk for me. The Lord talks *with* me. He talked with Shadrach, Meshach, and Abednego in the fiery furnace (Dan. 6:16–22). He talked with Paul on a stormy sea (Acts 27:13ff). He challenges us to talk with him.

We are challenged to talk with the Lord fervently (James 5:16), even as the Lord "was praying very fervently" in the Garden of Gethsemane (Luke 22:44). Likewise, in response to Peter's imprisonment, "prayer for him was being made fervently by the church" (Acts 12:5).

We are challenged to talk with the Lord boldly and with confidence. The writer of Hebrews encourages us to "draw near with confidence [the King James Version says, "come boldly"] to the throne of grace" (Heb. 4:16). Because it is a throne of grace we can go boldly. Were it any other kind of throne—of judgment, of punishment, of discipline—we could not go near. So we should go boldly, because of grace, to talk with the Lord.

How many times have we attempted to communicate with someone by phone only to get caught in the maze of an automated voice mail system. No matter how many keys we push we keep getting transferred to another automated voice. Because I'm a bit tenacious, I spent more than thirty minutes recently trying to talk with a live person on one phone call. I finally hung up—depressed and defeated.

The Lord does not own a voice mail system. When I call on him, he answers. Not only does he answer, he is available to talk with me. We can have instant access with the Lord. Since prayer is two-way communication the question is, does the Lord have instant access with us?

Oh, the privilege of personal prayer. He talks with *me*. I need personal prayer because often I am the one in need of the prayer. The old spiritual said:

> It's me, it's me, it's me O Lord
> Standing in the need of prayer.
> Not my brother, nor my sister,
> But it's me O Lord,
> Standing in the need of prayer.

When we think of how busy the Lord must be and how many requests must be addressed to him, isn't it amazing that at any moment, we can crawl up into the arms of our Abba, our Father, our Lord, and he will talk with us?

The Lord cares enough to talk with us. If we want to stay in shape spiritually, then we must communicate with the Lord. But communication does not stop there. The spiritually fit disciple will stay in shape as witness is shared with nonbelievers.

COMMUNICATING WITH NONBELIEVERS

Several years ago the following story was released by Associated Press:

> Trapped at the bottom of a highway embankment in a cold, dark, overturned van, her body wracked with pain, Linda Myers gave thanks for the little dog on her lap as she prayed for deliverance.
>
> But when Myers, who suffers from muscular dystrophy, finally managed to rig a makeshift radio powered by her wheelchair battery, she said more than twenty people ignored her calls for help.
>
> "I thought I was going to die," the forty-year-old woman said Friday as she recalled her twelve-hour predicament early

Thursday. "If it hadn't been for Honey, my little cockapoo, I would have lost my mind," she said as she lay in her hospital bed.

Her ordeal began as she drove her specially-equipped van east on State 2, returning home to Amston from visiting friends twenty miles away in New Britain. She said she was just south of Exit 11, in a remote area near Glastonbury, when she was cut off by a speeding truck.

"It was a flatbed and the driver cut back into my lane too soon, forcing me into the guardrail," she said. "I don't know if he did it on purpose but he never stopped, not even after my van went over the rail."

Myers said she blacked out during the descent. When she regained consciousness, she said, the van was lying on its side and she found herself sitting on the right-front passenger's window, dazed, cold and in pain.

"The van must have flipped ten times," she said. "The state police said it was 438 feet down the ravine."

As soon as she could, she reached for her cellular telephone to dial 911, but got a busy signal. "The state trooper told me later that I was in an area of the state that has poor reception for cellular phones."

Meanwhile, she said, the car lights died and its battery went dead, leaving her CB inoperative.

"I was left sitting there in the dark, with Honey asleep on my legs," she said. "My body hurt all over. I prayed and prayed that somebody would find me and help me get out of there. Honey kept my legs warm. I would have been pulling my hair out if it hadn't been for her."

Finally, dawn came and Myers, who says she can barely crawl because of her crippling disease, took stock.
"I had a knife," she said, "so I decided to try and splice the cord from the phone onto the leads of the CB, using my wheelchair battery for power."

In her weakened condition, it took nearly three hours to accomplish the hookup. Then, when the connection was complete, she began trying to contact motorists passing by on the highway up above her.

"I was calling on Channel 19, the truckers' band," she said. "I talked with I don't know how many people, it must have been at least twenty-five, but nobody would stop and help me.

"I remember one woman saying, "That little girl sounds like she needs help,' but the woman didn't stop. I don't know whether they didn't believe me or whether they just didn't want to get involved."

It was almost 11:30 A.M. Thursday, nearly ten hours after she went over the guardrail, when a trucker stopped to help.

"I was begging, crying and pleading with him to stop, telling him I was trapped and going to die. He finally believed me, thank God."

The trucker notified the state police of Myers' plight but it was nearly two more hours before medics could rescue her and the dog from the demolished van and bring them up the steep embankment.

Myers was covered with bruises and abrasions but apparently did not suffer any serious, lasting injuries, the hospital said. Don Hart, one of the emergency medical technicians who helped rescue Myers, said he was impressed by her resourcefulness.

"She helped herself as much as we did," Hart said. "If she hadn't figured out how to get that radio working, in that remote area it would have been days before she was found"

Many people are calling out to God in prayer. Some, like Linda Myers, are calling out to others for help. The spiritual help that nonbelievers are calling for is found in a personal relationship with Jesus Christ. For this reason and others, we ought to be talking about Jesus.

I have a tendency to talk about those things that are important in my life. If it is football season, I talk about football. If it is baseball season, I talk about baseball. In season and out of season, I talk about my family. I talk about my job and my church. These are items of importance to me, and they surface in my talk. When Jesus is real to me and I am following his model, I talk about him as part of my lifestyle.

There is a barrier to communication of the good news of Jesus Christ. In spite of all the factors I would like to blame, the one barrier to my communication is myself. It just may be true, that communication rises and falls with self-image. When I am confident of myself and my faith, I am more verbal about Christ. When I am unsure of myself and out of harmony with Christ, I do not talk about my faith as much. I have both experienced this personally and observed it in others. Let's explore self as the barrier to communication.

To explore self is to explore a complicated, yet challenging subject. True knowledge of self is possible only to the one who believes in God. In his "Essays on Man," Alexander Pope wrote, "Know thyself." Since persons are created in the image of God (Gen. 1:27), knowledge of self is only possible when we begin with knowledge of God. To know God is to know what we ought to be. To know self is to know that which keeps us from being what we ought to be. The barrier to verbalizing our faith in Jesus Christ is ourselves.

Since self is the barrier to communication, our excuses are numerous. Perhaps the number one excuse is the *fear*. We fear rejection, being made fun of, questions we can't answer, peer pressure; we fear a hundred things. We fear because people talk back. I'd fight the heavyweight champion of the world if he agreed not to fight back. I'd witness to everyone I met if they agreed not to talk back. But the world champion would not agree to that, nor would the non-Christian; so I must verbalize, knowing they will talk back. That makes me fear. But what is the real problem? Is it fear? "God has not given us a spirit of fear; but of power, and of love, and of a sound mind" (2 Tim. 1:7, NKJV). The real problem is self. We are afraid of being embarrassed, getting our ego bruised, or straining a relationship. A healthy self-image will go a long way in preventing fear from excusing our lack of communicating our faith.

A second excuse is *misplaced priorities*. We do so many good things; we just never get around to communicating. God called us to be "ambassadors for Christ" (2 Cor. 5:20), but misplaced priorities make us secret agents instead. The problem is not misplaced priorities, it is self, for I set my own priorities, at least for the time that is my own.

Some of us use *prejudice* as a third excuse for our limited sharing. We might be prejudiced against methods—tracts or memorized outlines; prejudiced against motives, some of which we suspect are false; prejudiced against people, some of whom we'd rather not talk to. The real problem is not prejudice but self. We determine our own prejudices, so we must deal with them, and conquer them for the sake of communicating the good news.

A fourth excuse that keeps us from communicating is *life styles that are not good enough*. We know that our life styles do not live up to our verbal witness. That's one reason mission trips have been so popular. I can easily get a group of Christians to go across the country or to another country to share their faith in Christ. But getting them to share their faith where they live is tough. In the far away place, the non-Christian can't compare my verbal witness with my life style, so it is easy to witness verbally. The closer one gets to home the harder it is to witness verbally if the life style and the verbal witness do not harmonize. The most difficult place of all to share our verbal witness is in the home where we are known best. But again, the real problem is not life style but self. The answer may lie in improving your life style, or it may lie in an awareness that you do not have to be perfect to share verbal witness. But nevertheless, we control our own life styles, thus self is the real barrier.

A fifth excuse is *lack of assurance*. With self as the real problem, we can deal with the lack of assurance by reading and applying 1 John 5:11–12: "God has given us eternal life, and this life is in His Son. He who has the Son has the life; he who does not have the Son of God does not have the life." If we invited the Son of God, Jesus Christ, into our lives, he is there to stay; and we can share him with others. If we have not invited him in, we can do so right now and begin to share him with others. Four times in Matthew, Jesus told his disciples that they had "little faith" (Matt. 6:30; 8:26; 14:31; 16:8); and each time it followed a failure on their part. Sometimes our faith is small. We can increase our faith through a renewed harmony with

Jesus Christ. Whether the excuse is lack of faith or little faith, we control the excuse because self is the real barrier.

Each excuse we make for failing to communicate our faith is directly related to the barrier of self. We must decide to witness in spite of self, if not in harmony with self. The Word, when shared, will not return void or empty (Isa. 55:11). And there is sufficient reason for our communication of the good news.

Just as there is only one barrier to communication (self), there is only one reason for verbalization—Jesus Christ. He must be the motivation for sharing; any other will be less than best. Some communicate out of fear of not pleasing another person, some communicate after the example of a respected friend, still others share in the temporary excitement of a spiritual mountaintop experience. They share best who communicate out of the motivation provided by Jesus himself.

There are at least three reasons for communicating Jesus with nonbelievers. The first reason is *the work of Jesus*. If, before this day is over, someone dies for us, could we keep it a secret? Just suppose that another person, whether intentionally or not, died in our place today. We should have been killed but another died instead. Could we go to work or to school or to church and not tell anyone about it? Could we sit through the next meal with our family and not breathe a word of it? I doubt if we could keep silent about something as meaningful as that. Yet, in spite of the fact that Jesus Christ died for us, we keep silent. Telling someone about the death of Jesus for us should be one of the most natural and enjoyable things we do. It seems to me we spend a great amount of time and energy making difficult that which God has made easy. Jesus not only died for us but also called us to be his witnesses.

A second reason is *the call of Jesus*. The last recorded words of Jesus to his disciples were, "You shall be My witnesses . . . to the remotest part of the earth" (Acts 1:8). That is not a multiple choice question or an optional extra. It is a statement of fact. If we are Christians, we are witnesses. We may be a good witness, a mediocre witness, a poor witness, or some other kind of witness. Whatever we do or say is a witness for Jesus Christ. His call assures us of that. Beyond his work and his call, Jesus and his followers set the example for verbalization.

A third reason for communicating the good news is *the example of Jesus and his followers*. We know about the model Jesus set and his consistency in sharing the good news, but what of his followers? According to the Gospel of John, Andrew heard about Jesus from the preaching of John the Baptist. In the very next verse, John wrote of Andrew, "He found first his own brother Simon and said to him, 'We have found the Messiah' (which translated means Christ). He brought him to Jesus" (John 1:41–42). When Jesus found Philip and instructed him to follow, it took John only two more verses to add, "Philip found Nathanael, and said to him, 'We have found Him of whom Moses in the Law and also the Prophets wrote, Jesus of Nazareth, the son of Joseph'" (John 1:45). After her own discovery, the woman of Samaria left the well and went into her village of Sychar to say to the people, "Come, see a man who told me all the things that I have done; this is not the Christ, is it?" (John 4:29). Those who first met Jesus set the example for us.

We have considered the barrier as well as the reason for communication. We must now turn to that which we are to communicate—the ingredients of the gospel. In addition to sharing what God has done for us in Jesus Christ (our testimony), we need to share what we know God can do for others. This knowledge comes to us not only from our own experience but also from God's Word. The Bible sets forth a plan of salvation. Even though we use our own terminology at times, we must not insist on all people responding exactly the same. It is possible for someone to become a Christian without using the same words that we used. The plan is the same; the words may differ. Out of my own Christian heritage, I use the following words to describe the biblical plan for obtaining new life, salvation.

The first ingredient of communication is *God's love and care for all persons*. The Bible begins with the God of love. Jesus said in his prayer to God, "You loved Me before the foundation of the world" (John 17:24). Before God ever created, God loved. Out of this love, God created all things, including humanity as the object of divine love (Gen. 1: 1–31). We have already seen that God loved the world so much that God "gave His only begotten Son, that whoever believes in Him shall not perish, but have eternal life" (John 3:16). Jesus further emphasized this when he said, "I came that they may have life, and have it abundantly" (John 10:10). It is good that God loves us, for sin has put us in need of this love.

The second ingredient of communication is *humanity's sinfulness*. It is best to begin with God's love, for most people will listen out of their own desire to be loved. To begin with sin is to risk not getting to your second point. To omit sin is to leave the plan incomplete. So we should emphasize that "all have sinned" (Rom. 3:23) and that "all of us like sheep have gone astray" (Isa. 53:6). Having identified ourselves as a sinful person, we are free to identify that person as having sinned. Tell him or her as did Isaiah, "It is because of your sins that he doesn't hear you. It is your sins that separate you from God when you try to worship him" (Isa. 59:2, GNB). Since "there is no one who does not sin" (2 Chron. 6:36, GNB), he or she is included in Paul's statement, "For the wages of sin is death, but the free gift of God is eternal life in Christ Jesus our Lord" (Rom. 6:23). Whereas there is no graceful way to tell people that they are sinners, by identifying with them we can show them how we found forgiveness and release in the person of Jesus Christ.

The third ingredient of communication is *the person and work of Jesus Christ*. Wherever you begin in the verbalization of the plan, go straight to the person and work of Jesus. The non-Christian needs to know that "God demonstrates His own love toward us, in that while we were yet sinners, Christ died for us" (Rom. 5:8), and that "because of our sins he was given over to die, and he was raised to life in order to put us right with God" (Rom. 4:25, GNB). Our friends who refuse to accept the New

Testament need to know that it was "because of our sins he was wounded, beaten because of the evil we did. We are healed by the punishment he suffered, made whole by the blows he received" (Isa. 53:5, GNB). Jesus said, "I am the resurrection and the life; he who believes in Me will live even if he dies, and everyone who lives and believes in Me shall never die" (John 11:25–26), and again, "I am the way, and the truth, and the life; no one comes to the Father, but through Me" (John 14:6). The non-Christian needs to know that "by the death of Christ we are set free, that is, our sins are forgiven" (Eph. 1:7, GNB). Part of our communication will be offering and encouraging a time of response on the part of the non-Christian.

The fourth ingredient of communication is *humanity's response in repentance, confession, and faith*. We should now inform the non-Christian, "If you confess with your mouth Jesus as Lord, and believe in your heart that God raised Him from the dead, you will be saved" (Rom. 10:9–10). Jesus instructed those who would follow him to "repent ['turn away from,' GNB]" (Mark 1:15). John wrote, "If we confess our sins, He is faithful and righteous to forgive us our sins and to cleanse us from all unrighteousness" (1 John 1:9). Isaiah encouraged those in Old Testament times to "Seek the Lord while He may be found; Call upon Him while He is near" (Isa. 55:6). The result of response is: "as many as received Him, to them He gave the right to become children of God, even to those who believe in His name" (John 1: 12). Having communicated concerning a response, the decision is up to the listener.

The fifth ingredient of communication is *humanity's decision*. The biblical record is clear when it says, "Believe in the Lord Jesus, and you will be saved" (Acts 16:31). It depicts Jesus standing at the door of a life, knocking, and saying, "if anyone hears My voice and opens the door, I will come in to him" (Rev. 3:20). You must press gently for a decision that is real. The answer is not true or false but yes or no. The decision does not call merely for intellectual assent but for a commitment of life. If the response of the non-Christian is a negative one, you should seek clarification. Be sure the person understood your presentation. Probe gently, but do not push. We must leave the door open for whoever might be used of God to verbalize the gospel to that person next. If the non-Christian's response is positive, we then lead him or her to invite Jesus Christ into his or her life and begin the follow-through.

The sixth ingredient of communication is *follow-through*. Jesus instructed his disciples not only to make disciples but to baptize them and teach them "to observe all that I commanded you" (Matt. 28:20). As a prelude to their own life style of evangelism, new Christians will need to know that they have now been "crucified with Christ; and it is no longer I who live, but Christ lives in me; and the life which I now live in the flesh I live by faith in the Son of God, who loved me, and gave Himself up for me" (Gal. 2:20). The apostle Paul believed in follow-through. Either he followed through himself or assigned the task to another or wrote letters back to the new converts. How we follow through is not as important as the fact that we do it. Would someone give birth to a newborn baby, then leave the baby in the hospital with only a wish for its well-being? Neither should we be a part of the spiritual birthing process only to walk off and leave the newborn believer to grow up on his or her own.

Our challenge is to begin to think positively about communicating the good news. Too much time is wasted on developing excuses, all of which relate to the same barrier of self. We must begin to think of the positive response that will be made by non-Christians as we share our faith. My friend Fred Akers, former head football coach at the University of Texas, shared how he motivated his players. He asked the entire team to picture in their minds what it would be like in the winning locker room after the game and how they would celebrate their victory. He specifically asked the running backs to picture what it would be like to break through the line and dash into the end zone for a touchdown. The wide receivers he asked to picture catching a pass for a first down. The defensive linemen he asked to picture sacking the opposing quarterback for a big loss on third down, and so on through the team. By the time the game started, the players had already tasted victory so much that they were determined to win. This positive planning will work in communicating our faith. We need to begin picturing in our minds the positive response people will make to our witness. We can begin now to celebrate the victory of new life in Christ on behalf of a non-Christian.

Staying in shape spiritually involves communication. Practice continual communication with God and faithful communication with nonbelievers. It is in communicating with God that we become better informed as to the content of our communication with nonbelievers. Likewise, communication with nonbelievers sends us back to communicate further with God. Francis R. Havergal said it well:

> Lord, speak to me, that I may speak
> In living echoes of Thy tone;
> As Thou hast sought, so let me seek
> Thy erring children lost and lone.

Now, a warning is in order—pace yourself.

EXERCISES FOR SPIRITUAL FITNESS

Day One   Check your recent prayers. Are your petitions self-ish or for God's ultimate glory? Explain: _____
_____
_____

Day Two   Prayer is two-way communication as the Lord talks with us. How much time have you spent recently listening in prayer? How could you increase your listening? _____
_____

Day Three As you listen to God what do you hear related to your communication with nonbelievers? What immediate steps do you need to take to respond to this? _____
_____

Day Four   What is your most frequently used excuse for not communicating with non-Christians more than you do? How could you take steps to remedy your excuse this week? _____
_____
_____

Day Five   Visualize sharing the gospel with a nonbeliever. Explain why your vision was positive or negative:
_____
_____

Scriptural strengths to remember:
1. Hebrews 7:32
2. Jeremiah 33:3
3. 2 Timothy 1:7
4. 2 Corinthians 5:20

WEEK EIGHT

Pacing

I WAS A DALLAS COWBOY FANATIC during the Tom Landry years. I watched with great interest as this master motivator prepared his team each week for the football game on Sunday. Because they were well prepared, they usually won. But for many seasons, they would falter at the end and fail during the playoffs. They couldn't seem to reach the championship game. Then I noticed they started losing a few games early in the season only to peak later and reach the championship like a well-tuned machine. Coach Landry had learned the secret of pacing. The season was long and much had to be saved for the last. The story is repeated in various athletic competitions with regularity. Poor pacing spells defeat.

Likewise in the spiritual arena, the disciple must understand and implement the principles of pacing if the journey is to be completed with pride and dignity. How then do spiritually fit disciples pace themselves? The answer is found in the way Jesus matured. Luke 2:52 says, "Jesus kept increasing in wisdom and stature, and in favor with God and men." Pacing involves the mental (wisdom), the physical (stature), the spiritual (God), and the social (men, or people).

Meditation has been lost as a spiritual practice in this day and the very reason for its absence is the reason it's needed. We discard meditation because our schedules are overcrowded with activity. There just is no time to be quiet and still before God. We begin to live with the assumption that quiet time is wasted time. Nothing could be further from the Biblical truth. Quiet time spent in meditation is not only Biblical, it is essential for spiritually fit disciples.

What is meditation? It is thought that is prolonged and focused. It is holding a spiritual thought or idea or scripture in your heart and mind until it affects every dimension of our lives. The meaning of the word *meditate* includes the ideas of depth, of purging, of analyzing. In other words, to meditate is not to be idle, but to go deeper in thought, in cleansing, and in investigation.

Is meditation Biblical? In Joshua 1:8, God says to Joshua, "This book of the law shall not depart from your mouth but you shall meditate on it day and night. . . ." Did Joshua simply have nothing else to do? A careful study of the context of this verse will show Joshua to be deeply involved in providing leadership for thousands of people. Perhaps he was busier than at any other time in his life and working under responsibility far greater than he could ever have imagined. In the midst of leadership challenges and battle campaigns, God instructed Joshua to meditate.

Psalms 1:1–2 says, "How blessed is the man who does not walk in the counsel of the wicked, Nor stand in the path of sinners, Nor sit in the seat of scoffers! But his delight is in the law of the Lord, And in His law he meditates day and night." These words are so familiar to most believers that the meaning has been lost. Continual meditation on the part of the disciple produces this promise from God: "in whatever he does, he prospers" (Ps. 1:3).

Finally, the aging apostle Paul wrote to young Timothy concerning the ingredients of his ministry and encouraged him to "meditate on these things" (1 Tim. 4:15 NKJV). It was Paul's desire that Timothy ponder on his instructions and then zealously put them into practice. It is not enough just to meditate. Meditation motivates one to ministry.

It is clear from these Biblical references that meditation for a believer is far different from that of a nonbeliever. The purpose of meditation in some of the Eastern religions is to empty and cleanse the mind. On the contrary, the purpose of Biblical meditation is not only to empty and cleanse the mind, but to refill it with the thoughts of God. For the believer meditation is not an end within itself. It is a means to an end—a mind in tune with the mind of God.

As to the argument that meditation began among the Eastern religions or the even more absurd idea that meditation is a New Age invention, consider that as early as Genesis 24:63 Isaac provided a role model for believers as he "went out to meditate in the field toward evening." Let no one accuse the disciple of practicing some Eastern religion discipline or even a New Age belief. Genuine meditation belongs to the people of God.

So, are we ready to pace ourselves using meditation? We will need at least two things initially: discipline and time. If we are like most, our agenda is full. We will need to make time and that takes discipline. Then we will need to keep that time faithfully; that also takes discipline.

Even though we may meditate on thoughts, images, ideas, and concepts other than scripture verses, scripture is really the heart of meditation. We can personalize the scripture through the use of our senses and our imagination. Think creative thoughts that go beyond descriptive words.

We might begin with Psalm 103:1–2: "Bless the Lord, O my soul and all that is within me, bless His holy name. Bless the

Lord, O my soul, and forget none of His benefits." As we bless the Lord, we meditate on his benefits. What about Proverbs 3:5–6: "Trust in the Lord with all your heart, and lean not on your own understanding; In all your ways acknowledge Him and He shall direct your paths" (NKJV). We can meditate on how we can trust the Lord more completely, on how to not lean on our own understandings, on how to better acknowledge him and then we can thank God for directing our paths.

From the New Testament we can meditate on Philippians 4:6–7: "Be anxious for nothing, but in everything by prayer and supplication with thanksgiving let your requests be made known to God. And the peace of God, which surpasses all comprehension, will guard your hearts and your minds in Christ Jesus." Can we be less anxious? What requests do we have for God? What does it mean for the peace of God to guard our hearts and minds? Consider also 2 Timothy 1:7: "For God has not given us a spirit of timidity, but of power and love and discipline." Where in our lives is there evidence of God's power, love, and discipline?

As we meditate, we can emphasize different words within the passage of scripture. We can ask questions such as who, what, where, when, why, and how. We can apply the passage to our lives by asking: What truth should I gain from this passage? Should I eliminate anything from my life? Should I change anything in my life? Should I begin anything new in my life? Finally, we should translate or paraphrase the passage of scripture into our own words.

Meditation is often hard work. Most pacing is difficult. But just like most pacing, the reward is worth the discipline. Meditation is mental pacing. But there is more to pacing than the mental.

PHYSICAL PACING: LIFE IN THE FAST LANE

Should we ever consider living in the fast lane? We've all driven in the fast lane of a freeway or been passed by someone else driving in the fast lane. What I'm talking about is living in the fast lane. No, not expensive cars, fine clothes, great food, outstanding entertainment, or money to burn. That may all be a part of life in one kind of fast lane, but not the one under consideration here. For this fast lane look at the words of the Lord through Joel the prophet, "Return to Me with all your heart, and with fasting, weeping and mourning" (Joel 2:12). Look also at the words of Jesus in his Sermon on the Mount, "Whenever you fast . . ." (Matt. 6:16). Jesus did not command fasting here, he assumed his disciples would fast.

So, what does it mean to fast? Fasting is an intentional self-denial for the purpose of gaining spiritual insight or becoming spiritually stronger. While most fasting is related to food and drink, it is not confined to these. Fasting is abstinence for a period of time from certain necessities of life such as food, drink, sleep, rest, association with other people, various forms of entertainment, sexual activity, etc. Fasting enables you to focus more strongly on the spiritual by renouncing for a time, that which may under other circumstances be both permissible and enjoyable.

Fasting is mentioned forty-four times in the Old Testament with Isaiah 58 being the most thorough treatment of the subject. There are thirty-one references in the New Testament to fasting. Among those who fasted in the Bible are Moses (Deut. 9:9, 18; Exod. 34:28), Joshua (Josh. 7:6), David (Ps. 35:13), Jehoshaphat (2 Chron. 20:17), Daniel (Dan. 10:3), Elijah (1 Kings 19:8), Anna (Luke 2:36–38), Jesus (Matt. 4:2), Paul (Acts 14:23; 9:9), and the leaders of the church in Antioch (Acts 13:2–3).

While modern believers generally prefer feasting, our history is punctuated with the fasting of Francis of Assisi, Martin Luther, John Calvin, John Knox, John Wesley, Jonathan Edwards, Charles Finney, Dwight Moody, Billy Graham, and many other less recognizable names.

While there are other ways than these, I would like to share four ways to participate in a Bible-based fast. *An absolute fast* involves abstaining from all food and drink for a time period not to exceed three days. This kind was practiced by Paul immediately after his encounter with the Lord on the road to Damascus. Acts 9:8–9 says, "Saul got up from the ground, and though his eyes were open, he could see nothing; and leading him by the hand, they brought him into Damascus. And he was three days without sight, and neither ate nor drank." To go beyond three days is medically unadvisable and in most cases impossible. However, both Moses and Elijah endured extended fasts for forty days (Deut. 9:9; 1 Kings 19:8). These extended, absolute fasts should be considered supernatural.

A second type of Bible-based fast is a *normal fast*. This is similar to the absolute fast, but water is allowed. While Moses and Elijah neither ate nor drank during their forty-day fast, Jesus abstained only from food during his forty-day fast (Luke 4:2). After his fast Jesus "became hungry" (Luke 4:2; Matt. 4:2), but neither Luke nor Matthew mentions his thirst even though the fast had been in the wilderness. We may assume then that Jesus had water available.

A third type of Bible-based fast is a *partial fast* which is simply a diet restriction. Daniel participated in such a fast for three weeks and described it as, "I did not eat any tasty food, nor did meat or wine enter my mouth, nor did I use any ointment at all, until the entire three weeks were completed" (Dan. 10:3). The King James Version of the Bible translates tasty food as "pleasant bread" while the New International Version translates it "choice food." We're not sure what Daniel deleted from his menu other than meat and wine, but he obviously participated in some type of diet-regulated fast. This is a good way for persons with certain medical conditions or persons on certain prescription medications to participate in a fast especially when their doctors discourage an absolute or normal fast.

Finally, we might choose to conduct *an other-than-food-and-drink fast*. We can abstain in another way than by diet—by eliminating something else from our lifestyles. Daniel not only abstained from tasty food, meat, and wine, he also refrained from using "any ointment at all" (Dan. 10:3). The use of salves or ointments was common in the East. In the warm climate this practice of anointing with these ointments contributed to health as well as made the skin smooth and tender. Daniel abstained from that which he ordinarily used as a means of personal comfort. With these four kinds of Bible-based fasts in mind, anyone can practice fasting.

We need to keep the purpose of our fast in mind. We do not fast for selfish reasons or even for church-related reasons. We fast for God's sake. We and our churches may benefit greatly from our fasting, but it is for God that we fast. Apparently the people of Zechariah's day got their purpose misplaced, and God asked, "When you fasted and mourned in the fifth and seventh months these seventy years, was it actually for Me that you fasted?" (Zech. 7:5). Remember that the call to fast is from God and for God (Joel 1:14; 2:15; Luke 5:33–35).

Are we ready to enter the fast lane? If we've never fasted from food and drink before, we should begin slowly by starting in the afternoon after a light lunch. The more difficult hours will pass during the night while we sleep. We can break the fast with breakfast (which means, break the all night fast). We will have completed approximately an eighteen-hour fast. We should break the fast gently with a light breakfast. If this goes well, we can try for a longer period next time. We can give God more waking hours to strengthen us through two-way communication. Once tried we may enjoy life in the fast lane.

SPIRITUAL PACING: TRAVELING BY THE BOOK

When traveling, I often look at a road map to see how many more miles I have to go. If I'm supposed to be at a given destination at a certain time, I have to pace myself in order to arrive on time—not too early nor too late. Likewise, in my spiritual journey I have a map, my Bible, to help pace me spiritually. The Psalmist, who traveled by foot rather than by motor vehicle, said, "Your word is a lamp to my feet, and a light to my path" (Ps. 119:105). If I will just travel by the book, my journey will be paced properly.

By this time we don't need someone to make a case for the validity of the Bible. Voltaire said in one hundred years from his day the Bible would be a relic of the past. To the day, one hundred years later, Voltaire's work sold for eleven cents and the Codex Sinaiticus copy of the Bible reportedly sold to the British Museum by the Czar of Russia for $400,000.

Besides taking it to church with us and leaving it on our bedside tables, what should we be doing with our Bibles? Perhaps the first experience we had with the Bible was hearing someone else read from it. We should continue to *hear the Bible* read. Paul said, "Faith comes by hearing, and hearing by the word" (Rom. 10:17). John said, "Blessed is he who reads and those who hear the words" (Rev. 1:3).

Tommy had been admitted to the AIDS ward of a local hospital, and he was dying. By a rather complicated set of circumstances, I was in his room meeting him for the first time and talking to him about his relationship to Jesus Christ. He kept the conversation going for some time by his questions, and then he said, "I can't read the Bible, you know. My eyes are getting so bad. I hear they have the Bible on cassette tape. Is that right?" Not only was it right, but within a few hours, Tommy had a cassette recorder and a set of tapes of the Bible. From the time he received them until he lapsed into a coma preceding death, no one was allowed to turn off the tapes. His parents told me that he wore out several sets of batteries. Hearing the Bible read at the end of the journey is comforting. Hearing it read at any time along the way is encouraging and strengthening.

In addition to hearing the Bible, we ought to *read the Bible* for ourselves. Peter wrote, "Like newborn babes, long for the pure milk of the word" (1 Pet. 2:2), and Paul wrote to Timothy, "Give attention to the public reading of scripture" (1 Tim. 4:13). We may read the Bible casually, at random, or we may read systematically, such as reading it through in one year. One year I read a Psalm a day beginning on January 1. That same spring I took a trip to Israel. On the day I arrived in Jerusalem, I read "Pray for the peace of Jerusalem" (Ps. 122:6). What a blessing I would have missed had I not been systematically reading the Bible.

What are some of the ways we can use our Bibles? We ought to *study the Bible*. Again Paul wrote Timothy, "Study to shew thyself approved unto God, a workman that needeth not to be ashamed, rightly dividing the word of truth" (2 Tim. 2:15, KJV). It was said of the early Christians, "They received the word with great eagerness, examining the Scriptures daily" (Acts 17:11). And Jesus spoke of searching the Scriptures (see John 5:39). In his book *Twelve Dynamic Bible Study Methods*, Rick Warren discusses proven methods of Bible study. They are:

1. *The Devotional Method.* Selecting a short portion of the Bible and prayerfully meditating on it until the Holy Spirit shows us a way to apply the truth to our lives. Then we can write out a personal application.

2. *The Chapter Summary Method.* Reading a chapter of a Bible book through at least five times; then writing a summary of the central thoughts we find in it.

3. *The Character Quality Method.* Choosing a character quality we would like to work on in our lives and studying what the Bible says about it.

4. *The Thematic Method.* Selecting a Bible theme to study, then thinking of three to five questions we'd like to have answered about that theme. Next we can study all the references we can find on that theme and record the answers to our questions.

5. *The Biographical Method.* Picking out a Bible character and researching all the verses about that person in order to study their life and characteristics. Then we can make notes on their attitudes, strengths, and weaknesses. Finally, we can apply what we have learned to our own lives.

6. *The Topical Method.* Collecting and comparing all the verses we find on a particular topic, then organizing our conclusions into outlines that we can share with others.

7. *The Word Study Method.* Studying the important words of the Bible and discovering how many times a word occurs in scripture and how it is used. This helps us ascertain the original meaning of the word.

8. *The Book Background Method.* Studying how history, geography, culture, science, and politics affected what happened in Bible times. Bible reference books are an aid to increasing our understanding of the Word.

9. *The Book Survey Method.* Surveying an entire book of the Bible by reading it through several times will give us a general overview of its contents. Next we can study the background of the book and make notes about its message.

10. *The Chapter Analysis Method.* Mastering the contents of a chapter from the Bible by taking an in-depth look at each verse in that chapter. This is done by dissecting each verse, word by word, observing every detail.

11. *The Book Synthesis Method.* Reading through a Bible book several times and then developing a summary and outline of that book. This method is best done after we have used a Book Survey Method and the Chapter Analysis Method on every chapter of that book.

12. *The Verse-by-Verse Analysis Method.* Selecting one passage of scripture and examining it in detail by asking questions, finding cross references, and paraphrasing each verse. The next step is to record a possible application of the verses we studied.

One of the most overlooked ways of using our Bibles is meditation. We ought to *meditate on the Bible.* Before daybreak, in a quiet place, it could be assumed that Jesus meditated on the Scriptures. Alone and in the dark, he set an example for us (Mark 1:35). Paul instructed Timothy to "Meditate on these things" (1 Tim. 4:15, NKJV). Mary, the mother of Jesus, remembered the word of God through the angel and "pondered [or meditated on] them in her heart" (Luke 2:19 NKJV). Continually, the Psalmist emphasized meditation (Ps. 1:2; 19:14; 49:3; 63:6; 77:12; 104:34; 119:15, 23, 48, 78, 97,148; 143:5). Since I have written on this subject earlier in this week's study, I will refrain from elaborating on meditation further. Suffice it to say, meditating on the Bible is an extremely important part of traveling by the Book.

There ought to be times in our Christian lives when we *memorize the Bible,* especially portions of it that are helpful to us. The Psalmist wrote, "Your word I have treasured in my heart, That I may not sin against You" (Ps. 119:11). Both in his temptation experience (Matt. 4:1–11; Deut. 8:3; 6:16; 6:13) and from the cross (Matt. 27:46; Ps. 22:1; Luke 23:46; Ps. 31:5), Jesus quoted from memory portions of scripture. If we commit portions of scripture to memory, Jesus promised the Holy Spirit will "bring to your remembrance all that I said to you" (John 14:26).

The human mind is more amazing than a computer at storing memorized information. I was riding with my host along Makaha Beach in Hawaii when he suddenly pulled off the road at a place where a man was selling shells from the back of his pickup truck. My host exclaimed, "I believe I see a chambered nautilus, and I've been looking for a good one." After I had purchased one of the beautiful shells myself, my host asked what interest I had in a chambered nautilus. At that point I began to quote for him from my own memory the last verse of "The Chambered Nautilus" by Oliver Wendell Holmes:

> Build thee more stately mansions, O my soul,
>   As the swift seasons roll!
> Leave thy low-vaulted past!

Let each new temple, nobler than the last,
Shut thee from heaven with a dome more vast,
    Till thou at length art free,
Leaving thine outgrown shell by life's unresting sea!

To the amazement of my host, I went on to explain to him that my twelfth-grade English teacher in high school had made us answer the roll by quoting verses of poetry from memory, and that was one verse I had memorized. The point is, it had been over twenty years since I had sat in the classroom at Reagan High School in Houston, Texas, and answered Miss Janie Belle Baten's roll call with that poem, and very few times in those years had I thought about it. Yet, once memorized, that poem had remained in my human computer brain. If the human mind can do such things, how much more can God do with our memorized verses of scripture?

Finally, we ought to *apply the Bible.* James wrote, "Prove yourselves doers of the word, and not merely hearers" (James 1:22). The writer of Hebrews indicated that those who progress from spiritual "milk" to spiritual "solid food" will do so, "because of practice [or application of the truths related to 'milk']" (Heb. 5:12–14). In teaching his followers, Jesus used an illustration that was preceded with a word of application. Before he told of a wise man who built his house upon a rock and a foolish man who built his house upon sand, Jesus likened the wise man to "Whoever hears these sayings of Mine, and does them" (Matt. 7:24 NKJV). It is good to hear, read, study, meditate upon, and even memorize God's Word, but it is of extreme importance to apply that Word to your own life and witness. What will happen if we do these things?

Having heard, read, studied, meditated upon, memorized, and applied the Bible, we will have a better understanding of the journey. We can be absolutely sure when we open our Bible and give it our undivided attention, God will communicate through the Word.

A word needs to be added here in regard to the role of the Holy Spirit in our use of the Bible for after all, the Holy Spirit was the mover or motivator of scripture. Peter said, "No prophecy was ever made by an act of human will, but men moved by the Holy Spirit spoke from God" (2 Pet. 1:21). The spiritually fit disciple, because of the indwelling Holy Spirit, can understand the Bible and follow its direction. Paul wrote, "A natural man does not accept the things of the Spirit of God, for they are foolishness to him; and he cannot understand them, because they are spiritually appraised. But he who is spiritual appraises all things, yet he himself is appraised by no one. For who has known the mind of the Lord, that he will instruct Him? But we have the mind of Christ" (1 Cor. 2:14–16).

We need to pace ourselves mentally, physically, and spiritually, but we can't stop yet. We must also pace ourselves socially.

SOCIAL PACING: THE SOUNDS OF SILENCE

God, who thunders from the heavens (2 Sam. 22:14) and who speaks and the earth shakes (Ps. 46:6), also can be heard in the sounds of silence. The Psalmist encouraged, "Be still, and know that I am God" (Ps. 46:10 NKJV), and Isaiah reported God saying, "In quietness and trust is your strength" (Isa. 30:15).

While most people will think of human interaction when they think of social pacing, we are to think here of the private introspection that precedes effective human interaction. Without the strength that comes from the quiet times of introspection, we can hardly endure the noisy times of interaction. Indeed the quiet time is the pacing that is necessary for proper social time.

Times if silence may be used to practice a number of constructive and positive disciplines. One of these disciplines is that of keeping a spiritual journal. While this will reflect directly on our relationship with God, it will also be a record of our social relationships and experiences. In both cases, journaling will assist us in our social pacing.

The University of Texas *Lifetime Health Letter* recently indicated several types of physical health benefits have been linked to journal writing. Researchers found evidence that writing about feelings can boost levels of certain disease fighting cells in the immune system, favorably affect blood pressure and heart rate, and help people cope with pain.

Journaling has also proved to assist emotional and social health, especially for those who have difficulty sharing their feelings with others and those who have no one with whom to share. Writing benefits those who are still living the experience about which they write. Thinking about it, dreaming about it, wanting to talk about it, learning from it are all beneficial experiences of keeping a journal.

Obviously journal keeping has spiritual benefits. While the Bible does not command journaling, much of the Bible is journaling. Writers from David to Jeremiah and from Luke to John, under the inspiration of God, recorded what they saw, heard, and felt.

A journal is a personal daily record of observations and experiences, a chronicle of lessons learned and perceptions gained. Many excellent journals and journal suggestions are available in Christian bookstores. Most include sections for personal Bible study notes, prayer requests and answers, items of praise, sermon or lecture notes and daily diary pages.

Keeping a journal will give balance to life's ups and downs. Looking back in your journal, we will be able to see trends of which we were unaware. We will see how God was constant whether we were up or down on a given day. A journal is like a mirror in which we see ourselves from a spiritual perspective. Likewise we will see who our real friends were and gain insight into social relationships over a period of time.

Here are some practical suggestions for keeping a journal:

1. Set a specific time each day for journaling. Perhaps the end of the day is ideal as it allows time to reflect back over the day's events and activities.
2. If possible, set a specific place for journaling, perhaps a chair beside the bed if journaling is done before sleep or in the same place where prayer time is kept.

3. Use various writing materials. A prepared journal may be purchased in a Christian bookstore, or loose-leaf paper, or index cards, or a computer program, or thoughts may be dictated for later typing into a journal.

4. Use various writing styles. Write for content rather than worrying about grammar, punctuation, spelling, etc.

5. Write in the first person. Forget formal, third person writing for now. This is personal.

6. Focus on more than facts. Write about feelings as well.

7. Look for the positive and negative in every experience, but don't go to the extreme in self-pity or excessive optimism.

8. Ask and answer key questions during the writing. Good questions include: What is happening? How does it relate? What feelings are present? Why? What is being learned? How does this impact the future?

9. Let writing flow freely. Don't force the writing in a particular direction.

10. Ask God to bless the journaling and use it for the development of greater spiritual fitness.

Jesus paced himself mentally, physically, spiritually, and socially. Often he would withdraw from the crowds (Matt. 4:1; 14:13, 23; 17:1–8; 26:36–46; Mark 6:31; Luke 5:15–16; 6:12). Sometimes he withdrew to pray, sometimes to train his disciples, often for personal renewal and strength, but always for a change of pace. This week we studied how we might pace ourselves in these same areas. We must pace ourselves before the pace gets faster.

DISCIPLESHAPE

EXERCISES FOR SPIRITUAL FITNESS

Day One Take one of the scripture passages suggested in this week's reading and meditate on it for fifteen-to-thirty minutes according to the suggestions given. What do you think God communicated to you during this meditation time? _____

Day Two Try the eighteen-hour fast suggested in this week's reading. Did you feel spiritually stronger or more focused on spiritual matters? Why or why not?

Day Three Read an extended passage of scripture three times today. What did you see the second and/or third time that you did not see on the first reading?

Day Four Find some truth in yesterday's reading to apply directly to your life today. What were the results?

Day Five What would it take for you to begin keeping a spiritual journal or improve the journaling you are already doing? _____

Scriptural strengths to remember:
1. Luke 2:52
2. Psalm 1:1
3. Joel 2:12–13
4. Psalm 119:11

Standing

WHILE MOST PHYSICAL FITNESS involves movement, there are times when we must simply stand. Sometimes athletes must stand against the opponent. Often the competitors stand prepared or equipped. Always the participants must stand strong. Finally the athlete may stand victorious. Likewise in the spiritual arena, the spiritually fit disciple must stand.

Three times in Ephesians 6, Paul instructs his readers to "stand" in the midst of conflict (Eph. 6:11, 13–14). The Greek word for stand is a military term. It has to do with the attitude of the soldier when facing the enemy. Transfer the confrontation of the soldier to the competition of the athlete and the word loses nothing. Like the soldier, the athlete must stand. Like the athlete, the disciple must also stand.

Not just in Ephesians, but throughout Paul's writings believers were encouraged to stand. In Romans 5:2 Paul speaks of "this grace in which we stand." In 1 Corinthians 15:1 Paul refers to the gospel "in which also you stand," and in 1 Corinthians 16:13 we are admonished to "stand firm in the faith." Speaking of freedom, Paul says in Galatians 5:1 "Keep standing firm and do not be subject again to a yoke of slavery." In Philippians 1:27, he wants to know that the believers in Philippi are "standing firm in one spirit" and so instructs them in Philippians 4:1 to "stand firm in the Lord." Using Epaphras as an example, in Colossians 4:12, Paul wants the believers in Colosse to "stand perfect and fully assured in all the will of God." Finally, Paul writes in 2 Thessalonians 2:15, "stand firm and hold to the traditions which you were taught."

We sing, "Standing on the promises of Christ my King" and "Stand up, stand up for Jesus, Ye soldiers of the cross" and "We are standing on holy ground. . . . We are standing in His presence on holy ground." We must stand, but how does a spiritually fit disciple do this?

STANDING AGAINST

One of the very reasons for standing is that there is an enemy set on defeating us. When God has something going, Satan will try to destroy it. Satan's very existence suggests opposition. Those who minister and serve must be prepared to encounter Satan and his forces on a consistent basis. Many times I have been assured that God was going to bless some engagement or assignment of mine because of the strong opposition I was feeling from Satan. Perhaps our failure to take our opponent seriously is one reason our ministry has not been more successful.

What is the nature of this foe? A look at the New Testament descriptions of Satan confirms the fact that there is a personal being of great power who carries on organized opposition to the activity of God. Actually, scripture has very little to say about the origin and apostasy of Satan. Several hints and clues are given but very few categorical statements are made about his existence. The name *Satan*, meaning adversary or opposer, is the most common name for the opposition. Among its fifty-six uses in the Scriptures is the statement by Paul that "Satan hindered us" (1 Thess. 2:18).

The Greek word *diabolos* is the New Testament word for devil, meaning slanderer or accuser. It is used thirty-five times. Peter referred to "your adversary, the devil" (1 Pet. 5:8). Both names appear in Revelation 12:9 with the idea of the serpent: "the serpent of old who is called the devil and Satan."

Paul described Satan as "the prince of the power of the air" (Eph. 2:2). According to the Bible, Satan's spirits must be somewhere, but not in heaven, and if in this present age they cannot be confined to hell, is it so unusual that Ephesians 2:2 refers to "the prince of the power of the air"?

The prince of evil is able, as far as God's providence permits, to carry on his work by sending his wicked army to our world and its surrounding atmosphere. Paul also referred to Satan as a "deceiver" (2 Cor. 11:3), an "angel of light" (2 Cor. 11:14), "the tempter" (1 Thess. 3:5), and "the god of this world" (2 Cor. 4:4).

Peter described Satan as "a roaring lion" (1 Pet. 5:8), and John described him as, "the accuser of our brethren" (Rev. 12:10) and as a "beast" (Rev. 19:19).

A modern idea depicts Satan as old, decrepit, and crafty. This image hardly inspires fear. In fact, we tend to revere those who are elderly and to seek their wisdom. A portrayal of Satan in this light tends to make us drop our guard against him.

Another modern image of Satan is that of the red creature with horns and a forked tail. Nonbelievers who think of Satan in this way may easily place him alongside the Easter bunny and the tooth-fairy as figments of imagination. This ridiculous image has its base more in the words of Dante and Milton than in the Bible. If Satan can convince us that he does not exist, there is no need for defense. Where there is no defense, we are vulnerable to every attack.

Rather than picture Satan as a red creature with horns and tail, or as an old, decrepit, crafty creature, we would do better to portray him as young, attractive, and creative. In our culture that worships youth, vitality, energy, creativity, and beauty, Satan takes on these forms.

Satan attempts to blind nonbelievers to the truth. In 2 Corinthians 4:4, Paul writes, "The god of this world has blinded the minds of the unbelieving, so that they might not see the light of the gospel of the glory of Christ." In his attempt to blind nonbelievers, Satan "snatches away what has been sown in his heart" (Matt. 13:19). He dilutes truth with error as he did with men in Jesus' day when he "sowed tares among the wheat" (Matt. 13:25). He tries to catch people in "the snare of the devil" (2 Tim. 2:26). Finally, he "deceives the whole world" (Rev. 12:9).

While Satan tries to blind unbelievers, he is also busy tempting believers. James 1:14 says, "Each one is tempted when he is carried away and enticed by his own lust." In tempting believers, Satan employs "the lust of the flesh and the lust of the eyes and the boastful pride of life" (1 John 2:16).

In his book *Dealing with the Devil*, C. S. Lovett gave the following "anti-Satan defense system":

1. Believe what God has said about the enemy.
2. Learn how the enemy operates.
3. Know of the enemy's weaknesses and strengths.
4. Have a definite plan for resisting the enemy.
5. Know how to use your own resources in Christ.
6. Go into action at the first hint of Satanic suggestion.

To the Pharisees, the religious leaders of their day, Jesus said, "You are of your father the devil, and you want to do the desires of your father. He was a murderer from the beginning, and does not stand in the truth because there is no truth in him. Whenever he speaks a lie, he speaks from his own nature, for he is a liar and the father of lies" (John 8:44). Be ready to stand against Satan's lies ten of which are listed below:

Lie 1: *God is not good.*
Defense: "Surely God is good to Israel, To those who are pure in heart!" (Ps. 73:1) "And we know that God causes all things to work together for good to those who love God, to those who are called according to His purpose" (Rom. 8:28).

Lie 2: *Your body is your own.*

Defense: "Or do you not know that your body is a temple of the Holy Spirit who is in you, whom you have from God, and that you are not your own? For you have been bought with a price: therefore glorify God in your body." (1 Cor. 6:19–20)

Lie 3: *Sinful living is beneficial.*

Defense: "Or do you not know that the unrighteous will not inherit the kingdom of God? Do not be deceived; neither fornicators, nor idolaters, nor adulterers, nor effeminate, nor homosexuals, nor thieves, nor the covetous, nor drunkards, nor revilers, nor swindlers, will inherit the kingdom of God. Such were some of you; but you were washed, but you were sanctified, but you were justified in the name of the Lord Jesus Christ and in the Spirit of our God." (1 Cor. 6:9–11) "But now having been freed from sin and enslaved to God, you derive your benefit, resulting in sanctification, and the outcome, eternal life. For the wages of sin is death, but the free gift of God is eternal life in Christ Jesus our Lord." (Rom. 6:22–23)

Lie 4: *God will forsake you.*

Defense: "Make sure that your character is free from the love of money, being content with what you have; for He Himself has said, 'I will never desert you, nor will I ever forsake you'." (Heb. 13:5) "Behold, I stand at the door and knock; if anyone hears My voice and opens the door, I will come in to him and will dine with him, and he with Me." (Rev. 3:20)

Lie 5: *This life is all you have.*

Defense: "Do not store up for yourselves treasures on earth, where moth and rust destroy, and where thieves break in and steal. But store up for yourselves treasures in heaven, where neither moth nor rust destroys, and where thieves do not break in or steal; for where your treasure is, there your heart will be also." (Matt. 6:19–21) "If you have been raised up with Christ, keep seeking the things above, where Christ is, seated at the right hand of God. Set your mind on the things above, not on the things that are on the earth. For you have died and your life is hidden with Christ in God. When Christ, who is our life, is revealed, then you also will be revealed with Him in glory." (Col. 3:1–4)

Lie 6: *You are what you make of yourself.*
Defense: "For we are His workmanship, created in Christ Jesus for good works, which God prepared beforehand so that we would walk in them." (Eph. 2:10)

Lie 7: *God doesn't love you.*
Defense: "For God so loved the world, that He gave His only begotten Son, that whoever believes in Him shall not perish, but have eternal life." (John 3:16) "But God demonstrates His own love toward us, in that while we were yet sinners, Christ died for us." (Rom. 5:8)

Lie 8: *Evil is to be feared.*
Defense: "Even though I walk through the valley of the shadow of death, I fear no evil; for You are with me" (Ps. 23:4). "For God has not given us a spirit of fear, but of power and of love and of a sound mind." (2 Tim. 1:7 NKJV)

Lie 9: *God doesn't keep promises.*
Defense: "The Lord is not slow about His promise, as some count slowness, but is patient toward you, not wishing for any to perish but for all to come to repentance. But the day of the Lord will come like a thief, in which the heavens will pass away with a roar and the elements will be destroyed with intense heat, and the earth and its works will be burned up. Since all these things are to be destroyed in this way, what sort of people ought you to be in holy conduct and godliness, looking for and hastening the coming of the day of God, because of which the heavens will be destroyed by burning, and the elements will melt with intense heat! But according to His promise we are looking for new heavens and a new earth, in which

righteousness dwells. Therefore, beloved, since you look for these things, be diligent to be found by Him in peace, spotless and blameless." (2 Pet. 3:9–14)

Lie 10: *There are many paths to God.*
Defense: "Jesus said to him, "I am the way, and the truth, and the life; no one comes to the Father, but through Me."" (John 14:6) "And there is salvation in no one else; for there is no other name under heaven that has been given among men by which we must be saved." (Acts 4:12)

Paul wants us to "resist" the devil (Eph. 6:13; James 4:7). To do so we will need to be properly equipped.

STANDING EQUIPPED

While Satan is strong, you were never meant to stand up to him unequipped. So Paul writes:

> Be strong in the Lord and in the strength of His might. Put on the full armor of God, so that you will be able to stand firm against the schemes of the devil. For our struggle is not against flesh and blood, but against the rulers, against the powers, against the world forces of this darkness, against the spiritual forces of wickedness in the heavenly places. Therefore, take up the full armor of God so that you will be able to resist in the evil day, and having done everything, to stand firm." (Eph. 6:10–13)

God has provided us with armor. Let's look at it.
Most of the armor of God is defensive equipment. That does not mean that we are to spend the majority of our time defending the faith. It simply implies that our one offensive weapon—the Word of God—is adequate for the encounter. But first, a look at the defensive armor.
"Stand firm therefore, having girded your loins with truth" (Eph. 6:14). On the surface, it would seem that armor would weigh us down in battle. However, Paul began with truth, for it is that

which sets us free (John 8:32). Our business as disciples is to set persons free from the bondage of sin. Truth will do just that, but it will also protect us. I would rather stand with a minority on the grounds of truth than stand with an overwhelming majority on the grounds of falsehood. Truth will win; in Christ, it has already won, regardless of the odds against it. Jesus Christ, the same yesterday, today, and forever, is truth. In that fact, we find security and safety. But not everyone agrees with this statement.

The prayer was not eloquent. In it I had made reference to a quote that bothered the speaker of the evening. It was the graduation ceremony at the University of Texas, and it was the Baptist's year to pray. So as the Baptist campus minister, it was my turn. As we marched in, dressed in our academic colors, looking for all the world like a funeral procession of peacocks, I was attracted to the words inscribed in marble over the doors to the main building. We would sit during the ceremony, just under that inscription, and face the students and guests seated on the lawn. The quote was from the Bible, "Ye shall know the truth, and the truth shall make you free" (John 8:32 KJV). I found it fitting to call attention to that quote in my invocation. I had a feeling very few eyes were closed anyway. Then I thanked God for sending Jesus Christ—the truth—to set us free. The commencement speaker was president of a southwest university noted for its academic standing and was, no doubt, an extremely well-educated man. I could tell that by his colors, since the colors on an academic robe represent various levels of achievement as well as signify disciplines of study. In his speech, just as most of the audience was falling asleep, this president turned to where I sat on the platform and said, "I must correct the Reverend Mr. Crawford's prayer of a few moments ago. Truth is relative! It is not embodied in any one person." I sat there and smiled. I knew two things: the Bible had told me he was mistaken, and I had the benediction in which to make a rebuttal. Truth is not relative. It finds its best expression in the Person of Jesus Christ and suits us well as our first piece of armor. But there is more.

"Stand firm therefore . . . having put on the breastplate of righteousness" (Eph. 6:14). As if truth were not enough security, the Psalmist said, "I have been young and now I am old, Yet I have not seen the righteous forsaken" (Ps. 37:25). Paul wrote to Timothy concerning a "crown of righteousness" (2 Tim. 4:8), and we sometimes sing, "dressed in his righteousness alone, Faultless to stand before the throne." Equipped with right-eousness we not only feel secure but we know that even in the end we will be found "faultless" and rewarded with a victor's crown. That's good news to the battle weary. But there is more.

"And having shod your feet with the preparation of the gospel of peace" (Eph. 6:15). Putting on peace allows one to relax in the midst of conflict because it is a different kind of peace than that which the world gives. Jesus said to his disciples, "Peace I leave with you; My peace I give to you; not as the world gives do I give to you" (John 14:27). God's peace, given to us by Jesus Christ, is peace with God, with others, and with self, and the world cannot comprehend it. It is indeed a peace "which sur-passes all comprehension"; and as defensive armor, it shall "guard your hearts and your minds in Christ Jesus" (Phil. 4:7). Yet there is more armor.

"In addition to all, taking up the shield of faith with which you will be able to extinguish all the flaming arrows of the evil one" (Eph. 6:16). The application and use of a shield is obvious, but a shield of faith will always look foolish to nonbelievers. Abraham was asked why he was packing for a journey and where he was going. His response was that he did not know. Now that looks foolish. You would not pack and prepare for a journey without knowing your destination, but that is exactly what Abraham did, and it looked foolish. God had told Abraham, "Go forth from your country, and from your relatives and from your father's house, to the land which I will show you" (Gen. 12:1). Abraham, as well as others, looked foolish when he employed his faith.

There is a fine line between faith and foolishness. What the believer sees as faith, the nonbeliever sees as foolishness.

Sometimes the truth is known only in retrospect. Noah looked foolish building an ark, miles from water. When asked where the water was coming from to float his boat, Noah probably told them what God had said—it was going to rain. Since rain falling from the sky had not been previously mentioned in history, Noah's friends must have had a good laugh at that prediction. But they quit laughing when it began to sprinkle: "The rain fell upon the earth for forty days and forty nights" (Gen. 7:12). Noah and his family survived through faith while the nonbelievers perished through foolishness.

The apostle Paul was thought to be foolish when in reality he was faithful. Here was a man who had already attained greatness. He was already the leader of the Jewish persecution of Christians. Had Paul never become a Christian, the probability is that he would still have been mentioned in history. Yet he gave up greatness, and all its benefits, for the lifestyle of a first-century Christian. Someone must have called him a fool, for Paul responded, "We are fools for Christ's sake" (1 Cor. 4:10). When we put on faith, we not only protect ourselves but also look foolish to nonbelievers. There is still one more piece of defensive armor.

"Take the helmet of salvation" (Eph. 6:17). The wording is significantly different for this piece of armor. All other pieces we put on or pick up, but the helmet of salvation we "take" or receive as one would receive a gift. Indeed, salvation is a gift from God (Eph. 2:8). So important is this helmet of salvation that even the Lord wears it. According to Isaiah, "He put . . . a helmet of salvation on His head" (Isa. 59:17). Equipped with this defensive armor, we are now ready to look at the one offensive weapon.

"And take . . . the sword of the Spirit, which is the word of God" (Eph. 6:17). The purpose of this sword is not to defend ourselves but rather to redeem the world. Reduced to a simple definition, the purpose of the Bible is the redemption of sinful humanity through the revelation of God. Redemption is not a difficult word to understand. My wife used to collect savings

stamps. There was a time when we were fanatics about them. We bought groceries only on Wednesday because that was double stamp day, and we bought gasoline only on Monday because that was double stamp day. We had a catalog of gifts that could be ours in return for the stamps. When we decided on a particular gift and collected the right number of books, we would take the stamps to a Redemption Center store. Inside we would "redeem" our stamps. The process of trading in one item of value, the stamps, for an item of greater value was called "redemption." The process is similar related to spiritual matters. One day I traded in my life for a life of greater value from God. We call it "new life" or "new birth," but it is in essence a replacement of the old life for the new. The process is called "redemption," and that is the purpose of the Bible, our sword.

This redemptive purpose runs throughout the Bible. In Genesis 1–2, *redemption* was *designed or planned*. Before God ever said, "Let there be . . ." there was a plan in place for the world, and that plan included redemption. In Genesis 3:1 to 11:26, redemption became required. Humanity sinned and thereby required a redemptive process to reunite the broken fellowship with God. In Genesis 11:27 to Malachi 4:6, *redemption* was *prepared for*. Through a people, then a nation, then a family, then the line of David, redemption was narrowed down to the focal point of all history: the birth of the Redeemer. In the Gospels—Matthew, Mark, Luke, and John—we have *redemption effected*. It was effected in the person of Jesus Christ. In the Book of Acts we have *redemption shared*. It was shared first with Jerusalem, then Judea and Samaria, and ultimately with the ends of the earth. In The New Testament letters, those of Paul as well as the general letters, we have *redemption explained*. Paul became the great explainer of redemption, joined by James, Peter, John, Jude, and the writer of Hebrews. In the Book of Revelation, we have *redemption realized*. Ultimately that which we know only in part will be known fully and that which "we see in a mirror, dimly" we shall see face-to-face (1 Cor. 13:12). Redemption will be realized. So from beginning to end, our sword—the Bible—has as its purpose the redemption of humanity. But even though Paul had listed the armor of God, he was not yet through with the subject of equipping.

A part of the armor or God's extra resource was noted by Paul in the equipping process: "With all prayer and petition pray at all times in the Spirit, and with this in view, be on the alert with all perseverance and petition for all the saints" (Eph. 6:18). We must always remember that the battle is not ours but God's: "Do not fear or be dismayed because of this great multitude, for the battle is not yours but God's" (2 Chron. 20:15). When we get the feeling that we are in the battle alone or that we can't fight off Satan any longer, remember that the battle is not between us and some other person or even between us and Satan. The battle is bigger than that; it is between God and Satan, and we are only participants. Because it is God's battle, continual, constant communication between us and God is essential.

The pattern of prayer is evident from the time Adam communicated with God in the Garden, to Enoch walking with God, to Abraham praying on the way to sacrifice Isaac, to the petitions of the Psalmist, to the intercessions of the Hebrew prophets, to Jesus praying in the garden, to Paul praying that all Israel might be saved, to John praying on Patmos. In no case did God delegate prayer to another, not to an angel, nor to a saint, nor to a spirit; but kept as personal the high privilege of prayerful communication with believers. If prayer is that important to God, we ought to practice its importance in our lives. Don't delegate this responsibility to another—this responsibility belongs to each one of us.

Prayer, in part, is asking God for what we desire. Jesus told his disciples to "ask the Father for anything" (John 16:23), and Paul said, "Be anxious for nothing, but in everything by prayer and supplication with thanksgiving let your requests be made known to God" (Phil. 4:6). The response from God may not always be what we want, but it will always be in keeping with God's will and for our best interests. We must pray! We must establish a disciplined prayer life so that we do not just pray when the mood hits us or the need overwhelms us. We must pray spontaneously, as we go. However we do it, we must pray, for the battle is God's, and communication is a must.

The fight is real, but we have a real Lord who has provided us with real armor. Paul wrote, "I box in such a way, as not beating the air." (1 Cor. 9:26). Like Paul, we must fight an actual enemy, Satan, and not swing at our own shadow. Satan is powerful and we will need strength as we stand against him.

STANDING STRONG

How can we stand strong before Satan? When Jesus was confronted by Satan, he resisted other methods which were within his power like force and retreat. Jesus simply quoted scripture to him—the Sword of the Spirit (Matt. 4:1–11; Luke 4:1–13). Jesus led from his strength and Satan fled.

Paul said one thing that was given to him was "a thorn in the flesh, a messenger of Satan to torment me" (2 Cor. 12:7). Notice that Paul did not go on the attack against Satan. He did not rebuke him, bind him, debate him, battle him, or even speak to him. He prayed. Specifically he asked God three times to remove the thorn. God's answer was to send sufficient grace (2 Cor. 12:8–9).

On yet another occasion Paul was hindered by Satan when he wanted to visit the believers in Thessalonica (1 Thess. 2:18). Again, Paul does not go on the attack trying to break Satan's strongholds or cast him down. Rather, he focuses on Jesus and on his fellow believers (1 Thess. 2:19–20).

How then can we stand strong against Satan? Paul told us in 2 Corinthians 10:3–4: "Though we walk in the flesh, we do not war according to the flesh, for the weapons of our warfare are not of the flesh, but divinely powerful for the destruction of fortresses." The key words are not "the destruction of fortresses" but "divinely powerful." We cannot war with Satan in our own strength. We must depend on divine power. While the results may well be "the destruction of fortresses," results are up to God.

Further Paul instructed Timothy to "fight the good fight, keeping faith and a good conscience" (1 Tim. 1:18–19). Again, the emphasis for the disciple is not fighting the devil, but "keeping faith." Our strength in the conflict will come from our faith in God, not from our skills in battle.

James added, "Submit therefore to God. Resist the devil and he will flee from you" (James 4:7). Here, we are told how to get Satan to leave us alone, at least temporarily—not command him or cast him out, but "resist" him.

How can we resist Satan? *Resist Satan by staying close to God through prayer and Bible study.* Three hundred graduates of a theological school were surveyed. All of them had committed some sexual sin. The one common answer was that none of them indicated that they had a private devotional/worship time with prayer and Bible study. While having such a private discipline is no guarantee of purity, failure to have such a discipline makes us extremely vulnerable to temptation.

Resist Satan by refuting temptation. While we are vulnerable in different areas, all are vulnerable to temptation at some point in their life. While we can't always control the temptations that come our way, we can control our response to them. Allowing our thoughts to run wild or even dwelling on a temptation is sowing seeds of our own destruction.

The Children of Israel, faced with the Red Sea in front of them and the Egyptian army behind them were tempted to run rather than refute. Some were tempted to run back to the Egyptians where, though slaves, they would have some sense of security. Others were tempted to run into the sea rather than allowing the Egyptians the privilege of killing them. Still others were tempted to run to the mountains where God had made no provision for them. But, refuting temptation they listened to Moses who said, "Do not fear! *Stand by* and see the salvation of the Lord which He will accomplish for you today" (Exod. 14:13, italics mine). Because they stood strong in refuting temptation they were able to "go forward" (Exod. 14:15) in victory.

Resist Satan by refusing to let him gain territory in your life. We must practice a healthy self-discipline of rejection and be accountable to others. As Paul said, "Make no provision for the flesh in regard to its lusts" (Rom. 13:14). Out of the seventeenth century comes the illustration from Madame Guyon of kneeling on serpents. The idea is if we kneel on Satan in prayer and worship, we need not rebuke him. When he becomes our kneeling bench in prayer, he can gain no other territory in our life.

Resist Satan by being creative. We must find new ways to win the victory over temptation. If Satan is continually discovering new ways to tempt us, we ought to be equally energetic in finding ways to resist and conquer. In the early 1960s Jean-Claude Killy was determined to win an Olympic gold medal for France. Daily he would run the ski slopes with his skis on and nightly he would lift weights. But he knew all the other skiers would be doing the same. He determined to discover a new way to win. He challenged the basic theories of racing. He tried different approaches. Finally, Killy discovered a new style exactly opposite of the traditional technique of his day. He learned to ski with his legs apart when he came to a turn, not together as others did. This explosive new style cut Killy's time considerably. In 1966 and 1967, he won virtually every major skiing trophy. In 1968 he won three gold medals at the Winter Olympics, a new record in ski racing. He was a winner because he dared to be creative. Spiritual creativity will likewise assist us in winning against the temptations of Satan.

Spiritually fit disciples are constantly being called upon to resist the temptations and assaults of the enemy. We have no choice. Enemy attack comes with the territory. When we successfully stand against the opposition, adequately equipped in God's armor, strengthened by God power, victory is reality.

STANDING VICTORIOUS

The truth is, in the midst of the conflict, the victory has already been won. We run the race having already won it. We fight this fight, not to win, but because we have already won. Our relationship with Satan will take on a completely different perspective when we realize that although he may tempt, torment, try, test, and trouble us, he cannot triumph over us.

After listing problems such as tribulation, distress, persecution, famine, nakedness, peril, and sword, Paul declared, "In all these things we overwhelmingly conquer through Him who loved us" (Rom. 8:37). In regard to difficulties coming from rulers and authorities, Paul said of Jesus, "He made a public display of them, having triumphed over them through Him" (Col. 2:15).

John exclaimed, "You are from God, little children, and have overcome them; because greater is He who is in you than he who is in the world" (1 John 4:4). Peter wrote that our Lord is "at the right hand of God, having gone into heaven, after angels and authorities and powers had been subjected to Him" (1 Pet. 3:22). Revelation exalts the ultimate defeat of Satan and eternal victory for God's people. Satan is a defeated foe and now lives in the interim between his sentence and his punishment while we live in the thrill of victory.

In the 1976 Olympic Games in Montreal, Bruce Jenner not only won a gold medal in the decathlon but became an American hero. Concerning the feeling, Jenner said, "When I crossed the finish line, I screamed so loud I thought I broke my vocal chords. It was the last meet of my life, and I'd known that for four years. Afterwards, I couldn't wipe the smile off my face."

As great as the joy that accompanies the winning of a gold medal, the spiritually fit disciple of Jesus Christ will someday stand on an even greater victory stand. Peter describes it this way, "In this you greatly rejoice, even though now for a little while, if necessary, you have been distressed by various trials, so that the proof of your faith, being more precious than gold which is perishable, even though tested by fire, may be found to result in praise and glory and honor at the revelation of Jesus Christ" (1 Pet. 1:6–7). George Duffield, Jr. wrote:

> Stand up, stand up for Jesus,
> The strife will not by long;
> This day the noise of battle,
> The next, the victor's song.
> To him that overcometh
> A crown of life shall be;
> He, with the King of glory,
> Shall reign eternally.

EXERCISES FOR SPIRITUAL FITNESS

Day One What is a recent experience where you had to "stand against" Satan and how well did you do?

_____

_____

_____

Day Two Of the five pieces of defensive armor mentioned in this chapter, which do you find is your most protective piece against Satan? Which is your least protective piece? _____

_____

_____

Day Three For what purpose have you used your Sword of the Spirit this week? _____

_____

_____

Day Four What does it mean to you to "stand strong"?

_____

_____

_____

Day Five What are three ways you have experienced standing victorious this week?

1. _____
2. _____
3. _____

Scriptural strengths to remember:
1. James 4:7
2. 2 Chronicles 20:15
3. 2 Corinthians 10:3–4
4. Romans 8:35–39

phase four

SERVING

IN SHAPE:

THE TEAMWORK

OF A DISCIPLE

WEEK TEN

Loving

THE TIME HAS COME to shift our thinking from personal spiritual fitness to how that fitness affects the team. While disciples should be concerned about their own spiritual fitness, they must also be concerned about the team. When, in the huddle, team members have only personal agendas, strange things are apt to happen, like in the following "sports report."

A strange thing happened at the stadium. After receiving the opening kickoff, the home team formed their huddle to get the play from the quarterback. They did not break the huddle, but for some reason stayed in it. A penalty flag was dropped and five yards stepped off for delay of the game. Still the team remained in the huddle. It seemed each player had ideas about how to improve the huddle itself. It was as if they had forgotten the object of the game. Officials dropped another flag and imposed another five-yard penalty. Word reached the coach that each player wanted all the other players to be just like him and adopt his ideas as to the design of the huddle. As the crowd became more amused the team changed the shape of their huddle from a circle to a diamond to an oval to a square. The referees tossed more penalty flags and assessed more yards lost. Several players moved from the huddle to the line of scrimmage in order to get back into the game. Once out of the huddle, they could not agree on the proper formation and when their teammates did not join them, they returned to the huddle. The amusement of the crowd gave way to frustration, then to anger. They booed until they were bored, but the team remained in the huddle. Finally the referee ruled the game had been forfeited and awarded the victory to the visiting team. The spectators left, but the players, still in the huddle, didn't seem to notice. Their individual preparation was never translated into serving as a team.

Serving well requires both personal preparation and teamwork. Summer Sanders prepared adequately for the 1992 Olympics in Barcelona, Spain, and won a gold and three other medals in swimming. But in 1996, she wasn't prepared. Coming out of retirement in order to compete again, Summer had qualified for the finals of the U.S. Olympic Swim Trials. The event was the 200-meter butterfly. For 150 meters, she was in the race, swimming with the leaders, then she fell back to a last place finish. "I guess ten and a half months wasn't enough in that last fifty meters," Sanders said.

When the preparation is inadequate, the participant does not serve their team well. In the spiritual waters, the same truth is seen. Spiritual fitness eventually leads us to serving as a part of a team. A spiritually fit disciple is not satisfied with personal spiritual growth alone. There must be teamwork. On the other hand the lack of spiritual fitness or the use of spiritual fitness for purely personal reasons sends a negative message to the team.

Everywhere you look people are wearing their message on their T-shirts. Increasingly the message I'm seeing concludes with the words, "No Fear!"

Even though we are born with only two fears, heights and loud noises, we acquire many more along the way. Eighty-one percent are afraid of flying, 74 percent are afraid of animals, 73 percent fear their house burning, 70 percent of us have a fear of being kidnaped. But God does not want us to be afraid. Three hundred sixty-six times in the Bible, God says, "Fear not." Specifically, in 1 John 4:18, we are told, "There is no fear in love; but perfect love casts out fear."

The more an athlete loves the competition, the less fear there is of the opposition. Love conquers fear and the spiritually fit disciple must understand love if he or she is going to succeed. Jesus told his disciples, "A new commandment I give to you, that you love one another, even as I have loved you, that you also love one another. By this all men will know that you are My disciples, if you have love for one another" (John 13:34–35). So, let's look at loving as a spiritual discipline.

Looking at love is a lot like looking through a kaleidoscope. In one end, there are different colored and shaped pieces of rock, plastic, or glass. When the cylinder turns the pieces tumble around, creating different formations. If we studied it long enough, we would understand that the ingredients never changed. It was our perspective that changed.

That's the way God's love is. The ingredients never change. It is always God's love, but every time we look at it, we get a different perspective. The following verses show three different perspectives of God's love:

Beloved, let us love one another, for love is from God; and everyone who loves is born of God, and knows God.

The one who does not love does not know God, for God is love.

By this the love of God was manifested in us, that God has sent His only begotten Son into the world so that we might live through Him.

In this is love, not that we loved God, but that He loved us and sent His Son to be the propitiation for our sins.

Beloved, if God so loved us, we also ought to love one another.

No one has seen God at any time; if we love one another, God abides in us, and His love is perfected in us.

By this we know that we abide in Him and He in us, because He has given us of His Spirit.

We have seen and testify that the Father has sent the Son to be the Savior of the world.

Whoever confesses that Jesus is the Son of God, God abides in him, and he in God.

We have come to know and have believed the love which God has for us. God is love, and the one who abides in love abides in God, and God abides in Him.

By this, love is perfected with us, so that we may have confidence in the day of judgment; because as He is, so also are we in this world.

There is no fear in love; but perfect love casts out fear, because fear involves punishment, and the one who fears is not perfected in love.

We love, because He first loved us.

If someone says, "I love God," and hates his brother, he is a liar; for the one who does not love his brother whom he has seen, cannot love God whom he has not seen.

And this commandment we have from Him, that the one who loves God should love his brother also. (1 John 4:7–21)

GOD LOVING YOU

A recent Gallup Poll revealed that nine out of ten Americans believe that God loves them. It is a seldom debated topic. *God loves us because God has always loved us.* Long before we knew it, long before we sang "Jesus Loves Me," long before we quoted John 3:16, God loved us. In fact, long before we were born God loved us. Jesus said the Father loved Him, "before the foundation of the world" (John 17:24).

At the center of all that exists is love. Why did God create? Because God loved. Why did God create us in the divine image? Because God loved. Before God ever said, "Let there be" (Gen. 1:3), God was love. God has always loved us. Love is the basis of the Godhead, the source of all that is.

The supreme demonstration of God's love is seen beautifully and meaningfully on the cross as God gives the only begotten

Son as an expression of divine love for all people. We can not find any page of history that reads, "God doesn't love." God initiated love, and God will love for eternity. God has always loved us.

There is a second fact about God's loving us. *God loves us as much as God loves anyone.* Now it gets complicated. You surely don't mean that God loves me as much as God loves so-and-so? Yes, that's what I mean.

God loves each of us as much as God loves anyone.

God loves each of us as much as God loved Abraham, the father of the faithful.

God loves each of us as much as God loved Moses who led the people out of bondage.

God loves each of us as much as God loved David, a man after God's own heart.

God loves each of us as much as God loved Hosea, a prophet of love.

God loves each of us as much as God loved John the Baptist, who prepared the way for the Son of God.

God loves each of us as much as God loved the apostle Paul, who walked all over the Mediterranean world sharing God's love.

We may understand more or less about love than someone else. We may appropriate more or less of it. We may know more, or feel more, or be able to share it better, or not as well, but we don't have any more or any less than anyone else. God loves each of us just as much as God loves anybody because God loves everybody one hundred percent. You see, when God gave Jesus Christ, he was given to everybody. God's love is not confined to one social group, one economic group, one ethnic group, or one denominational group.

Paul said, "There is neither Jew nor Greek, there is neither slave nor free man, there is neither male nor female, for you are all one in Christ Jesus" (Gal. 3:28).

The songwriter put it this way: "In Christ there is no east or west, in him no south nor north, but one great fellowship of love throughout the whole wide earth."

God loves everybody. If we think we experience God's love and we come away from that experience seeing human differences that divide people, then we haven't experienced God's love because God's love covers every person. God intends to love everyone, and God loves each of us just as much as anyone.

A third fact about God loving us is: *God will always love us.* The apostle Paul asked a multiple choice question: "Who will separate us from the love of Christ?" Then he gave multiple choices: "tribulation, or distress, or persecution, or famine, or nakedness, or peril, or sword," or none of the above? Paul is convinced that in all these things we "conquer through Him who loved us." Then he added, "I am convinced that neither death, nor life, nor angels, nor principalities, nor things present, nor things to come, nor powers, nor height, nor depth, nor any other created thing, will be able to separate us from the love of God, which is in Christ Jesus our Lord" (Rom. 8:35–39).

God is just going to keep on loving us. We can't rise so high professionally, socially, intellectually, or any other way that we rise above God's love. We can't sink so low emotionally, economically, mentally, or any other way that we sink below God's ability to love us. We can't get so far out that we are outside the reach of God's love.

God is going to keep on loving us. God is going to love us because of who we are, and God is going to love us in spite of who we are. There is nothing that can happen to us that will stop God from loving us. There is no circumstance of life that can come our way to negate God's love for us. There's not one thought we can think that will stop God from loving us. God is going to love us regardless of what we do—just like parents love children regardless of what they do. That doesn't mean God doesn't get disappointed just like parents do in children. It doesn't mean that God approves of everything we do any more than parents approve of everything their children do.

The reason is that God loves us not just for our benefit and not just for God's benefit. God loves us in order that some other folks can be loved through us. Knowing that about God's love brings about a crucial question: Are we a channel of God's love, or are we a reservoir of God's love?

George Matheson, the Scottish preacher, was deeply in love with his fiancé and planning their marriage. He was already one of the best preachers Scotland had ever known when it was determined that his eyesight was going bad and he would eventually turn blind. He shared this with his fiancé, and she immediately terminated their engagement. It crushed him and almost destroyed him.

Matheson went through weeks of gloom and despondency until his sister came to his assistance and became a source of strength and encouragement for him. As his eyesight gradually worsened, Matheson was determined that the people in his congregation would not know it. So this loving sister would sit with him on Saturday nights, listen to his sermons, speak them back to him, write them down, and read them back to him over and over again until he had memorized his sermon. He would stand in the pulpit on Sunday morning with an open Bible. Many in the congregation did not know he could not see one word on its pages.

Then one day this loving sister informed him that she was getting married, would be living in another town, and would no longer be available to be his source of strength. Again, he was almost destroyed by the news. Twice he had been crushed by those he had loved very deeply. He refused even to go to the wedding. But during the time the wedding was taking place in another town, George Matheson sat in his study and out of his despair penned the words:

> O, love that wilt not let me go,
> I rest my weary soul in thee.
> I give thee back the life I owe,
> That in thine ocean depths,
> It's flow may richer, fuller be.

George Matheson discovered what you and I need to discover: that while other loves may fail us and not live up to all our expectations, we can rest our weary souls in the certainty of God's love.

Now let's look at a second perspective on God's love.

YOU LOVING GOD

Remember the kaleidoscope? While the ingredients never change, every time we look into it, we find a fresh, new perspective. So it is every time we look at a passage of scripture that depicts God's love.

A little boy left a note for his mother one day. After he had gone to school she went in his room to see that everything was put in the right place, and there she found it. She read:

> Dear Mom:
> For making up my bed today—$1.00,
> For taking out the trash last night—$1.00,
> For hanging up my clothes—$1.00,
> For cleaning the tub after my bath—$1.00,
> Total charge—$4.00.
> P.S. Payable today.

When he got home from school, he found a note in his room. He read:

> Dear Son:
> For fixing your meals—no charge,
> For washing your clothes—no charge,
> For picking up after you are gone each day—no charge,
> For a hundred other things I do for you—no charge,
> Total—no charge.
> P.S. I love you.

That's the way God's love is. God gives so much to us we ought to desire to love in return without demands. If we loved God in return, it would allow God's love to be two-way.

The deadest thing in this world is a one-way love. I have seen the effects of it in families. I have counseled with those for whom the effect was a broken marriage. I have observed the effects of it in a church. One-way love has been responsible for divorces, disunity within families, splits in churches, and disrupted communities. The deadest thing I know of, in this world, is a one-way love.

If this devastation and destruction caused by one-way love is true on the human level, how much more true is it on a divine level? To allow God to love us again and again and again, and to somehow shake our fist back in God's face and say, "I refuse to love you" is not only unnatural—it's sinful.

The most natural thing for a person to do is love. That's the way God made us. If you don't believe love is natural, just try loving a young child. A child naturally loves back. They learn how to hate. They naturally love. God made us to not only be recipients of love, but to be responders to love.

There is something else about loving God that we need to have called to our attention, almost continually; love is not free. The world talks about a free love, but the Bible knows nothing at all about such a thing. It's a misnomer. If you have been misled to believe that loving God is free, or God loving you is free, then you are mistaken. Somebody has taken you down the wrong road. Somebody has read you the wrong chapter, if not indeed the wrong book. That just isn't the truth. Love is not free.

In fact, nothing is free. Everything has a price tag. Some of us learn that in harder ways than others. I think the first time I really learned it was within the first year of our marriage.

The doorbell rang. It was a salesman. He identified himself as being a representative of the XYZ Promotions Company. (I have changed the name to protect the guilty.) He wanted me to know that my name had been selected. I found out later that every person who lived in that apartment complex who was home that night had been selected. The way you got selected by that company was to have your name on the mailbox.

Nevertheless, I was selected—a winner. His company, as a special promotion, was going to give us three free magazine subscriptions. I invited him in. So far, I was pretty excited about that prospect. We hadn't been married but a few months and could hardly afford a magazine subscription of any kind. If it had not been for the church newsletter, we wouldn't have had any subscriptions. So the idea of having three magazine sub- scriptions at no charge to us was an exciting prospect. He showed me a list and said I could pick any three magazines, and I would begin immediately to get them free. I picked them. He decided he would give me a fourth one because he liked me. At least that is what he said. He had trouble remembering my name, but he liked me. About the time I picked a fourth magazine. my wife walked into the room. He decided almost immediately he liked her enough to give her a magazine. So, we now had five free magazine subscriptions. He asked me to sign a piece of paper.

Has anybody ever said anything to you and you didn't hear it until later? That's what happened that night. While I was signing my name, he said, "There will be a small postage and handling charge." I didn't hear that until later. The small postage and handling charge never registered in my mind. This "small charge" turned out to be $53.13. That was more than thirty years ago. Can you imagine with inflation what those free magazines would cost me if I won them today? I would be out several hundred dollars in postage and han- dling. That was my first experience with learning that every- thing in life has a price tag—even God's love.

When God loved us, it cost: "For God so loved the world, that he gave his only begotten Son" (John 3:16). The price tag on God's love is in the shape of a cross. When we choose to love God, it costs us also.

The Psalmist asks, "What shall I render to the Lord for all His benefits toward me?" (Ps. 116:12) He didn't answer it. The answer is service. To love God is to serve God. In the Bible, love and service are so interrelated they cannot really be separated.

What does it cost us to love God? It costs us at the point of service. That is a lesson we need to learn and be reminded of over and over again. The price tag on love is service. We somehow smooth over that when we talk about love.

I have often threatened to change the vows in a wedding ceremony to make them more up-to-date and meaningful. What I would really like to do is to have the groom promise the bride to take out the trash and help with the dishes. I would like it if the bride would promise the groom to wash his socks and clean the bathroom. I think it would be more realistic.

We can serve someone without loving them. There is a lot of that in this world. But we cannot love someone without being willing to serve them. So it is impossible (and John says it over and over) to say we love God and yet, not be willing to serve him.

That is what God was trying to demonstrate in the life of Abraham when he was instructed to take Isaac up on Mt. Moriah and build an altar; to take some wood, some rope, and a knife; to tie Isaac on that altar and sacrifice him (Gen. 22:1–19). We in our sophisticated culture look back at that scripture and wonder how in the world God could ask anything like that of anyone, much less Abraham.

Abraham committed himself to do whatever God wanted him to do. When God called, Abraham responded. He packed all that he had and set out for a land that God would show him. Over and over again God had demonstrated his love for Abraham. Now God orders Abraham to sacrifice Isaac on an altar. What a long journey up the mountain that must have been! Isaac kept asking about the lamb. Abraham kept believing God would provide. With Isaac tied to the altar and Abraham's blade hand lifted into the air, God provided. God always does.

But, God was asking of Abraham, if he was willing to do for his God what pagans were doing for their false gods? Child sacrifice was very prominent in that day. Since the nonbelievers were sacrificing their children to the gods who could not respond, God Almighty wanted to know if Abraham had enough love to do for his God what lesser men were willing to do for lesser gods? Abraham discovered, if he didn't know it already, that the price of loving God is serving God.

I think we have obscured this in our faith. We love God. We tell each other we love God. We sing that we love God. We can tell God that we love God. But we forget that love always comes with a price tag. The cost of loving God is being willing to serve God.

LOVING EACH OTHER

I have said already that looking at God's love is like looking through a spiritual kaleidoscope, in the sense that the ingredients never change but every time you look, the perspective changes.

The first perspective most often seen when we look at God's love is the fact that God loves us. The second perspective seen when we look at God's love is that we love God. That love for God is expressed in our service. The third perspective is that we ought to love each other.

We could and often do relate to each other without love. Paul expressed it in the thirteenth chapter of 1 Corinthians. He said if a man doesn't have love, he is as a "noisy gong or a clanging cymbal" (1 Cor. 13:1). He has no harmony, no melody. He has nothing. Today he might say: "Take a look at your life. Begin to add up everything you have that is yours, everything you could claim as 'owning', from material possessions to personality traits to health. When you get all of it listed on a piece of paper, give all of it some numerical value, and total it. If in that list, you do not have love, you have nothing. The bottom line is zero.

Paul said that if you have everything—abilities to understand, all knowledge, dreams, prophecies, and numerous other possessions but have not love, you have nothing (1 Cor. 13:1–3).

Sometimes we function in this world without love. When we do, we are spiritually out of shape.

There are some subtle substitutes for the kind of love that we are to express for each other as Christians. *One of those substitutes for love is reciprocity.* This means, "You scratch my back and I'll scratch your back." It's the idea someone sang about a long time ago: "I'll give to you, and you give to me, true love, true love." It's what we express sometimes by saying, "Let's don't go to their house because if we go over there, we'll have to invite them to our house." That's not love, but reciprocity. It's based on equal giving and taking. Sometimes we substitute that into our Christian experience. Instead of loving each other, we just swap pleasantries. We go around keeping score instead of really loving others.

Something else that is not love is fatalism. This is expressed by all of us at one time or another: "I fell in love." It sounds like falling into a trap. Fatalistically, it just happened. You didn't mean for it to happen. Nobody planned it. Nobody designed it. It just happened. That's not God's kind of love. We are not puppets on a string. We are people made in the image of God. Fatalism would say, "Love is blind." Not God's kind of love. Somebody else's love may be blind, but God's kind of love sees more clearly and discerns more carefully than any other kind of love. God's kind of love is not fatalistic, not blind. It doesn't just happen. It has a design, purpose, and plan behind it. We are a part of that design, purpose, and plan.

Still another thing that is not love is attraction. We mistake attraction, which is surface and short-term, for God's love which is deep and lasting. Attraction is that feeling which is expressed by the universal sign of nudging the person next to you with your elbow. Attraction occurs just before you do that. When we were younger, we would be standing in line and some girl would walk by and the elbow would go into the ribs of the person next to you. It's a universal action. It communicates without speaking. A nice car passes on the street and this nudge to the ribs happens. That's attraction. There's no depth to it. It usually doesn't last very long. Unfortunately, we sometimes substitute that in the Christian life. When we talk about loving each other, we really may only be attracted to each other.

Another substitute for love is emotion. This is not God's kind of love. Emotion just takes you where you let it. Go with the flow. Roll with the punches. Move along with the crowd—with the feeling. It's the current philosophy that whatever feels right is what we ought to do. That's not love. Love has within it a decision making ability. Emotion does not. Someone might lead us to do something emotionally, but they can't lead us to like it unless we want to, unless we decide to. I may get caught up in the emotion of the moment and do something that I think is really based on my love, but when it is analyzed, it's only the emotion of the moment. Love takes its time. Love evaluates.

The danger in these substitutes is not what they do in themselves because none of them are totally bad of themselves. There is a place for all of these. The danger is when we substitute these for love—God's kind of love that we ought to be expressing for each other.

I think the right kind of love is seen among the disciples who had every reason, humanly speaking, not to love each other. If we think through that disciple group, we can pick up very quickly on some reasons, humanly speaking, why they should not have loved each other.

Peter was loud and boisterous and sometimes obnoxious. Every time Jesus asked a question, it was Simon Peter who answered it. You don't have to have been in many groups with someone like Peter to know how old that gets. Peter was the kind of person we would have enjoyed being around for about five minutes at a time. After that, his personality would begin to wear a little thin.

In that disciple group was also a man by the name of John who was quiet and meditative, a disciple of love, a philosopher. When Jesus asked a question, Peter answered it. John was the kind who, when a question was posed, would want to go sit under a tree for a few days and think about it. He might answer and he might not, depending on what he thought while under that tree. Here are people with two totally different personalities working side by side and loving each other.

Consider Andrew, a man of untroubled faith. Translate that loosely and it translates "gullible." Andrew believed everything. One did not have to argue a point with Andrew. If Jesus said something, Andrew was ready to believe it. He didn't have to be talked into it. He was ready whenever Jesus was.

Within that disciple group there was Thomas, the doubter, who questioned everything. A man who would question that Jesus Christ was alive when he said he was going to be would question anything.

So here is one who never asks a question, who is always ready. He works alongside a man who asks questions about everything. Let Jesus ask a question and Simon Peter had an answer, John wants to be excused to go think about it, Andrew is putting his coat on ready to go, and Thomas has his hand up to ask a question. All these dynamics are going on in the group and still they love each other.

Need more? How about Simon, the Zealot? Do you know who the Zealots were? They were a political party whose purpose was the overthrow of the Roman government. That's who Simon was—a political revolutionary.

Within that group you find Matthew, a tax collector. One could not be any more part of the establishment than a tax collector. Everything Matthew stood for politically, Simon was committed to destroying. Yet they worked side by side in love.

Many reasons could be found, from a human perspective, why these disciples ought not love each other. But they learned a secret. They stopped looking at each other long enough to look together at Jesus. They learned that you we love people that we don't like. The person who has learned that has indeed learned a valuable lesson.

It was October of 1968. I was directing Baptist student ministries at Pan American University on the Texas-Mexico border (now the University of Texas at Pan American). Before daylight one Friday morning we were loading the bus to go to the Texas Baptist Student Convention. Two boys showed up to go with us on the bus. Neither had signed up, but we were far from turning people down just because they hadn't signed up. We invited them and welcomed them. Both were black which was a little unusual because that campus of seven thousand students was predominantly Hispanic.

As we made our way north for a couple hours and the morning naps ended, someone turned on their radio. The news reported the latest from the Olympic Games which were being held in Mexico City. John Carlos and Tommy Smith had finished first and third in their event. When they stood on the platform to receive their medals and to hear the playing of their national anthem, they had refused to stand at attention. In fact, one of them had stood with his fist raised in a symbol of black power with a black glove on his hand. The other had worn a black scarf around his neck. This news report started a discussion between these two black students about the role of the black person in society. The discussion became a debate. The debate became a fight. After a few minutes, we had to pull them apart and send them to opposite ends of the bus.

When we got to the Convention, Danny (one of the black students) told me he was not feeling well and did not want to stay with the group. He excused himself to spend the weekend with his aunt. He said he would see us on Sunday afternoon when it was time to leave.

On Sunday afternoon Danny was on the bus—under a blanket. I lifted the blanket just long enough to see who it was and to hear him say, "Leave me alone." I honored that request and left him alone. We made that long trip back to the Rio Grande Valley arriving after midnight. His family met him, took him home, and I didn't hear another word from him.

On Thursday night as we finished having supper with some friends, the phone rang. A girl's trembling voice asked: "Have you heard? Danny just died." I had not heard. After spending from Sunday night to Thursday night in bed, Danny had summoned enough strength to drive his own car to the hospital, walk into the emergency room and ask for help. Then he collapsed and died from infectious hepatitis.

I excused myself from our dinner guests and made my way across town to the funeral home and then to the home of his family. What little I could do was done. I started home through the campus and realized that lights were still on in the Baptist Student Center. It had been an emotion-filled evening. Danny was sports editor of the school paper. Word had spread quickly across the campus. I assumed that someone just forgot to turn off the lights. I pulled around behind the building, opened the back door, and reached in to switch off the lights when I heard voices. I walked down the hallway and saw on the carpeted lounge area of our Center about eight or ten students. They were kneeling on the floor praying. I started back down the hallway to leave, but I stayed in the building long enough to hear Donald (the other black student involved) pray what I think is probably the most beautiful prayer I have heard in my life. It was simple. This is what he prayed: "Oh God, give me one more chance to love."

I confess I have had to pray that prayer a few times—in those words and in other words. I think all of us have come to places along the way and will probably come to some more where we pray, "God, give me one more chance to love." One of the beautiful things about God is that this prayer is honored. God honored it for Donald, for the following summer Donald became a student missionary to the Watts area of Los Angeles.

What does loving have to do with spiritual fitness? Everything! Without love, you have nothing. Without love, you are nothing.

Earlier in the century, Albert C. Fisher, a well-known Methodist pastor and evangelist in Texas, wrote words that were appropriate for disciples of his day and likewise for ours:

Of the themes that men have known,
One supremely stands alone;
Thro' the ages it has shown,
'Tis His wonderful, wonderful love.

Love is the theme, love is supreme;
Sweeter it grows, glory bestows;
Bright as the sun ever it glows!
Love is the theme, eternal theme!

EXERCISES FOR SPIRITUAL FITNESS

Day One   How do you respond to the idea that God loves you as much as God has ever loved anyone?

_____

_____

_____

Day Two   What about the idea that God is going to keep on loving you regardless? _____

_____

_____

Day Three   What is one act of service you could perform this week that would demonstrate your love for God?

_____

_____

Day Four   Has anyone ever loved you in spite of your differences? Explain: _____ __

_____

_____

_____

Day Five   What could you do this week to show your love for other Christians, especially those different from you?

_____

_____

_____

_____

Scriptural strengths to remember:
1. John 13:34–35
2. 1 John 4:18
3. 1 Corinthians 13:1–2
4. Galatians 3:28

WEEK ELEVEN

Relating

ONE OF THE MOST EMOTIONAL moments in recent Olympic history was the performance of Kerry Strug of the United States women's gymnastics team in the 1996 Atlanta games. With her team holding the thinnest possible lead over the Russian team, Strug was the last to compete in the final rotation of the evening.

After falling and injuring her ankle on her first vault, all the pressure was on for her second and final vault. She was told, in order to guarantee a United States victory, she needed a score of 9.493. With her ankle hurting, she stared down the runway with four relationships in order.

Strug was in right relationship with her coach Bella Karolyi, who was encouraging her from the sideline. "You can do it!" he repeated over and over. She was in right relationship with her world—the audience—most of whom were shouting, "U.S.A.! U.S.A.!" She was in a right relationship with herself, knowing what she had to do and what she was able to do. And she was in right relationship with her peers—her teammates—who were cheering her on, knowing her unique gifts.

Down the runway Kerry ran, up and into the air she flew, landing on both feet, then quickly lifting her left foot in pain before collapsing on the mat. Her score: 9.712, insuring the first team gold medal ever for a United States Women's Olympic team. A coach celebrated, a crowd cheered, an athlete triumphed, and a team wore gold, all because of right relationships.

The spiritually fit disciple must have right relationships also. Right relationship with God is the highest priority. Right relationship with the world is a practical necessity. Right relationship to self is a crucial ingredient. Right relationship to the Body of Christ—the church—is a corporate absolute.

RELATING TO GOD

The apostle Paul wrote, "I urge you, brethren, by the mercies of God, to present your bodies a living and holy sacrifice, acceptable to God, which is your spiritual service of worship" (Rom. 12: 1). In our relationship to God there is a presentation, a condition, and a reason.

Although we sing, "All to Jesus I surrender, All to him I freely give," we content ourselves with giving only ten percent. We have assumed that if we just give some of our money, attend church somewhat regularly, and treat folks fairly, we are in right relationship with God. Paul indicated that God does not want just ten percent of our money or time nor even 99.44 percent, but he desires 100 percent. Paul wrote, "Present your bodies." That which is seen and represented by my "body" is all I really have to give to God because it is all that is really mine to give. That is exactly what God wants from me—a presentation of my "body"—my all. But there are some conditions to that presentation.

Paul often leaned back on his Old Testament concept of God to explain a New Testament truth. In Old Testament days, one related to God through a sacrificial system—the killing of animals. The New Testament truth is God wants no more dead sacrifices but rather "living" sacrifices from us. In addition we are to be a "holy" sacrifice, that is "set apart." We are "set apart" from the rest of the world, no longer to be like others, but now to be "acceptable to God." The thoroughness of our sacrificial presentation of self, although difficult, is based on good reason.

With so many demands on my life, why should I give all of myself to God? Paul indicated that it is my "spiritual service of worship" or, as the King James Version of the Bible says, "reasonable service." I give my all to God because it makes sense in a world where very little else makes sense. Giving all to God is reasonable, logical, and rational. In light of the fact that Jesus Christ, in the beginning with the Father, clothed this earth with flowers, grass, shrubs, and trees and yet was allowed to hang naked on a cross, giving all to God is reasonable. In light of the fact that Jesus said, "I am the Light of the world" (John 8:12) and yet hung on the cross in midday darkness, giving all to God is reasonable. In light of the fact that Jesus claimed to give "living water" (John 4:10) and yet cried out from the cross, "I am thirsty" (John 19:28), giving all to God is reasonable. In light of the fact that Jesus claimed, "All authority [power] has been given to Me in heaven and on earth" (Matt. 28:18) and yet was allowed to hang powerless on the cross, giving all to God is reasonable. Relating to God begins with giving all. One of the ways of relating to God is through worship.

Worship is a misunderstood and often misplaced basic of the Christian's relationship to God. Satan promised to give Jesus the kingdoms of the world if Jesus would only worship him. Jesus underlined the importance of worship by quoting an Old Testament scripture, "You shall worship Him [God], and swear by His name" (Deut. 6:13). Other biblical references to worship are found in David's saying, "In the morning, O LORD, You will hear my voice" (Ps. 5:3). Enoch walked with God (Gen. 5:24). Isaiah's calling was directly related to his worship of God (Isa. 6:1). Jacob worshiped alone (Gen. 28:15–17), and John worshiped on the Isle of Patmos (Rev. 1:10). Both biblical history and personal experience indicate that when the Christian fails to worship consistently, spiritual dryness follows. Worship must go beyond that which is experienced on Sunday.

Did you know that we can worship in ways and at times other than on Sunday? The Bible speaks of corporate worship, as what takes place (or should take place) when two or more are gathered in his name. Corporate worship is beyond the sum total of what we as individuals can offer to God and beyond the sum total of what we as individuals can receive from God. It is group involvement in the company of fellow Christians. The Bible speaks of corporate worship (Gen. 35:2–3; Exod. 24:10–12; Ps. 35:18; Matt. 18:20; Acts 4:31–33; Rom. 15:6; 1 Cor. 14:26; and Heb. 10:25) and encourages our participation in it.

As an expression of corporate worship, the Bible is filled with references to family worship. When Jesus becomes Lord of the family, a new authority is in place. Jesus claimed to have absolute authority over life. This authority guides us in the setting of the ideals of our lives and determines the standard of conduct as we live out these ideals. Responsibility to the authority of Jesus Christ is a higher responsibility than that of husband to wife or wife to husband or parent to child or child to parent. If any relationship within the family clashes with the individual's relationship with Jesus Christ, the result is faulty relationship with God. However else the chain of command works out in our families, Jesus had better be first.

But there is more to the worship of God than what we do in groups, however small or large. When a Christian stands alone before God, the potential of real worship is present. Regardless of the level of commitment, it is still possible for a Christian to fake worship for one hour on Sunday or even around the family altar; but when that Christian stands alone with God, all pretense and ritual disappear. Whereas faking it in a group may be possible, faking it one-to-one is extremely difficult. Arising a great while before day, Jesus placed a high value on private worship as a basic means of relating to God. In addition to the example of Jesus, the Bible speaks of private worship throughout (Gen. 5:24; 28:15–17; Ps. 5:3; Isa. 6:1;

Mark 1:35; Rev. 1:10). As important as relating to God through worship is, there is yet another relational basic to be considered for spiritual fitness.

RELATING TO THE WORLD

"We meet to worship. We depart to serve." That quote, or variations of it, has appeared in numerous church bulletins. The quote is precisely in keeping with what Jesus had in mind when he responded to Satan's "worship me" with the words: "You shall worship the Lord your God and serve Him only." Jesus knew that worship is not complete until it results in service. Thus, one of the basic ways you relate to God is through service to persons. What is service?

Service defined is more than work. It is that for which a person gives one's entire life. The broad base of Christian service is seen in 1 Peter 4:10–11, which indicates that anything that is a gift from God can be used in service. The discussion of spiritual gifts in 1 Corinthians 12 supports this fact. One reason God calls people is for service. Israel was selected by God to be a light to the nations. John the Baptist was selected to prepare the way for Jesus. Each disciple was chosen by Jesus with some special service in mind, as well as the overall service of sharing the gospel with the world. But just how important is service?

In comparison to other Christian doctrines, very little is written concerning service. Its importance may be seen in the fact that the same New Testament word translated *worship* is also translated *service*. That explains the various translations of Romans 12:1: "reasonable service", "spiritual service of worship," "spiritual worship," and "true worship." Service and worship are inseparable, and the biblical models are numerous.

Two great models of servanthood stand above the rest in the New Testament. When Jesus described servanthood, he pointed not to the scribe, who was the educated man of the day, nor to the priest, who was the religious man of the day. Jesus pointed to the servant and even claimed identity with him: "Who is greater, the one who reclines at the table or the one who serves? Is it not the one who reclines at table? But I am among you as the one who serves" (Luke 22:27). On another occasion Jesus told his disciples, "The greatest among you shall be your servant" (Matt. 23:11). And when the disciples refused to wash one another's feet in the upper room, Jesus looked for a bowl and a towel in order to perform the servant's duty of washing the feet of the disciples (John 13:4–17).

One New Testament personality, more than others, modeled the servant role of Jesus. Even though the world sees him in his greatness, the apostle Paul saw himself as a servant. Paul began his letter to the Romans by identifying himself as a "bond-servant" (Rom. 1:1). In 1 Corinthians Paul wrote, "For though I am free from all men, I have made myself a slave to all, so that I may win more" (1 Cor. 9:19). In 2 Corinthians Paul wrote, "We do not preach ourselves but Christ Jesus as Lord, and ourselves as your bond-servants for Jesus' sake" (2 Cor. 4:5). Galatians bears these words from Paul, "If I were still trying to please men, I would not be a bond-servant of Christ" (Gal. 1:10). In Ephesians, Paul went a step further and referred to himself as "the prisoner of Christ Jesus" (Eph. 3:1). Beginning his letter to the Philippians, Paul referred to himself, as well as Timothy, as "bond-servants of Christ Jesus" (Phil. 1:1). In Colossians Paul linked himself to servanthood through a reference to "Epaphras, our beloved fellow bond-servant" (Col. 1:7).

Continuing his self descriptions in the area of servanthood, the apostle Paul described himself as a "fellow worker in the gospel of Christ" with Timothy in 1 Thessalonians 3:2 and as serving among "perverse and evil men" in 2 Thessalonians 3:2. In 1 Timothy Paul wrote, "I thank Christ Jesus our Lord, who has strengthened me, because He considered me faithful, putting me into service" (1 Tim. 1:12). In 2 Timothy 1:3, Paul again thanked God "whom I serve with a clear conscience." In his letter to Titus, Paul called himself "a bond-servant of God" (Titus 1:1), and in his letter to Philemon he called himself a "prisoner of Christ Jesus" and Philemon "a fellow-worker" (Philem. 1). Thus, in all thirteen of Paul's letters, he made reference to his servanthood. While Jesus, Paul and others served other believers, they also served the non-believing world.

A tire manufacturer used to advertise the tires they sold with the caption, "Where the rubber meets the road." That is like my grandfather's saying, "Where the water meets the wheel." The real test of a product or of an idea is when it meets the test of application. A tire is of little use if it cannot meet the road and do its job. Water generates power when it meets the wheel. The acid test of discipleship comes when it meets the un-Christian world. It will either change that world or be changed by that world and its influence.

So how are we to live in relationship to this un-Christian world?

Let's begin with a definition of the world and an identification of its leader. The apostle Paul described the world as "dark" when he wrote, "For our struggle is not against flesh and blood, but against the rulers, against the powers, against the world forces of this darkness, against the spiritual forces of wickedness in the heavenly places" (Eph. 6:12). Earlier in that same Ephesian letter, Paul had identified Satan as "the prince of the power of the air" (Eph. 2:2). But what did Jesus have to say about this world and its leader?

Jesus knew the evils of this world and told his disciples, "Behold, I send you out as sheep in the midst of wolves" (Matt. 10:16). He likewise knew who was responsible for the evil in this world and pointed to Satan as "the ruler of this world" (John 12:31). On the surface, the prospect of living as "sheep" in a world of "wolves," especially where it is "dark," is not too exciting. But there is a way to relate to that kind of world.

Our relationship to the world was described by Paul in Romans 12:2: "Do not be conformed to this world, but be transformed by the renewing of your mind." Literally Paul is saying we should not let the world squeeze us into its own mold, but rather we should allow God to remold our minds from within. Our concept is found in this play on words: "mold/remold" or "conformed/transformed." The Greek words are *schema* and *morphe*. *Schema* refers to the outward, changeable aspect of something, whereas *morphe* refers to the inward, unchanging part. Let me illustrate.

In relation to *morphe* (from which we get our word *metamorphosis,* change by a supernatural means) I would refer to myself as a male. I had no personal choice in that matter, and I cannot of myself change my maleness. Part of my *morphe* is maleness. In relation to *schema* (from which we get our word "scheme," to form a plan as in the scheme of things) I would refer to myself as once being a male baby in diapers, a boy-male playing Little League baseball, a teenage male, a college male, a single adult male, a married male, a father male, a middle-age crisis male and now a grandfather male. The maleness (*morphe*) did not change, but the outward form (*schema*) according to the plan of God changed as I grew older. Now let's look again at what Paul said about relating to the world.

Paul said we are not to be conformed (*schema*) to the world, but we are to be transformed (*morphe*). That is, our priority in relating to the world is not to look like, walk like, talk like, or smell like the world but rather to be different on the inside where a miracle has taken place. God has changed that part of us that we cannot change. We are transformed in Christ, no longer conformed to the world. We are still in this world; but as believers in Jesus Christ, we are no longer of this world.

A word of caution is in order before proceeding. This is the same apostle Paul who, on another occasion, wrote, "I have become all things to all men, so that I may by all means save some" (1 Cor. 9:22). Paul did not want Christians conforming to the world; yet, at the same time, he did not want Christians to so withdraw that they lost their ability to communicate with and witness to the world. Withdrawal to the point of becoming weird is not transformation. Remember, we are still in this world, but in Christ we are no longer of this world.

Jesus had much to say about the believer's relationship to the un-Christian world. Jesus said of himself, "I am not of this world" (John 8:23), and of his disciples, "You are not of the world" (John 15:19); yet being in this world, he described his disciples as "salt" (Matt. 5:13) and "light" (Matt. 5:14) and the kingdom of heaven as "leaven" (Matt. 13:33). Salt, light, and leaven call no attention to themselves, but rather "glorify" that to which they relate. Our relationship to the un-Christian world is to glorify God through our Christlike servanthood.

RELATING TO SELF

The apostle Paul had a view of self that is worth noting. He challenged us to think sober, balanced thoughts about ourselves: "For through the grace given to me I say to everyone among you, not to think more highly of himself than he ought to think; but to think so as to have sound judgment, as God has allotted to each a measure of faith" (Rom. 12:3). The words "sound judgment" mean being mentally balanced or having a sound mind. Those to whom Paul was writing had a problem of thinking of themselves too highly. As I travel and meet many Christians, I am becoming increasingly convinced that this is not our problem. Whereas I have met some who think of themselves too highly, the vast majority of Christians today think too little of themselves. Since Paul used the word meaning "sound judgment" or mentally balanced, he implied that we were not to think thoughts of ourselves that were too high or too low but balanced.

Many Christians have a low self-image spiritually. When the call goes out for teachers in a church program, some people who might like to teach refuse because they don't think they have the proper training. When we invite persons to join the church's music ministry, some people who may have a secret desire to sing, don't because they have never had voice lessons. When the recruitment is made for workers in Vacation Bible School, many excuse themselves because they have never had any child psychology courses. The illustrations are endless. We do not respond in service because we are too busy putting ourselves down spiritually. When will we learn that God is not nearly as interested in our abilities as in our availability? The apostle Paul wrote that we should have balanced thoughts about ourselves. You are a creature made in the image of God with unlimited potential. God has a wonderful plan for your life regardless of your failures or successes. God's people are special. God told us that and demonstrated it.

That which God said to the people of Israel has application to the new Israel, the believers in Jesus Christ. One day God called to Moses from the mountain of Sinai and instructed him to tell the people—God's people—that they were God's special, treasured possessions: "If you will indeed obey My voice and keep My covenant, then you shall be My own possession among all peoples, for all the earth is Mine" (Exod. 19:5). In the place of "My own possession," other translations offer, "a peculiar treasure," "my treasured possession,"and "my chosen people." The specific word is *segula* and it has an exciting meaning. In those days, the kings owned everything—the house in which you lived, the clothes you wore, etc. When we own everything, what is special? Each king had in his palace a *segula*—a treasure chest of "special possessions" which might include a trophy of war or a gift from another king. To put it in our terminology, it was his shoe box under the bed. Special private possessions were kept there. The God who owns everything, whose brand is on the cattle on a thousand hills, whose copyright is on the bird's song—this great God said of the people, "You shall become my (*segula*) special (treasured) possession." You and I are special to God. We ought to act more like special possessions, especially in light of the New Testament demonstration of that specialness on the cross of Calvary.

That which God promised on Sinai, he demonstrated on Calvary. The magnitude of God's love, the depth of God's feeling for this special possession, was demonstrated in the giving of the only Son to die on a cross: "For God so loved the world, that He gave His only begotten Son, that whoever believes in Him shall not perish but have eternal life" (John 3:16).

A healthy relationship to self will include a proper self-love. Jesus said the second greatest commandment was "you shall love your neighbor as yourself" (Mark 12:31). Love of self is biblical, but be careful. Self-love is the last part of the second commandment. Prior to Jesus' words on loving self, he spoke of loving God and others. Still, self-love is biblical because a proper relationship to self is necessary to be a spiritually fit disciple.

Let me make some suggestions on how to relate to yourself with love. First, *be yourself*. For your own well-being, it is far better to be rejected for who you are than to be accepted for who you're not. The temptation is always to be something we're not. We aren't the first to face that. Jesus faced it constantly. Almost daily he faced some temptation that would lead him to be something he was not. It came from his family, from his friends, and certainly from his enemies. They were constantly trying to get him to compromise who he was. If he had just compromised, if he had just been something he wasn't, he could have been rich. He could have been popular. He could have been powerful. He could have lived to a ripe old age. But the most uncompromising figure in all of human history was Jesus Christ. He was true to who he was. Not one time did he deviate from who he was, regardless of the temptation that would lead him astray.

Relating to self continues with accepting self. Tragic is the sight of a person who is trying to fool themselves about who they are. You must accept your gifts, your talents, and your limitations.

We are frustrated by our limits. Sometimes when we reach our limits and start hating ourselves, we need to remember the difference between the Christian and the non-Christian. The non-Christian reaches his limits and is frustrated. The Christian reaches his limits and relaxes in the Lord. What the human mind can conceive, the power of God can achieve. We do have our limits, but our God has no limits. Paul said it this way: "I am what I am" (1 Cor. 15:10). He was not saying that out of arrogance, pride, false pride, or egotism. He was just stating a fact: "I am what I am." Self acceptance frees us to love ourselves. When you can be yourself, and accept yourself, you are on the road to loving yourself.

Relating to self grows with control of self. She was very beautiful. I remember sitting under a huge pine tree at a retreat center in Alabama talking with her between sessions of a conference. While beautiful on the outside, she was a mess on the inside. She was currently working through divorce, had lost her job, had gained extra weight, and couldn't speak without emotion in her voice. Occasionally her lip would tremble when she would talk about her former husband or former boss or friends who would no longer speak to her. It was obvious that she was out of control. Finally, in frustration she just blurted out, "Nobody up there likes me." She blamed herself; she blamed her employer; she blamed her former husband, and, finally, she blamed God. She was completely out of control. When you're out of control, it's hard to be in right relationship to yourself.

There is one other step. *We must be ourselves, accept ourselves, and control ourselves.* We must also realize *proper relationship to self culminates with the sharing of self.* In fact, if it doesn't reach the point of sharing self, then it is less than genuine Christ-centered love of self. Godly self-love culminates in sharing self. Otherwise, we have a spiritual problem. The scribes said, "What commandment is the foremost of all?" Jesus said, "Love the Lord your God . . . the second is this, you shall love your neighbor as yourself" (Mark 12:28–31). Now, we either have a commandment versus a commission—"love yourself" versus "be My witnesses" (Acts 1:8)—or we have a commandment and a commission—love yourself and share yourself with the world. I don't think for a minute that we have a commandment versus a commission, but rather we have a commandment *and* a commission. God loves us and enables us to love ourselves, then desires that we share that love with the world.

RELATING TO THE CHURCH

Of extreme importance in spiritual fitness is your relationship to the church, the body of Christ. When the apostle Paul likened the church to marriage, he was referring to a relationship of support and complement. Just as wives are to be subject to their husbands, so ought the church to be subject to Christ, its Head (Eph. 5:22–23). Paul said Christ loved the church and gave himself for her (Eph. 5:25) and wants the church to have "no spot or wrinkle or any such thing" but be "holy and blameless" (Eph. 5:27). But Paul also said, "We are members of His body" (Eph. 5:30), the church, and as members we ought to love the church.

We need to support the church and to be supported by it. Since the church is made up of people, I am saying we need to support people and be supported by people. Yet what I am seeing, with obvious exceptions, is a strong desire to do my own thing, to march to my own drummer, to cut my own path. That which happens among the churches also happens within the local church. Individualism has its place, but its place is not first. "I Did It My Way" was a popular song but it is not a hymn, nor is it biblical. We must do it God's way, and God's way is through the church.

Some churches remind me of the parable of the mudites and the anti-mudites. Two men met a great many years ago at a church meeting. They were mutually surprised, as they became better acquainted, to discover that both had formerly been completely blind, and that Jesus had opened their eyes and given them sight.

"Isn't it marvelous," said one, "how the Master makes mud, puts it into your eyes, and then tells you to go and wash? Then when you wash, your eyes are opened, and you can see?"

"Mud? Jesus doesn't use mud. He just speaks a word, and you can see!"

"Jesus does use mud!"

"He doesn't!"

"He does!"

"He does not! I ought to know. I was blind, and he opened my eyes, and now I can see!"

"He does use mud! If he didn't use mud, he didn't open your eyes. You can't see. You just think you can see. You're still blind, and I'll have nothing more to do with you. You have denied one of the fundamentals of our faith!"

And presently those whose blind eyes Jesus had opened with mud came together in an exclusive group, and excluded all others. And those whose eyes Jesus had opened without mud joined together also, and the two groups spent their time in rivalry between themselves, while the blind all around them groped through life, unaware of the One who came to bring light to all who walk in darkness.

It breaks my heart to see quarreling and fighting among the churches and within church memberships when we, of all people, should be supporting each other in spite of our differences. We need a rediscovery of the concept discussed by the apostle Paul in Romans 12.

There is both unity and diversity in our relationship to the body of Christ. Paul wrote, "Just as we have many members in one body and all the members do not have the same function, so we, who are many, are one body in Christ, and individually members one of another. Since we have gifts that differ according to the grace given to us, each of us is to exercise them accordingly" (Rom. 12:4–6).

As to the unity involved in our relationship to the body of Christ, Paul said we are "one body." The parallel is made to the human body. My body is one body, a united body. All the members of my body are connected. To accept the body is to accept all of its parts, and to reject the body is to reject all of its parts. Accept me, and you accept all of me; reject me, and you reject all of me. Likewise with the body of Christ, for it is "one body." In 1 Corinthians Paul mentioned various members of the human body—foot, hand, ear, eye, nose, and head—yet he concluded, "There may be no division in the body . . . you are Christ's body, and individually members of it" (1 Cor. 12:25–27).

As to the diversity involved in your relationship to the body of Christ, Paul said the "one body" has "many members" and "varieties of gifts." Although all the parts of my body are connected—united—they are not all equal, nor do any of them make up a majority. Each member of my body has its own function. If my ear decides that it no longer wants to hear and out of jealousy demands to see, how will I hear? And if the ear starts seeing, obviously not as good as the eye, the eyes may get fed up and refuse to function any longer. Now my body must function with no hearing and limited sight. Eventually other members of the body get upset, and their various reactions further upset the unity. Sounds like some churches doesn't it? That's the point! The church is not to be that way for "God has so composed the body . . . that there may be no division in the body, but that the members may have the same care one for another" (1 Cor. 12:24–25).

With many members and different gifts, the church must function with its diversity. Just as there are no majority parts to my physical body, there are no majority gifts in the spiritual body. But with our different gifts, we function as a unity. Each part of the body is crucial to the overall functioning of the body; and whereas not all the parts are seen, all are important. So, we must discover a balance to the unity and diversity of the body.

As to the balance involved in your relationship with the body of Christ, the proper relationship comes when each member understands his own spiritual gifts and appreciates the spiritual gifts of others. When I was fifteen years old, I was in an automobile accident, and my neck was broken at the second vertebra. Because I was not killed or paralyzed, as others had been with the same injury, the doctors didn't know what to do with me.

For nine months, I was a medical experiment. Numerous times during those months, things were done to my body that upset the balance. The bone began to heal, then stopped healing. Surgery was planned, then canceled. A body cast was made for me, then discarded. Parts of my body ceased to function properly because the neck and its supporting muscles were not functioning. It was only after complete healing and rehabilitation that my whole body functioned again as a united body. I have a feeling that parts of my body learned to appreciate other parts of me as they came to a greater awareness of their own function. If in the body of Christ we could understand our own gifts/function and begin to appreciate the gifts/function of others, we would have discovered a healthy balance. But before that happens, questions will have to be answered related to spiritual gifts.

The first question related to spiritual gifts is, *Where do spiritual gifts come from?* There is only one answer: spiritual gifts come from God. The church cannot bestow spiritual gifts on a member nor can the pastor or any other believer. God alone gives spiritual gifts.

A second question is, *Where are spiritual gifts mentioned in the Bible?* There are five lists of gifts in the New Testament—Romans 12:6–8; 1 Corinthians 12:7–11; 1 Corinthians 12:28; Ephesians 4:11–14; 1 Peter 4:7–11; and numerous other places where only one or two gifts are mentioned. Since the five lists are different, we may conclude that none of them is meant to be an exclusive or exhaustive list. Depending upon which scholar you choose to believe, there are more than twenty-five spiritual gifts identified in the New Testament. (There is some disagreement over the validity of a few of these gifts.)

A third question is, *What exactly is a spiritual gift?* A spiritual gift is a special ability given by the Holy Spirit to every believer according to the grace of God for building up the body of Christ.

Two related questions concerning spiritual gifts are: *who has spiritual gifts* and *why should that person try to discover what his or her gift(s) is?* According to the New Testament, only believers in Jesus Christ have spiritual gifts. The conversion experience and the accompanying activation of the Holy Spirit in the new life bring about spiritual gifts. The discovery of that gift (or those gifts) may come much later as the new Christian matures in the faith and is introduced to the concept. Spiritual gifts must be discovered since they are given rather than earned and since they cannot be developed until their presence is known to the believer.

The final question for consideration is, *What is the proper view of spiritual gifts?* A spiritual gift is from God. But to worship the gift rather than the Giver is in reality a kind of idolatry. Anything that is worshiped in the place of God—spiritual gifts, a building, a pastor, a version of the Bible, or a time of day—is idolatry. Some idolatry is not as easily identified since it has the appearance of spirituality. We must keep the focus on the Giver of the gifts and let the gifts themselves be seen and used in the proper perspective. Since God gives believers just what he wants them to have, it is wrong for me to desire or demand a certain gift for you. But for me to encourage you to be in a right relationship to God and thereby understand and use your spiritual gift is right and desirable. By keeping our focus on God, the Giver and gift will be revealed and applied properly.

Possible spiritual gifts should be tested, if at all feasible. If you believe you have the gift of teaching, try teaching. If everyone goes to sleep as you teach, you might try another gift you suspect you have. Often other Christians will see the gift in you before you discover it. Spiritual gifts should be affirmed by fellow believers and confirmed by trusted Christian friends. If you are the only person who thinks you have a particular gift, you may be mistaken. It was an exciting time for me as a young minister, even before understanding spiritual gifts, to try certain things. Those faithful folks whom I pastored kept telling me they enjoyed my teaching. Years later, I was delighted to discover that I had a teaching gift. In fact, my discoveries have shown that God's gifts have been in areas where I enjoy serving and function naturally. I can function in other areas and have done so with some degree of success, but it has taken much more commitment and discipline. The excitement of testing spiritual gifts is exceeded only by the excitement of discovery and implementation.

DISCIPLESHAPE

Below is a list of the more widely agreed upon spiritual gifts with scripture references so we can begin to study, test, and discover our spiritual gifts. I honor your right to add to the list gifts you feel I have omitted or omit gifts you feel should not be listed. This is a representative list, not meant to be exhaustive:

Gifts mentioned in Romans 12:6–8
1. *Prophecy/Preaching*: 1 Cor. 12:10, 28; Eph 4:11–14; Luke 7:26; Acts 15:32, 21:9–11; 1 Peter 4:11.
2. *Service*: 2 Tim. 1:16–18; Acts 6:1–7; Titus 3:14; Gal. 6:2, 10; 1 Peter 4:11.
3. *Teaching*: 1 Cor. 12:28; Eph. 4:11–14; Acts 18:24–28, 20:20–28.
4. *Exhortation/Encouragement*: 1 Tim. 4:13; Heb. 10:25; Acts 14:22.
5. *Giving*: 2 Cor. 8:1–7, 9:2–8; Mark 12:41–44.
6. *Leadership*: 2 Tim. 5:17; Acts 7:10, 15:7–11; Heb. 13:17; Luke 9:51.
7. *Mercy*: Mark 9:41; Acts 16:33–34; Luke 10:33–35; Matt. 20:29–34, 25:34–40; Acts 11:28–30.

Additional gifts mentioned in 1 Corinthians 12:7–11
8. *Wisdom*: 1 Cor. 2:1–13; Acts 6:3, 10; James 1:5–6; 2 Peter 3:15.
9. *Knowledge*: 1 Cor. 2:14; Acts 5:1–11; Col. 2:2–3; 2 Cor. 11:6.
10. *Faith*: Acts 11:22–24, 27:21–25; Heb. 11; Rom. 4:18–21.
11. *Healing*: 1 Cor. 12:28; Acts 3:1–10, 5:12–16, 9:32–35, 28:7–10.
12. *Miracles*: 1 Cor. 12:28; Acts 9:36–42, 19:11–20, 20:7–12; Rom. 15;18–19; 2 Cor. 12:12.
13. *Discerning of Spirits*: Acts 5:1–11, 16:16–18; 1 John 4:1–6; Matt. 16:21–23.
14. *Tongues*: 1 Cor. 12:28, 14:13–19; Acts 10:44–46, 19:1–7; Mark 16:17.
15. *Interpretation of Tongues:* 1 Cor. 12:30, 14:13, 26–28.

Additional gifts mentioned in 1 Corinthians 12:28

16. *Apostle*: 2 Cor. 12:12; Eph. 3:1–9, 4:11–14; Acts 15:1–2; Gal. 2:7–10.

17. *Helps*: Rom.16:1–2; Acts 9:36; Luke 8:2–3; Mark 15:40–41.

18. *Administration/Organization*: Acts 6:1–7, 27:11; Luke 14:28–30.

Additional gifts mentioned in Ephesians 4:11–14

19. *Evangelist*: 2 Tim. 4:5; Acts 8:5–6, 26–40, 14:21,21:8.

20. *Pastor/Shepherd*: 1 Tim. 3:1–7; John 10:1–18; 1 Peter 5:1–3.

Additional gifts mentioned in 1 Peter 4:7–11

21. *Hospitality*: Rom. 12:13, 16:23; Acts 16:14–15; Heb. 13:1–2.

Others some consider to be "spiritual gifts"

22. *Intercession*: James 5:14–16; 1 Tim. 2:1–2; Col. 1:9–12, 4:12–13; Acts 12:12; Luke 22:41–44.

23. *Missionary*: 1 Cor. 9:19–23; Acts 8:4, 13:2–3, 22:21; Rom. 10:15.

24. *Celibacy*: 1 Cor. 7:7–8; Matt. 19:10–12.

25. *Martyrdom*: 1 Cor. 13:3; Acts 5:27–41, 7:54–60, 12:1–5; 2 Cor. 11:21–30, 12:9–10.

The purpose of spiritual gifts is the "building up of the body of Christ" (Eph. 4:12). There are two ways to build up a body—internally and externally. We build up the body of Christ internally as we use our gifts to minister to and support each other. It is to this end that Paul wrote, "the members may have the same care for one another, and if one member suffers, all the members suffer with it; if one member is honored, all the members rejoice with it" (1 Cor. 12:25–26). But we also build up the spiritual body externally as we add others to it. Spiritual gifts are to be used within the context of the body. The New

Testament references to spiritual gifts are primarily addressed to the church, not to individuals. But part of that use within the context of the body is to assist each other in adding new members to the body.

The apostle Paul wrote, "Now concerning spiritual gifts, brethren, I do not want you to be unaware" (I Cor. 12:1). Neither should we be unaware of this tremendous, effective method of fulfilling our spiritual fitness.

We hear much these days about the importance of relationships. Most of what we hear is true. We must begin with a right relationship to God, continue with a proper relationship to our world, focus on a healthy relationship to self, and function within a sound relationship to the church. With these relationships in order, we will be more spiritually fit for a ministry of serving.

EXERCISES FOR SPIRITUAL FITNESS

Day One What steps do you need to take this week to improve your corporate worship, family worship, and private worship? _____

_____

_____

Day Two What is one act of service you could perform this week that would encourage and strengthen another believer? A nonbeliever? _____

_____

_____

Day Three What does it mean for you to "not be conformed" to this world? _____

_____

_____

Day Four What are some sound, balanced thoughts about who you are? _____

_____

_____

Day Five How can you use your spiritual gifts this week to build up the body of Christ internally? Externally?

_____

_____

_____

Scriptural strengths to remember:
1. Romans 12:1–6a
2. Exodus 19:5
3. 1 Corinthians 12:24–27
4. Ephesians 4:12

Envisioning

BEFORE THE DISCOVERY OF AMERICA, the Spanish coins of the fifteenth century bore the inscription under the Straits of Gibraltar, *Ne Plus Ultra*, which means, "Nothing more beyond!" Then, in 1492, Christopher Columbus, with the blessing of Spain's King Ferdinand and Queen Isabella, sailed across the Atlantic Ocean and discovered America. Now the coin inscription was incorrect and had to be changed. With the discovery of America, the new Spanish coins bore the inscription *Plus Ultra*, which means "more beyond." With God, there is always more beyond.

One day Jesus' disciples had a "Ne Plus Ultra" experience. Response had been good in Capernaum in the early days of Jesus' public ministry. In the synagogue, the people were amazed at his authoritative teaching. There Jesus had cast an unclean spirit out of a man. Afterwards he went to the home of Peter's mother-in-law, and he found her to be ill with a fever. Jesus healed her and restored her strength. Many sick and demon-possessed were brought to Jesus later that same day and Jesus healed them.

The next morning the disciples found Jesus in a solitary, lonely place praying. In their excitement over his healings they exclaimed, "Everyone is looking for You" (Mark 1:37). They were ready to settle down in Capernaum as though there was nothing more beyond. Jesus, with vision greater than theirs, replied, "Let us go somewhere else to the towns nearby, so that I may preach there also; for that is what I came for" (Mark 1:38). Jesus understood what the disciples would learn. While glancing back is sometimes beneficial, it is never permanent. Vision thrusts us beyond ourselves and into the future.

Even with all the disciplines we've discovered in this book, we are incomplete and ultimately ineffective without vision. Remember the words from Proverbs 29:18: "Where there is no vision, the people are unrestrained."

ENVISIONING THE PAST: GLANCE BUT DON'T TARRY

When the children of Israel pleaded with Moses to turn back to Egypt rather than die in the wilderness (Exod. 14:10–12), they set a pattern for the future. The danger of looking back is that we may decide to go back when God is instructing us to go forward.

Jesus had to deal with looking back. On an occasion, his mother and brothers arrived where he was ministering. The call from the past was to go to his family, yet the call of the present and future was that of ministry to the masses. Putting the past, present, and future in balance, Jesus responded:

> Answering them, He said, "Who are My mother and My brothers?" Looking about on those who were sitting around Him, He said, "Behold, My mother and My brothers!" (Mark 3:33–35)

In looking back Jesus was respectful of the past and yet challenged by the future. Faced with the familiar and comfortable music of home, Jesus chose the unfamiliar and compelling beat of another drum. While many of his parables are drawn from well-loved incidents of home and some of his prayers were those taught to him as a child at home, Jesus, nevertheless, looked beyond the past and so must we.

It happened in the 400-meter race at the Regional High School Track Meet in Lubbock, Texas. The runner, who just two weeks earlier had run the fastest time in the state as he won the district championship, got a good start out of the blocks, and ran a good race ahead of the others. However, there are several lines on a college track that are not always on high school tracks. Thinking he had already finished and won the race, the runner slowed down and looked back. When he did his rival passed him for first place.

We can learn some valuable lessons by looking back; unfortunately the time spent looking back is deducted from the time we could spend looking forward. But a glance back is often in order. Looking back can give us perspective on our present situation. Looking back can provide insight for our present problems. Remembering the positives of our past can pave the way for a more pleasant and productive future.

Memory is a valued possession. Why then did Paul write, "Forgetting what lies behind and reaching forward to what lies ahead, I press on toward the goal (Phil. 3:13–14)? And why did Joseph say, "God has made me forget (Gen. 41:51)? Because, as valuable as memory is, the power to forget is no less valuable. Following are some things we need to forget if we would be spiritually fit.

Forget our past sins. When we sought God's forgiveness, God not only forgave us but removed our sin "as far as the east is from the west" (Ps. 103:12). If God has removed our sin that far, why do we wish to remember it? God further made a promise to "forgive their iniquity, and their sin I will remember no more" (Jer. 31:34). If God forgets it, why would we want to remember it?

Forget sins that have been committed against us. In his model prayer, Jesus taught disciples to pray for forgiveness when he said, "As we also have forgiven our debtors" (Matt. 6:12). Are we harboring hurts from a sin against us and hoping for revenge? For God's sake and for our sake, we must forget it. Otherwise it will destroy us from the inside like a slow-spreading cancer. However justified we think our feelings are, we must forget them. Reconcile if we can. If we can not, then move on to the future.

These are only two areas where the gift of forgetfulness will serve you well. There are obviously others. We must forget that which bears no value to our present and future and begin to look beyond.

ENVISIONING BEYOND: MISSION POSSIBLE

Our commission is not just to become a spiritually fit disciple, but to "make disciples of all the nations" (Matt. 28:19). Can we envision the sharing of our faith beyond our immediate circle of influence? We must. Our mission is to see beyond and it is a mission that is possible.

When a lawyer asked Jesus, "Who is my neighbor?" (Luke 10:29), Jesus replied with a parable of a man who was befriended in his time of need by a Samaritan after being rejected by a priest and a Levite. The assistance from the unlikely and hated Samaritan drove home the point Jesus wanted to make that neighbors range from the ones near us and like us to the ones living to ends of the earth. When Jesus returned the question, "Which of these three do you think proved to be a neighbor to the man who fell into the robbers' hands" (Luke 10:36), the answer was easy to give, but difficult to live.

The outreach of Christians must go beyond their friendships and their neighborhoods even as did the witness of Crispus, a Synagogue ruler. When Crispus and his household believed in the Lord "many of the Corinthians when they heard were believing and being baptized (Acts 18:8). Corinth was a center of corruption and immorality as well as a political center of southern Greece. It was a Greek city under Roman rule, meaning there was a diverse mixture of people in Corinth. As a commercial center, the city sold products from Arabia, Egypt, Phoenicia, Lybia, Babylon, Cicilia, Lyconia, and Phrygia. There the citizens were a mixture of poor and rich with extremes of both. Corinth has been described as "the Vanity Fair of the Roman Empire, at once the London and the Paris of the first century after Christ."

While in Corinth, Paul wrote to believers in Rome, describing the worldliness he saw in this city:

> Professing to be wise, they became fools, and exchanged the glory of the incorruptible God for an image in the form of corruptible man and of birds and four-footed animals and crawling creatures. Therefore God gave them over in the lusts of their hearts to impurity, that their bodies would be dishonored among them. For they exchanged the truth of God for a lie, and worshiped and served the creature rather than the Creator, who is blessed forever. Amen. For this reason God gave them over to degrading passions; for their women exchanged the natural function for that which is unnatural, and in the same way also the men abandoned the natural function of the woman and burned in their desire toward one another, men with men committing indecent acts and receiving in their own persons the due penalty for their error. And just as they did not see fit to acknowledge God any longer, God gave them over to a depraved mind, to do those things that are not proper, being filled with all unrighteousness, wickedness, greed, evil; full of envy, murder, strife, deceit, malice; they are gossips, slanderers, haters of God, insolent, arrogant, boastful, inventors of evil, disobedient to parents, without understanding, untrustworthy, unloving, unmerciful. (Rom. 1:22–36)

What a composite picture of our world today! Yet, regardless of the nature of the people, God said of Corinth, even as God says of our wicked world today, "I have many people in this city" (Acts 18:10).

One of those people was Titus Justus (Acts 18:7ff). Titus opened his home to Paul and apparently invited a group of his friends, among them a Synagogue ruler named Crispus. Once converted, Crispus, through his influence and God's power, influenced "many of the Corinthians." No doubt in this cosmopolitan city, "many" included people from all walks of life and from every segment of the Corinthian society. So are we to reach beyond our neighborhood and our friends to a diverse, complex world.

There is an "allness" about the gospel that does not allow us to discuss any discipleship strategy without including the whole world. For what begins in a life should ultimately, like ripples in a pond, reach the ends of the earth. When the angels announced the birth of Jesus to the shepherds they said, "I bring you good news of a great joy which will be for *all* the people" (Luke 2:10). As Jesus talked with his disciples, predicting his own death, he said, "I, if I am lifted up from the earth, will draw *all* men to Myself" (John 12:32). In His high priestly prayer Jesus prayed for his future disciples "that they may *all* be one" (John 17:21). In His Great Commission, our Lord challenged his disciples to "go therefore and make disciples of *all* the nations" (Matt. 28:19). Jesus modeled and taught that we are to keep on reaching out until we have reached to the ends of the earth.

John envisioned in heaven, "A great multitude which no one could count, from every nation and *all* tribes and peoples and tongues, standing before the throne" (Rev. 7:9). Look closely at that crowd. Look at the individuals: some with eyes of oriental slant, some with slender brown faces, some with dark-skinned faces, some with pronounced features. What a diversity in unity! How will this diverse crowd get to heaven? They will get there as spiritually fit disciples reach out to their friends and neighbors and as that reaching reaches to all nations, tribes, peoples, and language groups. Discipleship by its very nature knows no boundaries. None were included in the commission of our Lord to make disciples to the ends of the earth and no boundaries should be included in our modern application of that commission. Thus, no adequate strategy of spiritual fitness can end without including the whole world, remembering that our task is not to change the world but to bring about change in people whose lives, collectively, will change the world.

Does making disciples really need to go beyond friends, family and neighbors? The commission of our Lord instructed his disciples to bear witness both in Jerusalem, where they were and unto the ends of the earth (Acts 1:8). This is a reference to only one witness. This witness is to be shared from the home, from the pulpit, from the work place to the ends of the earth. There is to be no break, no detour anywhere along the way. This means all programs of outreach should be both local and worldwide.

Jesus Christ knows no other kind of strategy than one which reaches to the ends of the earth. He did not give one commission to an individual, another commission to the Christian family, still another commission to the local church, and yet another commission to Christianity as a whole. There is just one commission for all people and groups. It is the same commission in each case. What Jesus said to one, he said to everyone. Therefore, there should be no lines drawn between our neighborhood, our city, and the ends of the earth. No Christian should ever feel that their mission is exclusively their immediate surroundings. While it begins there, it reaches beyond. Anything contrary to this idea is contrary to the teaching of the New Testament.

Why must we reach beyond? We live in a large world. The Pacific Ocean covers more than sixty-four million square miles; the Atlantic Ocean covers more than thirty-three million square miles; the continent of Asia fills more than seventeen million square miles; Africa, eleven-and-a-half million square miles; North America, nine million square miles. We often forget in this large world that we who are Christians and who live in North America not only occupy a small portion of the world's space, but make up a small percentage of the world's population. The degree to which we limit our outreach is the degree to which the world grows increasingly pagan. David Barrett, speaking on behalf of the Southern Baptist International Mission Board, estimated that by the year 2000 there will be 4.3 billion non-Christians in the world, living in countries where Christian missionaries cannot go. We must reach out far and we must reach out soon if the world is to know Jesus Christ by faith.

What do I need to know about the people beyond? Those people who live beyond us are also people for whom Christ died. Whether these people be among the two hundred ethnic groups living in our own country or whether they be of some language group across the sea, Jesus Christ had them in mind when he offered salvation to the world.

They are also people with pressures. Sometimes their pressures relate to the family, just as ours do. Other times pressures are financial, cultural, or relational, but they are people who are like us with pressures. Likewise, they are people with problems. Their problems vary from person to person, but like us, they are people who face problems daily in their lives.

We need to know that there is a procedure by which these people can come to know Jesus Christ as Lord and Savior. It is not a hopeless situation, even though some of them live where Christian witness can not legally be shared. Perhaps more than anything else we need to know the possibilities of people becoming Christians to the ends of the earth. Thirty-three percent of the world's population claim to be Christian. Forty-one percent of the world's population have been evangelized; they have heard the gospel presentation and faced an opportunity to respond but do not claim to be Christian. Twenty-six percent of the world's population have yet to hear the gospel in a manner by which they could respond in faith. We need to know that our commission is yet to be fulfilled.

I was surprised when the art student to whom I was witnessing responded, "We have heard about Jesus, but no one has told us what to do to become Christians." I could have been in Russia, or India, or Yemen, or Kazakhstan, or Guatemala, or Spain. For that matter, I could have been on a major university campus or in an international business community somewhere in the United States. Or anywhere unreached people gather. I happened to be in western China. The truth is there are still many people who have not heard about Jesus Christ and many others who have heard about him but not accepted his offer of salvation. On the surface, they appear to be beyond our reach.

But isn't reaching beyond just for missionaries? The Great Commission of our Lord, like every other command he gave, is directed to the individual. It is given to a corporate group such as a church or a denomination, only because that group is made up of individual believers. Thus the primary source of all action in the Kingdom of God is through the individual believer. The believer is the primary unit of life. Every program must involve him or her.

The key to reaching beyond is the individual believer. While some of these individual believers hear and respond to God's call to a life-time of vocational service beyond, every believer in Christ is commissioned to bear witness both in their Jerusalem and to the ends of the earth. No individual Christian escapes that command. It is as all-inclusive as is the sky over us or the air around us. Those who profess faith in Jesus Christ can no sooner avoid the responsibility of witnessing to the ends of the earth than they can avoid the very presence of God. No matter what the church may believe or no matter what the denomination may do, the individual believer in Jesus Christ is obligated and commissioned to bear witness in all the world. While some, such as vocational missionaries, may reach beyond with their physical presence, all believers must reach beyond.

All believers can financially support a witness beyond their neighborhood and their borders. The financial program of the New Testament church was such that it did not stop with a tithe but insisted that persons give their all to Jesus Christ. The pattern was set that all New Testament giving would be somewhere between all that one had and a tithe of one's income. This is a foundational principle in New Testament times for financing the spread of gospel to the ends of the earth.

While we may not have the privilege of being present in every place, certainly we have the challenge of giving of our resources in support of reaching out beyond ourselves. While it is not the privilege of every believer to be called into vocational missions it is the privilege of every believer to be involved in missions.

Occasionally, we may have opportunity to relate to those classified as "beyond." What do we need to know about reaching out to these? Generally speaking there are four things we need to remember in reaching beyond. First, *we must seek to understand the person to whom we are reaching*. Their lifestyle and thought pattern may be completely different from ours. If we expect them to understand what we share, we must take the initiative in understanding them.

Second, *we must work hard at cultivating a friendly relationship with the person*. Because there are barriers, work is necessary for communication. The friendship, perhaps, will take more time than any other friendship we have. Therefore, we must be patient in cultivating this friendship.

Third, *we should engage in dialogue with the person*. Even though their speech may be different from ours, we need to continue to engage in dialogue. Even though their thinking and verbalizing may be strange to us, we must keep engaging in dialogue. If the gospel is going to be shared verbally, there must be verbal communication. Therefore, it is extremely important that we continue to dialogue with the person.

Finally, *we must not hesitate to share our faith in Jesus Christ with the person*. We cannot yield to the temptation that says we may offend them if we share our faith. As they get to know us and we get to know them, they are interested in what we think and believe, as we are in their thoughts and beliefs. Therefore, it will seem unnatural to them if we do not share our deepest faith.

What specifically can we do to communicate in order to reach those who might be classified as "beyond"? Let's approach the answer to this question by discussing some specific *do's* and *don'ts*. First, there are several *must nots* in witnessing to people of other persuasions. The following is a partial list:

1. We must not tell our friend that their ideas about Christianity are all wrong. Beliefs are important to people and even though you may feel that they are wrong you should not express that to them. Have a sincere respect for their beliefs.

2. We must not criticize or argue. Remember that the most sincere sharing of faith is affected negatively by criticism and argument.

3. We must not dominate the conversation. Sometimes this is done as you seek opportunities to speak about Jesus Christ. It will be better to rely on the leadership of the Holy Spirit in creating that opportunity.

4. We must not apologize for our faith or present Christianity from a negative viewpoint.

5. We must not use theological language which our friend may not understand. Be careful to clarify all terminology used.

6. We must not witness to this person just to be able to tell our Christian friends that we have witnessed to a non-Christian. Remember that this person is also a creature made in the image of God and needs his forgiveness.

7. We must not betray the confidence of our friend. Because there will be characteristics about them that are different from what you believe to be the norm, it's often easy to share these contrasts with other friends. Do not yield to the temptation and betray their confidences.

8. We must not force a decision on the part of our friend. There may be many barriers to cross with those who are considered "beyond." Allow them to respond in their own time and at their own level of understanding. Trust the Holy Spirit to be in charge of the witness.

There are some *positive suggestions* for bearing witness to those who are considered to be "beyond":

1. Because they are different from us, there will be some interest in our testimony. There is always interest in the personal, but this interest will be intensified by the differences.

2. We must explain that our relationship with Jesus Christ is different from all other approaches to religious faith. This is a relationship built completely upon love and grace.

3. We must respect their feelings and their evaluation of Christianity. Nothing will endanger our witness faster than a feeling on the part of our friends that we are disrespectful of what he or she believes.

4. We must answer all questions as adequately and as honestly as we know how. We should not be afraid to share that we do not have an adequate answer to their question. Assure them that we will find the answer and get back with it.

5. We must be ready to admit that not all Christians live up to the teachings of Jesus Christ. However, point out that we are not to measure ourselves by other persons, but by Jesus Christ himself. Their response is to Jesus Christ, not to the faulty lifestyles of some Christians.

6. We must remember that conversation even about spiritual matters is always two-way. We need to learn to listen as well as speak.

ENVISIONING LEADERSHIP: THE VIEW FROM UP FRONT

University of California Sociologist Robert Bellah, an expert on civil religion, has stated, "A society can be changed when two percent of its population has a new vision." Obviously that two percent will, by virtue of their vision, become leaders. On his motivational videotape, *The Power of Vision*, futurist Joel Barker lists four ingredients of successful vision. The first is, "leader initiated." Just as it is true, "Where there is no vision, the people perish" (Prov. 29:18 KJV), so it is likewise true, where there is no visionary leader, the people perish. Every successful venture has a visionary leader in its developmental stages.

How does this apply to spiritually fit discipleship? Either we will be a visionary leader or we will follow one. We must determine to be a leader. We must learn to envision goals so large that if God is not in them, they will fail. We must remember, we can lead people where we have never been before, but we cannot lead them where we have never dared to envision.

Consider the vision passed on to Moses and his leadership team: "Then Moses went up with Aaron, Nadab and Abihu, and seventy of the elders of Israel" (Exod. 24:9–10).

They were confused. These leaders of Israel had been called out, but now their marching orders were muddled. No new nation yet existed. The Promised Land was still a dream. The people were unsure. Yet these leaders "saw the God of Israel" (Exod. 24:10).

Many times, when our circumstances begin to get the best of us, we find ourselves needing a fresh vision of God. In the case of Moses and his fellow leaders, this vision resulted in several things.

First was *a new understanding of God*. They had recently experienced the wrath of God as well as the distrust of their followers. Now they experienced a communication based on love and trust rather than fear and uncertainly. The Bible says that God "did not stretch out His hand against the nobles of the sons of Israel" (Exod. 24:11).

Second was *a new relationship between themselves*. So at peace were they with each other that "they ate and drank" (Exod. 24:11). We can usually eat and drink with our peers when we are at peace with them. Seemingly, a new vision of God always leads to a deeper fellowship of the faithful.

Third was *the entering into of a new covenant*. In those days, the meal confirmed the covenant. So in fellowship were they with God and with each other, that they responded, "All that the Lord has spoken we will do, and we will be obedient!" (Exod. 24:7).

As a visionary leader there are at least five things we must possess. First *we must possess the insight to build our vision on a solid foundation*. We are not talking about idle dreamers. Dreamers often build on dreams. Visionaries build on reality.

The Eddystone Lighthouse off the coast of Plymouth is to England what the Statue of Liberty is to the U.S. The first beacon light was placed in this lighthouse over two hundred years ago. An architect named Winstanley was so confident of the stability of his lighthouse, he wrote on the cornerstone, "Blow, O ye winds! Rise O ocean! Break forth, ye elements, and try my work!" Within three years of its construction the lighthouse was destroyed by a storm. Along with the lighthouse, Winstanley and others who were making repairs at the time, were also destroyed.

Years later an early leader in civil engineering, John Smeaton, envisioned a new lighthouse and rebuilt on a new site, on solid rock. A committed Christian, Smeaton wrote on the new cornerstone, "Except the Lord build the house, they labor in vain that build it." The second lighthouse has weathered many a storm through the years and stands today as a testimony of vision based on a solid foundation.

Second, *a visionary leader must possess the patience to work within the limitations given to him or her.* I remember my first Tinkertoy set. On the cover of the cylinder-shaped box was a lot of "neat stuff" that I hoped to be able to put together. There was a Ferris wheel that would go around, a drawbridge that would actually raise up and down, and an airplane with a propeller that would actually spin. I took the top off the box and dumped the contents out on the floor and started putting pieces together, making one of those objects. All of a sudden I realized I didn't have a drawbridge, or a Ferris wheel, or an airplane. I had a little car with round wheels. I picked up the instructions and looked at them again. The $1.98 set wouldn't build what was on the cover. What I needed was the X126 box which cost $19.95. Then if I wanted the bridge to rise up, the wheel to turn, or the propeller to go around, I needed something else that contained a motor. That cost $14.95. Suddenly I realized the limitations which I had been given. I had two choices. I could be content with what I had, enjoy that little car, and envision building more, or I could be frustrated because I didn't have more. A visionary leader understands the limitations and practices patience.

Third, *a visionary leader must possess the assurance of success.* Tony Volpentest was born without hands or feet, but not without heart. Following a solid high school track career, he became a two-time national champion at the 1992 Handicap Sports Amputee Games. In the 1992 Summer Olympics in Barcelona, Volpentest won gold medals in the men's 100-meter and 200-meter races setting world records in both. About envisioning success, Volpentest says, "If someone challenges me, saying, 'you can't do that,' I always want to show them I can. If you can dream it, you can do it." Tony's coach told him he needed five things to win: vision, focus, persistence, discipline, and commitment. Visionary leaders likewise start their list of needed qualities with vision.

Fourth, *a visionary leader must possess a realistic view of God's resources.* When the enemy surrounded the city of

Dothan during the night, Elisha's servant awoke Elisha in fear. "What shall we do?" he cried. Elisha, whose vision of God's resources was greater than that of the servant, replied, "Do not fear, for those who are with us are more than those who are with them" (2 Kings 6:16). Since the servant did not see with God's vision, he could not see God's resources. So, Elisha prayed, "O Lord, I pray, open his eyes that he may see." Our eyes, like those of the servant, tend to see only the visible, while God sees the invisible. When God opened the servant's eyes he saw "the mountain was full of horses and chariots of fire" (2 Kings 6:17). We must allow God to open our eyes to divine resources as we seek to lead others.

Fifth, *a visionary leader must possess the blessing of God upon his or her ventures.* Fermin Ruiz would have been the first to admit he was not a favorite to win the gold medal at the Barcelona Olympic Games in 1992, but now he was in front of his fellow countrymen as he ran the 1500-meter race. As he reached the final turn, he was in the pack of runners up front. He decided to run as hard as he could for as long as he could just to see what would happen. He broke in front of the pack and with just a few meters to go was well out in front. "The crowd made the loudest noise I had ever heard in my life," he said. "As I crossed the finish line, I looked up at King Juan Carlos, and he was smiling and waving at me. It completed my dream." We, too, must envision our King, cheering us on, and blessing our leadership.

God prophesied through Joel that a day was coming when "old men will dream dreams" and "young men will see visions" (Joel 2:28). You don't have to be old to dream dreams or be young to see visions, but you do have to be visionary to lead. The ancient Irish poem says:

> Be Thou my vision, O Lord of my heart;
> Naught be all else to me, save that Thou art;
> Thou my best thought, by day or by night,
> Walking or sleeping, Thy presence my light.

EXERCISES FOR SPIRITUAL FITNESS

Day One   In your life, what idea or task has recently changed from *Ne Plus Ultra* (nothing more beyond) to *Plus Ultra* (more beyond)? _____

_____

_____

Day Two   Have you looked back lately and if so what happened? Did you draw strength from the past, get behind in the present, gain perspective for the future, or some of each? _____

_____

_____

Day Three   What does your "vision beyond" include? _____

_____

_____

Day Four   Evaluate your financial support of ministry beyond your neighborhood and surroundings. Could you do more? Should you do more? _____

_____

_____

Day Five   Have you had a fresh vision from God recently? If so, how have you used it to lead others? If not, why do you think you have not? _____

_____

_____

Scriptural strengths to remember:
1. Proverbs 29:18
2. Psalm 103:12
3. Acts 1:8
4. 2 Kings 6:16

Conclusion

You now have the basic training needed to be a spiritually fit disciple of Jesus Christ. In my introduction, I shared that my inspiration for the book came from my son's Marine Boot Camp experience. James is now a Sergeant in the U.S. Marine Corps, assigned to a reserve sniper unit while he completes his college education. Not long ago he wrote concerning his job as a sniper: "Success is based on the amount of confidence you have in yourself and your abilities. . . . If my commander asks me, 'How do you feel about this mission you are about to encounter?' I must reply, 'I have no doubt that I can do it!' If I were to say, 'I hope I can do it,' my commander would definitely get someone else for the job."

When God calls us to a mission, an assignment, or a task, how do we respond? Does God have to look for someone else to do our job? We have been trained to be spiritually fit and ready. We must respond with confidence. We must respond faithfully. We must remember perfection and maturity are not the goal. Faithfulness is. It is now time to be faithful to what God has taught us.

The Atlanta Olympic Games of 1996 were preceded by a torch relay across America. Men and women, boys and girls, old and young, red, yellow, black, and white participated by carrying the torch for a portion of the journey. Some ran; others walked. As they neared Tacoma, Washington, Harley Sheffield carried the torch as he rode his bike. But while crossing a bridge, Harley's rear tire blew out. The accident sent Harley and the torch flying over the handle bars and onto the pavement. A gasp went through the crowd. Harley's face and hands were cut, but worse—the torch had gone out. It was quickly re-lit from the "mother torch" carried in the van that was following.

You and I may never carry the Olympic torch like Harley Sheffield, but we have been commissioned to carry the light of the Lord. That is why we are in fitness training—spiritually. Undoubtedly, there will be times when we will stumble and fall. There may even be times when our torch goes out. But we must never, never give up. We are the Lord's torchbearers and he is depending upon each one of us.

Fortunately, spiritual fitness is not one-sided—for God involves himself in our training. We can find comfort and strength in the day-in and day-out goal for perfection by committing to memory these words from Paul: "I am confident of this very thing, that He who began a good work in you will perfect it until the day of Christ Jesus" (Phil. 1:6).

BIBLIOGRAPHIES

BIBLIOGRAPHIES

PHASE ONE BIBLIOGRAPHY

Allen, Charles L. *The Sermon on the Mount*. Westwood, NJ: Fleming H. Revell Co., 1966.

Allen, J. P. *The Sermon on the Mount: the Kingdom of God*. Nashville, Broadman Press, 1959.

Allen, R. Earl. *Divine Dividends*. Nashville: Thomas Nelson, 1974.

Augsburger, Myron S. *The Expanded Life*. Nashville: Abingdon Press, 1972.

Barclay, William. *The Beatitudes and The Lord's Prayer for Everyman*. New York: Harper and Row Publishers, 1963.

Boice, James M. *The Sermon on the Mount*. Grand Rapids: Zondervan Publishing House, 1972.

Carson, D. A. *The Sermon on the Mount*. Grand Rapids: Baker Book House, 1978.

Chambers, Oswald. *Studies in the Sermon on the Mount*. London: Marshall, Morgan & Scott, reprint, 1955.

Chappell, Clovis G. *The Sermon on the Mount*. Nashville: Cokesbury Press. 1930; Grand Rapids: Baker Book House, 1975.

Davis, William David. *The Sermon on the Mount*. Cambridge: University Press, 1966.

Eddleman, H. Leo. *Teachings of Jesus in Matthew 5–7*. Nashville: Convention Press, 1955.

Fisher, Fred L. *The Sermon on the Mount*. Nashville: Broadman Press, 1976.

Graham, Billy. *The Secret of Happiness*. Garden City, NY: Doubleday Inc., 1955.

Guelich, Robert A. *The Sermon on the Mount*. Dallas: Word Publishing, 1982.

Hargrove, H. H. *At the Master's Feet*. Nashville: Broadman Press, 1944.

Hastings, Robert J. *Take Heaven Now*. Nashville: Broadman Press, 1968.

Hendricks, Herman. *The Sermon on the Mount*. London: Geoffrey Chapman, 1979.

Henson, William E. *The Inaugural Message of the King*. New York: Vantage Press, 1954.

Hunter, Archibald M. *A Pattern for Life*. Philadelphia: Westminster Press, 1953. Reprint 1965.

Jones, E. Stanley. *The Christ of the Mountain*. New York: Abingdon Press, 1931

Lloyd–Jones, D. Martyn. *Studies in the Sermon on the Mount*. Grand Rapids: Wm. B. Eerdmans Publishing Company, 1959.

MacArthur, John, Jr. *The Mac Arthur New Testament Commentary Matthew 1–7*. Winona Lakes, IN: BMH Books, 1985.

Meyers, F. B. *Blessed Are Ye*. Grand Rapids: Baker Book House, 1955.

McEachern, Alton H. *From the Mountain*. Nashville: Broadman Press, 1983.

Montizambert, Eric. *The Flame of Life*. Greenwich, CT: Seabury Press, 1955.

Paker, Hankins Fred. Earth's Greatest Sermon. Orlando: Christ for the World, 1973.

Pentecost, J. Dwight. *Design for Living*. Chicago: Moody Press, 1975.

Pink Arthur, W. *An Exposition of the Sermon on the Mount*. Grand Rapids: Baker Book House, 1950

Price, Nelson. *Supreme Happiness*. Nashville: Broadman Press, 1979.

Shinn, Roger Lincoln. *The Sermon on the Mount*. Philadelphia: United Church Press, 1962.

Stott, John R. W. *The Message of the Sermon on the Mount.* Downers Grove: Inter Varsity Press,1978.

————. *Sermon on the Mount: 13 Studies for Individuals or Groups.* Downers Grove: Inter Varsity Press, 1987.

Thompson, Ernest Trice. *The Sermon on the Mount.* Richmond: John Knox Press, 1946.

Tolar, William B. *Teaching Guide for Matthew 5–7.* Nashville: Convention Press, 1992.

Trench, Richard Chevevix. *Exposition of the Sermon on the Mount drawn from the Writings of St. Augustine.* London: Mac Millian and Company, 1869.

West, Edward, N. *God's Image in Us.* New York: The World Publishing Company, 1960.

PHASE TWO BIBLIOGRAPHY

Walking Through Want: Conviction

Allen, Diogenes. *Christian Belief in a Postmodern World: The Full Wealth of Conviction.* Louisville: Westminster/John Knox Press, 1989.

Farmer, Herbert Henry. *Experience of God: A Brief Enquiry into the Grounds of Christian Conviction.* London: Student Christian Movement, 1929.

James, William. *Varieties of Religious Experience.* New York: Modern Library, 1902.

McCheyne, Robert Murray. *Conviction of Sin,* 1997.

Walking To Decision: Conversion

Barclay, William. *Turning to God: A Study of Conversion in the Book of Acts and Today.* Philadelphia: Westminster Press, 1964.

Chamberlain, Eugene. *When Can a Child Believe?* Nashville: Broadman Press, 1993.

Gaventa, Beverly Roberts. *From Darkness to Light: Aspects of Conversion in the New Testament.* Philadelphia: Fortress Press, 1986.

Jones, E. Stanley. *Conversion*. New York: Abingdon Press, 1959.

Robinson, Darrell W. *The Doctrine of Salvation*. Nashville: Convention Press, 1992.

Dead Men Walking

Aycock, Don M. *Walking Straight in a Crooked World*. Nashville: Broadman Press, 1987.

Healy, Kilian. *Walking with God*. New York: D.X. McMullen Co, 1948.

Hobbs., Herschel H. *New Men in Christ*. Waco: Word Books, 1974.

Poe, Harry Lee. *The Fruit of Christ's Presence*. Nashville: Broadman Press, 1990.

Warren, Richard. *The Power to Change Your Life*. Wheaton: Victor Books, 1990.

Walking the Talk: Testimony

Christian Will and Testimony Kit, 1993.

Kerr, Hugh T. and John M. Mulder, eds. *Conversions: The Christian Experience*. Grand Rapids: Wm. B. Eerdmans Publishing Co., 1983.

Miller, Calvin. *Walking With Saints*. Nashville: Thomas Nelson Publishers, 1995.

Running Ahead: Decision Making

Floyd, Ronnie W. *Choices: Making Sure Your Decisions Move You Closer to God*. Nashville: Broadman & Holman, 1994.

Mullen, John Douglas. *Decision-Making: Its Logic and Practice*. Savage, MD: Rowman & Littlefield, 1991.

O'Flaherty, Vincent M. *How to Make Up Your Mind*. Statan Island, NY: Alba House, 1969.

Russo, J. Edward. *Decision Traps*. New York: Simon and Schuster, 1990.

Schaller, Lyle E. *The Decision-Makers*. Nashville: Abingdon Press, 1974.

BIBLIOGRAPHIES

Running Behind: Following God's Will

Blackaby, Henry T. and Henry Brandt with Kerry L. Skinner. *The Power of the Call*. Nashville: Broadman & Holman, 1997.

Maston, T. B. *God's Will and Your Life*. Nashville: Broadman Press, 1964.

McEachern, Alton H. *Set Apart for Service*. Nashville: Broadman Press, 1980.

Montgomery, E. *Pursuing God's Call: Choosing a Vocation in Ministry*. Nashville: Convention Press, 1981.

Whitlock, Glenn E. *From Call to Service: The Making of a Minister*. Philadelphia: Westminister Press, 1968.

Running With: Fellowship

Maritian, Jacques. *Truth and Human Fellowship*. Princeton: Princeton University Press, 1957.

Milne, Bruce. *We Belong Together*. Downers Grove: InterVarsity Press, 1978.

Panikulam, G. *Koinonia in the New Testament*. Rome: Biblical Institute Press, 1979.

Phillips, Jim. *One Another*. Nashville: Broadman Press, 1981.

White, Jerry E. *Friends and Friendship*. Colorado Springs: Navpress, 1982.

Running in Place: Rest

Cadenhead, Al. *Hurry Up and Rest*. Nashville: Broadman Press, 1989.

Carson, D. A. *A Call to Spiritual Reformation: Priorities from Paul and His Prayers*. Grand Rapids: Baker Book House, 1992.

Collins, Gary. *You Can Profit from Stress*. Santa Ana: Vision House Publishers, 1977.

Hansel, Tim. *When I Relax, I Feel Guilty*. Elgin, Il: Life Journey Books, 1979.

Oates, Wayne Edward. *Your Right to Rest*. Philadelphia: Westminster Press, 1984.

Rhodes, Tricia McCary. *The Soul at Rest*. Minneapolis: Bethany House, 1996.

BIBLIOGRAPHIES

Pressing Through Priorities

Banks, Robert J. *The Tyranny of Time*. Downers Grove: InterVarsity Press, 1983.

Erickson, Kenneth A. *Christian Time Management*. St. Louis: Concordia Press, 1987.

Lakein, Alan. *How to Get Control of Your Time and Life*. New York: New American Library, 1974.

Pressing With Power

Green, Michael. *I Believe in the Holy Spirit*. Grand Rapids: Wm. B. Eerdmans Publishing Co., 1985.

Gordon, A. J. *The Ministry of the Spirit*. Grand Rapdis: Baker Book House, 1964.

Lindsell, Harold. *The Holy Spirit in the Latter Days*. Nashville: Thomas Nelson Publishers, 1983.

Ockenga, Harold John. *Power Through Pentecost*. Grand Rapids: Wm. B. Eerdmans Publishing Co., 1959.

Packer, J .I. *Keep in Step with the Spirit*. Old Tappan, NJ: Fleming H. Revell Co., 1984.

Pressing Toward the Finish

Duewel, Wesley. *Measure Your Life*. Grand Rapids: Zondervan Publishing House, 1992.

Hargrove, Terry D. *Finishing Well*. New York: Brummer/Mazel, 1992.

Marden, Orison Swett. *Do It to the Finish*. New York: T.Y. Crowell, 1909.

Shibley, David. *Heavenly Incentives for Earthly Living*. Old Tappan, NJ: Chosen Books, 1988.

Summers, Ray. *The Life Beyond*. Nashville: Broadman Press, 1959.

BIBLIOGRAPHIES

PHASE THREE BIBLIOGRAPHY

Communicating with God

Crawford, Dan R. *Connecting with God.* Fort Worth: Scripta Publishing Co., 1994.

Duewel, Wesley, L. *Touch the World through Prayer.* Grand Rapids: Francis Asbury Press, 1986.

Eastman, Dick. *The Hour that Changes the World.* Grand Rapids: Baker Book House, 1978.

Foster, Richard. *Prayer: Finding the Heart's True Home.* San Francisco: Harper, 1992.

Lockyear, Herbert. *All the Prayers of the Bible.* Grand Rapids: Zondervan Publishing House, 1959.

Communicating with Non-Believers

Coleman, Robert E. *The Master Plan of Evangelism.* Grand Rapids: Baker Book House, 1993.

Crawford, Dan R. *EvangeLife: A Guide to Lifestyle Evangelism.* Nashville: Broadman Press, 1984.

Johnson, Ronald W. *How Will They Hear If We Don't Listen?* Nashville: Broadman & Holman, 1994.

Robinson, Darrell W. *People Sharing Jesus.* Nashville: Thomas Nelson Publishers, 1995.

Thomason, W. Oscar. *Concentric Circles of Concern.* Nashville: Broadman Press, 1981.

Mental Pacing: Think About It

Bonhoeffer, Dietrich. *Meditating on the Word.* Cambridge: Cowley, 1986.

Boylan, M. Eugene. *Difficulties in Mental Prayer.* Westminster, MD: Newman Press, 1965.

Toon, Peter, *The Art of Meditating on Scripture.* Grand Rapids: Zondervan Publishing House, 1993.

McCormick, Thomas. *Meditation: A Practical Guide to a Spirit.* Downers Grove: InterVarsity Press, 1993.

BIBLIOGRAPHIES

Physical Pacing: Life in the Fast Lane.

Anderson, Andy. *Fasting Changed My Life.* Nashville: Broadman Press, 1977.

Baird, John. *What the Bible Says about Fasting.* Joplin, MO: College Press, 1984.

Bright, Bill. *The Coming Revival: America's Call to Fast, Pray, and "Seek God's Face."* Orlando: New Life Publications, 1995.

Prince, Derek. *Shaping History through Prayer and Fasting.* Old Tappan, NJ: Fleming H. Revell, Co, 1973.

Wallis, Arthur. *God's Chosen Fast.* Fort Washington, PA: Christian Literature Crusade, 1968.

Spiritual Pacing: Traveling By the Book

Drakeford, John W. *Experiential Bible Study.* Nashville: Broadman Press, 1974.

Jensen, Irving Lester. *Enjoy Your Bible.* Chicago: Moody Press, 1992.

Job, John B. *How to Study the Bible.* Downers Grove: InterVarsity Press, 1972.

Warren Richard. *Twelve Dynamic Bible Study Methods.* Wheaton: Victor Books, 1986.

Social Pacing: The Sounds of Silence

Klug, Ron. *How to Keep a Spiritual Journal* Minneapolis: Augsburg Books, 1993.

Merton, Thomas. *The Solitary Life.* Lexington: Stamperia del Santuecio, 1960.

Miller, Calvin. *The Table of Inwardness.* Downers Grove: InterVarsity Press, 1984.

Peace, Richard. *Spiritual Journaling.* Colorado Springs: Navpress, 1995.

Stand Against

Chafer, Lewis Sperry. *Satan: His Motive and Methods.* Grand Rapids: Zondervan Publishing House, 1919.

Lockyear, Herbert. *Satan: His Purpose and Power.* Waco: Word Books, 1980.

Lovett, C. S. *Dealing With the Devil.* Baldwin Park, CA: Personal Christianity, 1967.

Sanders, J. Oswald. *Satan Is No Myth.* Chicago: Moody Press, 1975.

Standing Equipped: Armor of God

Heine, Max, *Equipping Men for Spiritual Battle.* Ann Arbor: Servant Publications, 1994.

Lloyd-Jones, D. M. *The Christian Soldier.* Grand Rapids: Baker Book House, 1977.

Malone, George. *Arming for Spiritual Warfare.* Downers Grove: InterVarsity Press, 1991.

Moreau, A. Scott. *Essentials of Spiritual Warfare: Equipped for Battle.* Wheaton: Harold Shaw Publishers, 1997.

Standing Strong

Andrew, Brother. *Is Life So Dear? Key Issues in Spiritual Warfare.* Nashville: Thomas Nelson Publishers, 1985.

Gross, Edward N. *Miracles, Demons & Spiritual Warfare.* Grand Rapids: Baker Book House, 1990.

Mac Arthur, John. *How to Meet the Enemy.* Wheaton: Victor Books, 1992.

Sirotnak, Tom. *Warriors.* Nashville: Broadman & Holman, 1995.

Standing Victorious

Murray, Andrew. *Triumph in the Inner Life.* Wetchester, IL: Good News Publishers, 1959.

Stedman, Ray C. *Spiritual Warfare: Winning the Daily Battle with Satan.* Portland: Multnomah Press, 1985.

Taylor, Jack. *Victory Over the Devil.* Nashville: Broadman Press, 1973.

Warner, Timothy Marcus. *Spiritual Warfare: Victory Over the Power of This Dark World.* Wheaton: Crossway Books, 1991.

BIBLIOGRAPHIES

PHASE FOUR BIBLIOGRAPHY

God Loving You

Baxter, J. Sidlow. *For God So Loved.* Grand Rapids: Kregel Publications, 1995.

Dean, William D. *Love Before the Fall.* Philadelphia: Westminster Press, 1976.

Durland, Francis Caldwell. *Growing in God's Love.* Nashville: Broadman Press, 1982.

Lefebre, Georges. *The Mystery of God's Love.* New York: Sheed & Ward, 1961.

You Loving God

Baker, Benjamin, S. *Feeding the Sheep.* Nashville: Broadman Press, 1985.

Johnson, Ralph M. *The Great Commandment: Love Canon.* Minneapolis: Augsburg Press, 1988.

Huey, F. B., Jr. *Obedience: The Biblical Key to Happiness.* Nashville: Broadman Press, 1990.

Swindall, Charles R. *Improving Your Serve.* Waco: Word Books, 1981.

Loving Each Other

Arn, Win, Carroll Nyguist and Charles Arn. *Who Cares About Love?* Pasadena, CA: Church Growth Press, 1986.

Chapman, Gary D. *The Five Love Languages.* Chicago: Northfield Publishers, 1992.

Lewis C. S. *The Four Loves.* New York: Harcourt, Brace and Company, 1960.

Powell, John J. *Why Am I Afraid to Love?* Chicago: Argus Communications, 1967.

Cook, Jerry. *Love, Acceptance & Forgiveness.* Ventura: Regal Books, 1979.

Relating to God

Allen, J. P. *Reality in Worship.* Nashville: Convention Press, 1965.

Segler, Franklin M. *Christian Worship: Its Theology and Practice.* Nashville: Broadman Press, 1967.

BIBLIOGRAPHIES

Tozer, A. W. *The Knowledge of the Holy.* New York: Harper & Brothers, 1961.

Webber, Robert E. *Worship is a Verb.* Waco: Word Books, 1985.

Yates, Miles Lowell. *God in Us: The Theology and Practice of Christian Devotion.* Greenwich, CT: Seabury Press, 1959.

Relating to the World

Augsburger, David. *Caring Enough to Confront.* Glendale, CA: Regal Books, 1973.

Bakke, Ray. *The Urban Christian.* Downers Grove: InterVarsity Press, 1987.

Emmons, Michael L. *Accepting Each Other.* San Luis Obispo: Impact Publishers, 1991.

Ford, Kevin Graham. *Jesus for a New Generation.* Downers Grove: InterVarsity Press, 1995.

Hunter, George C. *How to Reach Secular People.* Nashville: Abingdon Press, 1992.

Relating to Self

Ashford, Ray. *Loving Ourselves.* Philadelphia: Fortress Press, 1977.

May, Rollo. *Man's Search for Himself.* New York. Norton, 1953.

Price, Nelson L. *How to Find Out Who You Are?* Nashville: Broadman Press, 1977.

Scroggs, James R. *Letting Love In.* Englewood Cliffs, NJ: Prentice Hall, 1978.

Relating to the Church

Bridge, Donald & David Phypers. *Spiritual Gifts & The Church.* Downers Grove: InterVarsity Press, 1973.

Gangel, Kenneth O. *Unwrap Your Spiritual Gifts.* Wheaton: Victor Books, 1983.

Getz, Gene A. *Building Up One Another.* Wheaton: Victor Books, 1976.

Hemphill, Kenneth S. *Spiritual Gifts: Empowering the New Testament Church.* Nashville: Broadman Press, 1988.

Wagner, C. Peter. *Your Spiritual Gifts Can Help Your Church Grow.* Ventura, CA: Regal Books, 1979.

BIBLIOGRAPHIES

Envisioning the Past: Glance But Don't Tarry

Edman, V. Raymond. *They Found the Secret*. Grand Rapids: Zondervan Publishing House, 1960.

Miller, Calvin. *Walking With Saints*. Nashville: Thomas Nelson Publishers, 1995

Winter, David. *100 Days in the Arena*. Wheaton: Harold Shaw Publishers, 1977.

Envisioning Beyond: Mission Possible

Crawley, Winston. *Biblical Light for the Global Task*. Nashville: Convention Press, 1989.

Eckland, Bobby and Terry Austin. *Partners With God: Bible Truths About Giving*. Nashville: Convention Press,1994.

Guder, Darrell L. *Be My Witness*. Grand Rapids: Wm. B. Eerdmans Publishing Co., 1985.

Goerner, H. Cornell. *All Nation's in God's Purpose*. Nashville: Broadman Press, 1979.

Tanner, William G., Compiler. *From Sea to Shining Sea*. Nashville: Broadman Press, 1986.

Envisioning Leadership: The View From Up Front

Dobbins, Gaines S. *Learning to Lead*. Nashville: Broadman Press, 1968.

Eims, Leroy. *Be The Leader You Were Meant to Be*. Wheaton: Victor Books, 1975.

Hayford, Jack. *Pastors of Promise*. Ventura: Regal Press, 1997.

Kenzes, James M. *Credibility: How Leaders Gain and Lose It: Why People Demand It*. San Francisco: Jossey-Bass Publishers, 1993.

Nanus, Bert. *Visionary Leadership: Creating a Compelling Sense of Direction for Your Organization*. San Francisco: Jossey-Bass Publishers, 1992.

Schaller, Lyle E. *The Change Agent*. Nashville: Abindon Press, 1972.

BIBLIOGRAPHIES

GENERAL DISCIPLESHIP BIBLIOGRAPHY

Adsit, Christopher, B. *Personal Disciple-Making*. San Bernardino: Here's Life Publishers, 1988.

Barnett, Max D. *A Guide for Making Disciples on College Campuses*. Nashville: Sunday School Board of the Southern Baptist Convention, 1990.

Boice, James Montgomery. *Christ's Call to Discipleship*. Chicago: Moody Press, 1986.

Bonhoeffer, Dietrich. *The Cost of Discipleship*. New York: MacMillian and Company, 1953.

Coppedge, Allan. *The Biblical Principles of Discipleship*. Grand Rapids: Asbury Press, 1989.

Cosgrove, Francis M. *The Essentials of Discipleship*. Colorado Springs: NavPress, 1982.

Downs, P. *Teaching for Spiritual Growth*. Grand Rapids: Zondervan Publishing House, 1994.

Evans, Donald D. *Spirituality and Human Nature*. Albany: State University of New York Press, 1993.

Foster Richard J. *The Celebration of Discipline*. San Francisco: Harper & Row, 1978.

——— . *The Challenge of the Disciplined Life*. San Francisco: Harper & Row, 1985.

Gangel, Kenneth O. and James C. Wilhout., eds. *The Christian Educator's Handbook on Spiritual Formation*. Wheaton: Victor Books, 1994.

Griffiths, Michael. *The Example of Jesus*. Downers Grove: InterVarsity Press, 1985.

Guibert, Joseph. *The Theology of the Spiritual Life*. New York: Sheed and Ward, 1953.

Helminiak, Daniel A. *Spiritual Development*. Chicago: Loyola University Press, 1987.

Hendrix, John and Lloyd Householder, eds. *The Equipping of Disciples*. Nashville: Broadman Press, 1977.

Holcomb, Daniel. *Costly Commitment.* Nashville: Convention Press, 1978. Revised, 1987.

Hughes, R. K. *Disciplines of a Godly Man.* Wheaton: Crossway Books, 1991.

Hull, Bill. *Jesus Christ Disciplemaker.* Colorado Springs: NavPress, 1984.

Hunter, John Edward. *Let Us Go On to Maturity.* Grand Rapids: Zondervan Publishing House, 1967.

MacArthur, John. *Our Sufficiency in Christ.* Dallas: Word Publishing, 1991.

Marsh, F. E. *Living God's Way.* Grand Rapids: Kregel Publications, 1981.

Maston, T.B. *Walk As He Walked.* Nashville: Broadman Press, 1985.

Miles, Margaret Ruth. *Practicing Christianity.* New York: Crossroad, 1988.

Moore, Waylon B. *New Testament Follow-Up.* Grand Rapids: Wm. B. Eerdmans Publishing Company, 1963.

Murray, Andrew. *Abide in Christ.* New York: Hurst & Co., 1984.

Nee, Watchman. *The Spiritual Man.* New York: Christian Fellowship Publishers, 1977.

O'Conner, Elizabeth. *Journey Inward, Journey Outward.* New York: Harper & Row Publishers, 1968.

Ortiz, Juan Carlos. *Disciple.* Carol Stream, IL: Creation House, 1975.

Pink, Arthur W. *Spiritual Growth.* Grand Rapids: Baker Book House, 1976.

Richards, Larry. *Living in Touch with God.* Grand Rapids: Zondervan Publishing House, 1988.

————. *A Practical Theology of Spirituality.* Grand Rapids: Zondervan Publishing House, 1987.

Sanders, J. Oswald. *The Best That I Can Be.* London: OMF Books, 1976.

Schaeffer, Francis A. *True Spirituality.* Wheaton: Tyndale House Publishers, 1972.

————. *The New Super-Spirituality.* Downers Grove: InterVarsity Press, 1972.

Schweizer, Eduard. *Lordship and Discipleship.* London: SCM Press, LTD., 1960.

Segovia, F., ed. *Discipleship in the New Testament.* Philadelphia: Fortress Press, 1985.

Swindall, Charles R. *Discipleship: Ministry Up Close and Personal.* Fullerton: Insight for Living, 1990.

Thiele, William Edward. *Fruitful Discipleship.* New Orleans: Insight Press, 1994.

Thornton, Martin. *Spiritual Direction.* USA: Cowley, 1984.

Thurian, Max. *Modern Man and Spiritual Life.* New York: Association Press, 1963.

Tozer, A. W. *The Pursuit of God.* Harrisburg, PA: Christian Publications, 1948,

Underhill, Evelyn. *Concerning the Inner Life.* London: Methuen, 1947.

———. *The Spiritual Life.* London: Hodder & Stoughton, 1937, 1955.

Watson, David. *Called and Committed: World Changing Discipleship.* Wheaton: Harold Shaw Publishers, 1982.

Webb, Lance. *Disciplines for Life.* Nashville: The Upper Room, 1986.

Whitney, Donald S. *Spiritual Disciplines for the Christian Life.* Colorado Springs: NavPress, 1991.

Wilkins, Michael J. *Following the Master.* Grand Rapids: Zondervan Publishing House, 1992.

Willard, Dallas. *The Spirit of the Disciplines.* San Francisco: Harper & Row, 1988.